# Advertising Research

# Advertising Research

Javed Shaikh

RANDOM PUBLICATIONS
NEW DELHI (INDIA)

**Advertising Research**

---

ISBN 978-93-5111-212-9



Published in 2013 in India by

**RANDOM PUBLICATIONS**

4376-A/4B, Gali Murari Lal, Ansari Road
New Delhi-110 002
Phone : +91-11-43580356, +91-11-23289044
e-mail: randomexports@gmail.com, sales@randompublications.com,
info@randompublications.com

Reprinted 2021

*Type Setting by* : Keystoneprintads, Delhi-110051
*Digitally Printed at* : Replika Press Pvt. Ltd.

# Preface

What makes us buy some products and not others? Why do we prefer some brands over others? Do print ads and TV commercials actually influence our behavior? In an effort to answer these questions, advertisers look to research. At present, diverse research strategies-psychological, social, and cultural-help advertisers understand consumers and assess the effectiveness of advertising messages directed to them. The particular kinds of research conducted in an advertising campaign are always tailored to serve the needs of those who produce the ads as well as the interests of the clients whose products are promoted. A client who seeks to direct messages to a very specific group of consumers needs to know if the ads are effective with that group. For example, milk producers may want to encourage adults to consume milk. Thus, they need ads that position milk as an adult beverage. Another client may need assistance determining which groups of consumers are most likely to buy the products they offer. For example, an MP3 manufacturer wants to determine which consumers make up its potential market and needs research to help define the market. A third client may ask for detailed information about what consumers recall about the company's ads. For example, a pet food company wants to know if consumers who watched its TV commercials remember the brand name and have positive associations with the brand. Advertising research is directed toward answering such questions as these. Because the questions differ from campaign to campaign, no single research strategy can work for every situation.

Advertising is a form of communication intended to persuade its viewers, readers, or listeners to take some action. It usually includes the name of a product or service and how that product or service could benefit the consumer, to persuade potential customers to purchase or to consume that particular brand. Modern advertising developed with the rise of mass production in the late 19th and early 20th centuries. Commercial advertisers often seek to generate increased consumption of their products or services through branding, which involves the repetition of an image or product name in an effort to associate related qualities with the brand in the minds of consumers. Different types of media can be used to deliver these messages, including traditional media such as newspapers, magazines, television, radio, outdoor or direct mail. Advertising may be placed by an advertising agency on behalf of a company or other organization. Organizations that spend money on advertising promoting items other than a consumer product or service include political parties, interest groups, religious organizations, and governmental agencies. Nonprofit organizations may rely on free modes of persuasion, such as a public service announcement. Money spent on advertising has declined in recent years. In 2007, spending on advertising was estimated at more than $150 billion in the United States and $385 billion worldwide, and the latter to exceed $450 billion by 2010. Perhaps the best known example of this is the United Kingdom's public broadcaster, the BBC, whose domestic networks do not carry commercials. Instead, the BBC, in common with most other public broadcasters in Europe, is funded by a television license fee levied on the owners of all television sets. The Senate of Canada suggested that the country's public broadcaster, the Canadian Broadcasting Corporation, be funded sufficiently by the federal government so that it could air without any advertising

This book examines some of the kinds of research conducted in the service of advertising. The actual variety of methods and techniques used in advertising research is so great that it would be impossible to discuss them all. The research strategies discussed here are indicative of this great variety and represent some of the most common types of research. For convenience, they will be organized and discussed as research conducted before, during, and after the production of an advertisement

I thank all members of my team who have helped in the preparation of the book. My special thanks go to "Random Publications" who have published the book.

*– Javed Shaikh*

# Contents

# 1

# Advertising and the Media

Counter-advertising commonly is used to balance the effects that alcohol advertising may have on alcohol consumption and alcohol-related problems. Such measures can take the form of print or broadcast advertisements (e.g., public service announcements [PSAs]) as well as product warning labels. The effectiveness of both types of counter-advertising is reviewed using the Elaboration Likelihood Model as a theoretical framework.

For print and broadcast counter-advertisements, such factors as their emotional appeal and the credibility of the source, as well as audience factors, can influence their effectiveness. Further, brewer-sponsored counter-advertisements are evaluated and received differently than are the more conventional PSA counter-advertisements. For warning labels, both the content and design of the label influence their effectiveness, as do audience factors. The effectiveness of those labels is evaluated in terms of the extent to which they impact cognitive and affective processes as well as drinking behaviour.

Widespread concern exists among policymakers and the public about the potential effects of alcohol advertising on alcohol consumption and problems, especially among children and adolescents. It is especially important to counter the potential effects of advertising on young people because these age groups may be more susceptible to those effects. Children are less able to discriminate between advertising and other media content and are less critical of commercial messages than are adults.

Moreover, recent studies of children and adolescents have shown that attention to and liking of alcohol advertising are related to:

- Greater knowledge about alcohol slogans and beer brands,
- More favorable beliefs about drinking,
- Increased intentions to drink as an adult,
- Increased drinking.

Similarly, it may be important to counter the potential effects of alcohol advertising on young adults, and especially college students, who frequently are at risk for heavy and problematic drinking. A recent national survey indicates that 67 per cent of adults in the United States support banning liquor advertisements on television and 61 per cent favour banning beer and wine advertisements in this medium. Similarly, public health advocates routinely call for the strict regulation or even elimination of alcohol advertising, and initiatives at the community level frequently focus on reducing local alcohol advertising. In part, concerns about alcohol advertising result from its pervasiveness.

In 1999, the alcoholic beverage industry spent $1.24 billion on alcohol advertising. Most of these expenditures ($796.3 million) were concentrated on television and radio commercials; among beverage types, beer advertising accounted for the majority of the spending ($799.7 million). Consistent with these data, studies document that alcohol advertising, and particularly beer advertising, is a relatively frequent occurrence on television, especially in sports programming.

For example, approximately two alcohol advertisements appear in each hour of major professional sports programming, compared with approximately one alcohol advertisement in every 4 hours of entertainment programming. To address and counteract the pervasiveness of alcohol advertising, policymakers can take several approaches. In addition to the restrictions on alcohol advertising discussed above, counter-advertising--the presentation of factual information and persuasive messages through the media--is such an approach.

It primarily takes two forms: (1) broadcast (e.g., television and radio), outdoor (e.g., billboard), and print counter-advertisements, and (2) product warning labels. This chapter reviews the effectiveness of these two general types of counter-advertising in changing drinking-related beliefs, intentions, and behaviors. First, however, it presents a useful model for understanding and assessing media persuasion effects and the relative endurance and direction of such effects--the Elaboration Likelihood Model (ELM).

## THE ELABORATION LIKELIHOOD MODEL

The ELM distinguishes two routes through which counter-advertising may persuade target audiences to change their attitudes and behaviors--a central route and a peripheral route. The central route involves a high level of issue-relevant thinking. This means that message recipients are likely to carefully attend to the content of the message; scrutinize and elaborate upon this content in light of their own knowledge; decide on the merits of its arguments; and consequently derive an overall evaluation, or attitude, toward that message. Through this effortful reasoning process, the recipients integrate the provided information into their own belief structures, which then may result in attitude change. In contrast, the peripheral route involves a less effortful reasoning process that does not rely on scrutinizing the content and merits of the message. Here, attitudes are formed based on relatively simple cues without issue-relevant thinking.

For example, the very nature of a communicator being highly credible and/or attractive may be enough to automatically lead the message recipient to accept the recommendation without giving the provided arguments any serious thought.

The ELM posits that attitude change mediated through the more effortful central route will be longer lasting, more resistant, and more predictive of behaviour than change mediated through the peripheral route. According to this model, the goal of prevention experts in designing effective counter-advertisements and warning labels therefore should be to induce change through the central route.

The model also specifies that audience members must be both able and motivated to take the more lasting and effortful central route. In situations where the audience may only be moderately interested in a topic, factors that otherwise might act as peripheral cues (e.g., source credibility and source attractiveness) can also affect whether audience members engage in the more effortful central route. For example, college students, particularly fraternity members, who may be only moderately interested in messages about abstinence or responsible drinking might be more likely to deeply process a message delivered by a favourite athlete. Yet even central processing of a message does not guarantee that the message will result in attitude change in the intended direction.

Once people process information through the central route, the effect of the message depends upon how each person responds to it. For example, a heavy drinker could react defensively with his or her own set of biased thoughts to the provided counter-advertisement, doubting the merits of the information provided and becoming even more convinced of the legitimacy of his or her initial heavy drinking stance. In such a case, the persuasion attempt would thus backfire and further polarize an already pro-drinking attitude.

## EFFECTIVENESS OF BROADCAST AND PRINT COUNTER-ADVERTISING

Counter-advertisements that recommend responsible alcohol use generally are conveyed to the public through television, radio, outdoor, or print media. These messages can be either produced by government agencies or community action groups, or they can be industry-sponsored.

The broadcast of counter-advertisements also can be either donated (e.g., public service announcements [PSAs]) or purchased (e.g., social marketing). The issue of drinking and driving has been a primary target of counter-advertising campaigns. Following a rigorous analysis of the contents of drinking-and-driving PSAs, Slater identified the most common strategy in such campaigns as the informational/testimonial approach, which provides basic facts or simply exhorts appropriate behaviour. The information may be delivered as a testimonial by a celebrity or a person on the street, or in a more educational format as simple information to be learned. This approach neither does nor employs strong elements of the other four common strategies identified by Slater.

*These other strategies are those that*:

- Model appropriate behaviour (e.g., giving up car keys after drinking),
- Employ positive appeals (e.g., depicting enjoyable social situations without drinking),
- Evoke alcohol-related fear (e.g., of accidental death),
- Evoke empathy (e.g., for victims of drunk drivers).

The most common informational/testimonial approach assumes that providing information will increase audience knowledge and awareness of the drunk-driving issue and eventually impact the targeted behaviour.

When analysed from the perspective of the ELM, however, such messages are not always designed in a way that optimizes their long-term effectiveness. For example, although informational/testimonial PSAs provide relevant information that people can integrate into their belief systems, these PSAs are not necessarily appealing in their design and therefore are less likely to interest and motivate people to process them more carefully through the central route. Recently, Austin and colleagues compared the effectiveness of antidrinking PSAs to the alcohol advertisements that they were supposed to counter. In that study, college students rated both PSAs (e.g.,"Friends don't let friends drive drunk") and alcohol advertisements (e.g., for Bud Lite) on dimensions related to whether they would attract interest and motivate people to process them.

In general, the college students rated the PSAs as less enjoyable and appealing but also as more realistic, honest, and effective. The investigators also examined to what extent the frequency with which college students consumed alcohol influenced their ratings of the alcohol advertisements and PSAs. This analysis found that even though alcohol advertisements were generally rated as less effective than the PSAs, the more frequently college students reportedly consumed alcohol, the more favorably they responded to the alcohol advertisements.

For example, more frequent drinkers rated the alcohol advertisements as more effec tive, identified with their portrayals more, and rated those portrayals as more desirable compared with others. More frequent drinkers also rated the PSAs as less effective than did other students. The investigators concluded that an overemphasis on logic-based realistic and honest appeals in conventional PSAs, at the expense of the more emotion-based appeal of alcohol advertisements, can compromise the PSAs' effectiveness. Future research still must determine, however, whether the appealing features of the alcohol advertisements translate, over time, into a deep central processing of such advertisements with an enduring attitude and behaviour change, or whether these features contribute only to peripheral-route processing.

The influence of a person's drinking level in this process should also be examined. Designers of alcohol counter-advertisements should then employ those advertising features that best promote central processing for heavy drinkers, light drinkers, and nondrinkers alike. Another set of analyses of alcohol counter-advertising was conducted after a 1988 Surgeon General's workshop on drunk driving called for mass communication campaigns directed at the prevention of alcohol-related traffic deaths. To examine the impact of such campaigns, Dejong and Atkin analysed the contents of PSAs aired nationally between 1987 and 1992.

This analysis identified two dominant types of PSAs in the campaign that correspond to classic peripheral factors of influence posited by the ELM:

- Celebrity endorsements with a"talking head" format (e.g., Magic Johnson stating that a designated driver is the most valued player)
- Emotional appeals attempting to evoke fear, anger, and empathy (e.g., PSAs by Mothers Against Drunk Driving [MADD] expressing both anger at drunk drivers and sympathy for their innocent victims).

The main objective of these PSAs was to encourage the adoption of more responsible drinking-related behaviors, such as using designated drivers and intervening to prevent alcohol-impaired people from driving. Indeed, after the campaign, Gallup surveys offered strong evidence of a sharp drop in the number of impaired drivers on the road. In addition, a remarkable decline in the number of U.S. alcohol-related traffic deaths occurred between 1982 and 1996. To some extent, these decreases might be attributable to the PSA campaign. Yet, as Dejong and Hingson warn, determining the unique contribution of any single initiative to such favorable outcomes is fraught with methodological difficulties.

Several simultaneous legal and programmatic initiatives within the broader drunk-driving campaign (e.g., sobriety checkpoints, increased minimum legal drinking age, and responsible beverage service) as well as other shifts in regulations affecting risky driving behaviors (i.e., speeding laws) also contributed to the observed effects. Accordingly, future research must determine whether, and by what processes, the classic celebrity endorsement and emotional-appeal PSAs uniquely contribute to attitude and behaviour change. For example, celebrity endorsements could promote a shallower peripheral processing of a PSA, with a more temporary attitude and behaviour change, simply because the messages of well-liked and credible celebrities may go unchallenged without ever motivating viewers to think deeply about the message content. Conversely, celebrities could promote a deeper central processing and more enduring attitude change by attracting the attention of those viewers who initially were only mildly interested and motivate those viewers enough to carefully process and accept their messages.

## BREWERY-SPONSORED COUNTER-ADVERTISEMENTS

Some counter-advertisements also have been sponsored by beer brewers, and researchers have compared the reactions, particularly of young viewers (i.e., ages 16-22 years) to these brewer-sponsored messages with more conventional PSA counter-advertisements. The brewer-sponsored counter-advertisements studied were from Anheuser-Busch's"Know when to say when" and Coors'"Now, not now" campaigns, both of which were purportedly created to promote safe and responsible drinking.

According to the researchers, their content reflects a hybrid of commercial, public relations, and public service persuasion strategies. Thus, these brewer-sponsored counter-advertisements tend to be"soft sell" versions of traditional PSAs. In contrast, nonindustry PSAs (e.g., those sponsored by MADD or the Ad Council) tend to be straightforward fear appeals that have more explicit guidelines and are generally slower-paced and less entertaining.

Study participants rated the brewer-sponsored counter-advertisements as less informative, believable, on-target, and effective than the conventional PSAs. Furthermore, when asked to rank the motives for the brewer-sponsored counter-advertisements, the study participants rated the prevention of drunk driving only third, behind improvement of the company's image and selling its beer. Thus, these young viewers received the brewer-sponsored PSAs with skepticism. The young study participants also viewed the brewer-sponsored counter-advertisements as permitting liberal alcohol consumption, even in risky situations. This latter effect may result from the use of strategic ambiguity, which sends an unclear message about how much to limit one's drinking. This means that the messages sanction an acceptable level of drinking but leave it to the viewer to decide what that level is.

For example, in the"Know when to say when" counter-advertisements, the"when" and how to"know when" are never defined. Even with less ambiguous messages (e.g., a NASCAR Budweiser driver stating"Please, don't drink and drive") or with messages directly modeling choosing a designated driver, other cues in the advertisements may create ambiguity or even serve as peripheral cues in promoting pro-drinking attitudes. Such cues may include Budweiser logos promoting beer sales or people at a party enjoying alcoholic beverages.

Another problem associated with brewery-sponsored counter-advertising is that by the very act of airing a communication that promotes restricted alcohol use, the alcohol industry seemingly argues against its own interest and paradoxically may increase its credibility and persuasive power through peripheral processing mechanisms.

Indeed, despite the evidence for some skepticism toward brewer-sponsored PSAs, youth rated the beer industry as respectable, responsible, and caring after viewing the industry-sponsored counter-advertisements. The researchers concluded that, taken together, these findings suggest an unfortunate effect of brewer-sponsored counter-advertisements when compared to more conventional PSAs--that despite their initial intent, for youth, the brewer-sponsored advertisements may justify drinking in risky situations and promote alcohol sales more generally.

## THE INFLUENCE OF AUDIENCE FACTORS

Audience factors also can affect the extent to which counter-advertising leads to attitude and behaviour change. For example, videotaped alcohol counter-advertisements are most effective when the communicator is of the same gender as the viewer, and they have a greater influence on lighter than on heavier drinkers. Consistent with the previously discussed finding that heavy drinkers rated PSAs as less effective than did lighter drinkers, this latter observation suggests that heavier or problematic drinkers may be particularly resistant to counter-advertising. For this reason, Isaac recommended that drunk-driving media campaigns not target at-risk drinkers but rather urge the intervention by friends who are more likely to be respected and be listened to by resistant drinkers.

Nonetheless, even young people with a"sensation-seeking" personality who are prone to alcohol and other drug abuse can be directly influenced with properly designed counter-advertising. For example, such people are more likely to call a hot line mentioned in an anti-drug PSA when the PSA is high in sensation value (i.e., fast-paced, upbeat, and suspenseful). Conversely, young people with a less sensation-seeking personality are more responsive to PSAs with lower sensation value.

The optimal design of counter-advertisements for changing problematic behaviour also may depend upon what stage a person has reached in being able to recognize his or her own behaviour as problematic. For example, people who do not yet recognize that their drinking and driving is problematic and have a limited motivation to think about the issue likely will ignore a purely logic-based message unless it has appealing features (e.g., is dramatic enough to attract attention or is communicated by a well-liked celebrity).

For people who are already motivated to change, however, messages modeling the desired behaviors (e.g., how to tactfully refuse drinks at a party) could facilitate the translation of the drinkers' intentions into the desired behaviors by providing specific information on how to enact those behaviors.

Taken together, the research on message, source, and audience factors indicates that part of the success of counter-advertising will depend on how these factors interact. Based on the ELM, which predicts that central route processing leads to more durable attitude and behaviour change, it appears critical that counter-advertisements include strong logical arguments for audience members to integrate into their belief structures. Yet, for those audience members who are not motivated to attend to these messages, peripheral factors (e.g., appeal, celebrity endorsements, and sensational content) should be employed as well to maximize the likelihood that all audience members are attracted to and process the rich message content. Indeed, consistent with the ELM, Slater's analysis suggests that counter-advertisements should employ both peripheral factors to ensure that the advertisements are appealing and motivate the audience to process them and strong logical information that can be integrated into belief systems to ensure a lasting change.

## EFFECTIVENESS OF WARNING LABELS

The second form of counter-advertising is alcoholic beverage warning labels and posters. Health warning label legislation was implemented in the United States in 1989. This legislation requires all alcoholic beverage containers to bear a government warning of the risks associated with consuming alcohol while pregnant, driving a car, or operating machinery. Similarly, since the 1980s several States have mandated the display of health warning posters at places where alcohol is sold.

Of primary importance in studying the effectiveness of warning labels is the most basic research question--do people even notice the labels? Several studies have explored message-design factors that influence whether the labels are noticed. In three separate experiments, Laughery and colleagues measured how quickly people could locate warning labels on alcoholic beverage containers.

The investigators concluded that the typical alcohol warning labels are not particularly noticeable because they blend in with their backgrounds. Several factors, such as clutter on the labels themselves, their vertical placement on the container, and placement other than on the front of the container, make the warning less noticeable. Further, the use of pictorials, icons, and colour improve the labels' noticeability. From the perspective of the ELM, these findings indicate that the first critical step in designing effective warning labels should be to ensure that audience me mbers can notice and thus further process the labels.

Once a warning label is noticed, its content becomes of paramount importance. To identify the factors influencing the effectiveness of alcohol warning labels, MacKinnon and colleagues systematically varied several features of warning labels, such as their length, the use of qualifier words (e.g., may cause cancer), and the specific risks mentioned (e.g., birth defects, health risks, or cancer). To determine whether certain bottle warning labels would be more successful in leading people to avoid those bottles, participants were asked to imagine that they were in a supermarket and had to choose between two different bottles.

This test was repeated with several pairs of bottles, with bottles in each pair displaying one of the possible warning labels and a blank label. When participants chose the bottle with the blank label within each pair instead of the bottle with the experimental warning label, this signaled that the experimental warning label effectively led people to avoid or not choose the bottle on which it was displayed. For both college and high school students, the study had the following results:

- The specific risks mentioned on the label were more important in determining choices than was the label length.
- Bottles with labels containing qualifier words were avoided less than were bottles without such words.
- Whiskey bottles with warning labels were avoided more than were beer bottles with warning labels.
- Alternative warnings containing the words"poison" and"cancer" elicited more avoidance than did the currently used Surgeon General's alcohol warning label.

Together, these findings indicate that research participants under these experimental conditions noticed the content of the warning labels and processed that content at some minimal level. At the same time, the results point to a less thought-engaging and more peripheral process potentially underlying effective counter-advertising. That is, the alternative warning labels presumably worked by producing a visceral avoidance response.

The mere association of a bottled product with negative words (e.g.,"poison") may have effectively generated an automatic repulsive avoidance of the product, consistent with classical conditioning() mechanisms. It would be of interest to determine in future research whether the obtained findings would also generalize to other young adults not in college as well as to older adults. Whereas this experimental research examined the influence of the content of an alcohol warning label on its ability to evoke avoidance responses, later research has evaluated how deeply warning labels are being processed and whether they influence drinking behaviour. Various studies document that the general public's awareness of warning labels and posters is high.

A more recent study focused on 10th and 12th grade students' responses to warning labels during the first 5 years that those labels were required. Despite the fact that it is illegal for adolescents to drink alcohol, experimentation with alcohol typically begins in adolescence, and many attitudes regarding alcohol use are established during this period. It is therefore instructive to study how this population processes these labels.

This study found that the initial positive effects of the warning labels on adol escents' awareness of, exposure to, and recognition of these warnings were beginning to level off over the course of the study. Taken together, the accumulated evidence suggests that the warning labels are being noticed and their content is remembered. The findings are less clear, however, as to what people are learning or comprehending from these labels, how different people react to these labels, and whether people's behaviour is affected as intended.

For example, evidence concerning how deeply the information content of the warning labels is processed and to what extent readers comprehend and accept the risks communicated (e.g., pregnancy complications and drunk-driving risks) is mixed. Some researchers have argued that a"ceiling effect" exists--that warning labels are ineffective in teaching the general public anything new about the targeted drinking-related risks because the readers already know about these risks.

Furthermore, the aforementioned study on warning label effects in adolescents found no beneficial change in terms of alcohol-related beliefs, consumption, or driving after drinking that was attributable to the labels. Other studies also found evidence that alcohol warning labels do not affect drinking behaviour.

Some more recent evidence suggests, however, that warning labels may have delayed behavioral effects. Specifically, Greenfield found that a person's ability to recall the drinking-and-driving message on alcohol warning labels predicted the self-reported likelihood to limit both driving after drinking and drinking when planning on driving. Further, Hankin and colleagues documented that in a traditionally hard-to-reach population of pregnant, inner-city African American women, alcohol consumption among low-risk drinkers declined after the introduction of warning labels.

Experimental research that varies exposure to alcohol warnings to address the question of how these warnings affect people similarly has found mixed results for their effectiveness. MacKinnon's review raises the potential for"overwarning" effects--that people become overly accustomed to warnings and, as a result, ignore them or, worse yet, react to them unfavorably.

A study by Snyder and Blood found some evidence for such an effect. In that study, college student drinkers exposed to the Surgeon General's alcohol warning in a printed alcohol advertisement perceived greater benefits from drinking than did college student drinkers exposed to the same advertisement without the warning. In addition, male drinkers exposed to the warning expressed greater intentions to drink than did those exposed to the same advertisement without the warning.

Other researchers failed to replicate these effects in two separate experiments, however, leading them to conclude that the earlier observed effect was based o n inappropriate statistical comparisons and confounding factors. Slater and Domenech also have pointed to the weak nature of the warning employed by Snyder and Blood, which may have influenced the results. From the perspective of the ELM, the effect of a warning message will depend upon how its audience reacts to it. For a warning to effectively counter an alcohol advertisement, it must receive favorable reactions and generate supportive thoughts. For example, Slater and Domenech demonstrated that repeated exposure to alcohol warnings that were embedded within beer advertisements elicits negative beliefs to counter-argue those advertisements and leads viewers to be less confident about the benefits of beer drinking. Further, Andrews indicated that one's own conscious thoughts elicited in response to the warning labels (i.e., one's cognitive responses) mediate approximately three-quarters of the effects that warning labels have on how favorably the labels are evaluated. Thus, self-generated thoughts in response to reading warning labels are important intermediate variables in determining whether the warning labels will be persuasive.

Together, this research indicates that investigators and policym akers must understand how people cognitively react to alcohol warnings so as to design warnings that produce the intended antidrinking attitudes or at least erode the confidence of pro-drinking beliefs.

Several audience factors also predict the depth to which people process alcohol warning labels and whether they react favorably or unfavorably to them. For example, researchers found that the ability to recall container warning label messages is highest among younger respondents, heavier drinkers, and purchasers of alcohol. This finding suggests that the messages do indeed reach the target groups. Yet, although heavy drinkers are aware of drinking risks, they also discount warning labels and perceive them less favorably and as less believable than do light drinkers.

Similarly, in the study of pregnant, inner-city African American women, only the lighter drinkers who were less at risk of having children with alcohol-related birth defects heeded warning labels. Finally, younger, pregnant, inner-city African American women were more aware of and more likely to believe the birth defects warning and limit their drinking than were their older peers, despite the fact that the risks for alcohol-related birth defects increase with age. These findings indicate that although the people most in need of adopting alcohol warnings are aware of and can recall the information in warning labels, these same people are least likely to accept the warnings. Taken together, the research on the design and content of warning label factors as well as on audience factors indicates that the effectiveness of warning labels on drinking behaviour depends on how these factors initially impact underlying cognitive and affective processes.

First, design factors influence whether warning labels are even initially noticed. Second, the specific content of warning labels could influence the labels' potential for evoking visceral avoidance responses. Third, audience factors predict differential memory for, processing of, and reactions to alcohol warning labels. These audience effects can then modify drinking behaviour.

To dilute the influence of alcohol advertising. broadcast and print counter-advertising and warning labels present factual information and persuasive messages to the public. Some evidence supports the effectiveness of these strategies, although the findings are mixed and typically qualified by message, source, and audience factors. To predict the conditions under which various counter-advertising approaches will work, researchers must understand the processes contributing to or limiting their effectiveness. The ELM provides a useful framework for integrating the emerging findings and for predicting when counter-advertising and warning labels will lead to a more durable attitude change and ultimately affect the behaviors they target.

- Definitions of drinking severity (e.g., heavy drinking or moderate drinking) and drinking frequency (e.g., frequent drinker) vary among studies. Therefore, the terms are used in this chapter as they were in the original studies cited.
- The definitions associated With different levels of alcohol use varied across Bochner's three studies. In study 1, participants were classified as heavy versus light/moderate drinkers, contrasting those who had a drink at least once or twice a week (heavy) to all other participants, including those who never drank (light/moderate). In both studies 2 and 3, participants were classified as moderate/heavy versus light drinkers, contrasting those who had a drink at least once or twice a month (moderate/heavy) to all other participants, including those who never drank (light).
- Sensation-seeking is characterized by a willingness to take risks for the sake of varied, novel, and intense experiences. It is also associated with alcohol and other drug use.
- Classical conditioning allows for an initially neutral stimulus (e.g., new consumer product) to eventually elicit a positive or negative response on its own after repeated associations with an already valued stimulus.

# 2

# Approaches and Applications of Advertising Research

## SCOPE OF ADVERTISING RESEARCH

Homo sapiens are constantly inquisitive to search out the information about the surroundings, alongwith persistently keen to explore novel ideas and generate fresh knowledge related to various phenomenon. The process of knowledge formation involves various practices such as observations, experiments, and constant readings to comprehend new notions. Nevertheless, the most significant approach to engender factual and verifiable knowledge is research as it applies scientific and systematic methods. Pure and applied sciences, social sciences, language and management, all the disciplines employ scientific research methods to postulate new theories, and the lengthy voyage of human evolution took place. Growth of industrialization *escorted* the demand and supply phenomenon, and new discipline *marketing* has coined in the preceding century.

Marketing is a process to execute and plan the conception, pricing, promotions, and the distribution of products (goods, services, people, and ideas). Out of so many activities, research is one of the important fascinating facets of marketing. Prior to making the market strategy, market managers conduct research, to make out the needs and wants of customers, and to evaluate the market environment called *marketing research.* Market Research is "a systematic, objective collection and analysis of data about a particular target market, competition, and/or environment.

It always incorporates some form of data collection whether it is secondary research or primary research which is collected direct from a respondent". It is a systematic process of gathering, recording and analyzing information about customers and prospects. Marketing research performs a couple of functions it helps identify consumer needs and market segments, also provides information necessary for developing new products and creating market strategies. Marketing research is helpful for market managers to evaluate the effectiveness of market strategy and promotional activities. It is also significant in financial planning and economic forecasting and quality control of product. Since the expansion of global market, advertising research has become an imperative field of marketing research to measure the efficacy of advertising. Advertising research is a specialized area of marketing research. Marketing research identifies the information required to take marketing decisions, while advertising research explores the facts essential to take advertising decisions. Advertising research helps entrepreneurs to categorize the needs and wants of target customers as well as their social, psychological, and economical background.

Advertising, in eighteenth century, was a form of communication to inform people with a very simple way of presentation in print media. But with the advancement of technology and expansion of market, advertising and promotional activities have become a major tool of marketing. At present, advertising is one of the biggest revenue generating industries in the world. Millions and billions of currency are being spent on marketing communication to grab the attention of new market and to encourage and influence the decisions of target consumers. Top ten companies of the world contributed 25 -29 billion dollars approximately by in advertising and other promotional activities in 2008-2009. Moreover, new communication technologies are bringing a revolution and providing a more interactive and competitive environment for the market.

Online newspapers and magazines, podcasts, Wi-Max, new video formats, internet streaming etc. are helpful to introduce innovative techniques and provide better options for advertisers. In addition, digitalization in TV homes through DTH, cable and IPTV are helping bring better quality to consumers who can pay for the same. Better ways of presentation and high quality of techniques are used to create the advertising message. Huge money is being spent on production and dissemination of advertisements. Advertisers investing in marketing communication are keen to measure the effectiveness of advertising message on consumers.

As the marketing communication and advertising industry grew up, the field of advertising research emerged on a wide scale playing a very important role in marketing research. In addition, growth of media industry encouraged the expansion of advertising industry as well advertising research. FICCI has reported that Indian Media Industry will be at heights with its growth estimated at ₹ 1.57 trillion 2012. Growth of Media and entertainment industry, estimated at ₹ 513 billion in 2007, has increased and is estimated at ₹ 584 billion in 2008. Print, electronic, outdoor and new media bestow new opportunities to advertising industry. The overall breakup of the total share of advertising turnover in 2008 is:

- Television ₹ 240.5 billion
- Print ₹ 172.6 billion
- Film ₹ 109.3 billion

- Animation ₹ 17.4 billion
- Radio ₹ 8.4 billion
- Music ₹ 7.3 billion
- Gaming ₹ 6.5 billion
- Internet ₹ 6.2 billion

As the marketers spend big amount on integrated marketing communication, the need to determine the impact of promotion programmes becomes significant. Henceforth advertising research will allow the clients as well as 'ad' agencies to evaluate the performance of promotional programmes. As the advertising and promotional campaigns are started with specific objectives, advertising research helps whether the 'ad' campaign is accomplishing its objectives or not. Advertising research incorporates research approaches of various subjects such as sociology, psychology, economics and anthropology to know the target consumers' perception regarding product, brand image and audience behavior.

Dimensions of advertising research are vast as it is conducted in different areas such as audience analysis, motivational studies, and consumer behavioral studies. Audience profile, preference, brand attention, emotional appeal, likings, and disliking evaluation of campaigns are the recent trends of advertising research. Dominick and Wimmer (2006) have stated three dimensions of advertising research— Copy research, media research and campaign assessment research in which qualitative and quantitative research approaches are used to assess the effectiveness of advertisement. Four groups of people conduct advertising research: 'Ad' agency people conduct research to evaluate campaign or to get information about the audience, Syndicators conduct advertising research to study the market and to get information about the product and the market. Marketing managers conduct advertising research to support their market strategies. The fourth group, namely, academics, conduct advertising research to obtain new knowledge and to postulate theories related to advertising.

## OBJECTIVES OF ADVERTISING RESEARCH

Advantages of advertising research are many. For example, just to avoid the slip-ups investors spend a large amount over advertising and promotional activities. As 'ad' agencies have many strategies, the best is considered after conducting ad research. Due to cut-throat competition among marketeers, advertisers need to create the best creative message that requires lot of planning and research-based information. Objectives of advertising research are clustered in four categories based on information needs.

## ADVERTISING STRATEGY RESEARCH

Advertisers conduct research before the beginning of the creative work. Advertising companies need to get information about the creative mix:

product concept, the target audience, the communication media, and the creative message. During research, all the information related to product and brand is gathered. Different features of brand, brand image and position, product usage etc. are well defined and explained. To determine the psychographic, demographic, and geographic profile of audience, 'ad' strategy research is very helpful besides helping build relationship between brand and consumers. Audience's purchasing motives are identified, so that advertisers can decide the appeals to persuade them.

Different media have different characteristics and audience of every media is diverse in nature. It is very important for advertisers to select appropriate media to communicate with target audience. Reach– access and effectiveness of communication media are studied during media research. Companies want to create most persuasive message to influence the target audience's buying decisions. They study the likings and dislikings of 'ad' messages. Message element study is helpful to decide the theme of advertising campaigns. Techniques used in research: Consumer attitude study, consumer usage of product, study of market behavior and study of competitors' brands, descriptive analysis of media access and reach; TRP and readership surveys being held to study the popularity of media

## CREATIVE CONCEPT RESEARCH

The aim of advertising creative development and the goal of advertising testing is to identify the elements and ideas essential to advertising effectiveness, and then to make sure that those elements and ideas are consistently communicated by the entire advertising executives. Once the advertising research study develops, advertising agency begins work on creative concept. To develop the creative concept, research is conducted before the production of advertising message.

Qualities, which can lead the brand position, include: how the consumers perceive the brand and what should be the appeal for creative concept analysis. Concept testing research evaluates advertising concepts, 'ad' theme, concept, appeal, pricing, brand concepts, brand names, and positioning strategy concepts. Concept testing research studies identify the product, advertising, or branding concepts according to marketing strategy and market opportunity. Both qualitative and quantitative research approaches are employed to develop the creative concept. Survey, in-depth interviews, and online surveys are some popular techniques to get information about the brand image, equity, and consumers reactions.

## AUDIENCE ANALYSIS AND PROFILE STUDY

To determine the audience profile and their needs and wants, the advertisers conduct audience profile studies before launching the advertising campaigns. Audience psychographic, demographic, and geographic analysis is done to understand the behavior. In marketing research, this is a very popular trend to get information about the consumer so that product can be designed according to the requirement and needs of the consumers. Audience analysis bequeaths a profound insight about the nature, characteristics, and life style of target consumer. Psychological approaches are used to examine the attitude, behavior, and nature of the target consumer. Scale measurement techniques are very popular to study the audience profile. Motivational and behavioral studies are conducted to identify the psychographic characteristics of audience.

## MEDIA EXPOSURE AND EFFECTIVENESS

Expansion and growth of media industry pave the way to media research to examine the popularity ratings of channels and media. Based on the Television Rating Points and gross rating points, advertisers choose the media to disseminate the 'ad' message. Now a days, media research is one of the utmost popular and significant trends of advertising research to determine the rates of exposure and popularity of a particular media among audience. Media research is also conducted to measure the frequency and reach of different media available for the audience. Reach is the exposure of 'ad' message in total number of households and total number of people exposed to message received is frequency. Advertisers examine frequency and reach to decide the budget and requirement of message exposure in particular media. Concept of demassification has extended the horizons of media research in advertising. Specific media for specific audience based on specific subjects available has increased the concept of selectivity. Another dimension of media research is to find out the effectiveness and likings of a particular media among target audience.

## PRE-TESTING OF 'ADS'

Research is conducted in many phases– before launching the advertisement in media it is called pretesting and research and after the campaign it is called post-testing. Pre-testing is held to measure the effectiveness of message. Pre-testing may occur many times from idea generation to final production of advertising message. Copy and visuals of the advertisement are tested through various methods. One of the models considered very important is posed by *Leckenby and Weding* (1982), who put forward three dimensions of effect on audience while copy testing.

Cognitive is mapping the understanding level of audience before, during and after the 'ad' campaign e.g. how audience perceive the ad message, what are the rates of recall and recognition, are they aware of 'ad' etc.? Second dimension measures the attitude of consumer toward the particular product. Whether the attitude has changed after the exposure of 'ad' campaign, and what determines the likings and dislikings about the product. Consumers brand preferences and uses, frequency of purchasing and reasons of purchasing decisions are measured to know actual use of product advertised by the marketeer.

## LECKENBY AND WEDING (1982)

During pre-testing, target audience (consumer) and specialized persons are shown the 'ad' message prepared for testing and asked about the visuals and copy. In pre-testing many techniques like *tachistoscope,* cameras to pick the movements, are used to determine the attention level and stimulation of consumers during the advertisement message testing. With the help of electric instruments, different methods are applied to study the pulse frequency, eye tracking movements, facial expressions, interest, and attention of selected target consumers.

Audience liking, disliking, recall, and recognition rates of 'ad' message are discovered with the help of questionnaire and interview methods. Sometimes, audience is asked to complete the sentences shown in the 'ad' message or asked the key words used in the 'ad' to test the effectiveness and recall rates of copy. Pre-testing of advertisement helps advertisers to judge the actual response of audience, and according to the response, they can change the message. Pretesting save time and money of advertisers as it is beneficial to improve their message before launching the advertisement in media. Methods applied to conduct pre-test may vary. Both laboratory methods and field methods are employed to conduct pre-test research.

## POST-TESTING AND EVALUATION OF CAMPAIGN

Post-testing is another trend of advertising research which is conducted after launching advertising campaign in media to determine the effectiveness, actual purchasing behavior and product awareness among target consumer. Different methods of research have been used to evaluate the effectiveness of advertisements. To find out the awareness of brand after the advertising campaign and to scale the attitude of target audience toward the product advertised, survey, depth interviews, focus groups and observation methods are applied to measure the motivational factors of target audience. Psychological approaches are applied to test the liking scale of consumers with the help of attitude measurement scales and techniques.

Direct response of consumer is measured by using buying intention scale. At the point of purchase, actual behavior is judged by asking questions about the product. Exposure of advertisement message (copy and visuals), recall of advertisement, attitude change after the exposure and rationale of purchasing the products are examined during post testing research. Post testing research is advantageous as it determines whether the 'ad' campaign is successful in making a favorable image of product in the market. It is also helpful to notice the likings and exposure of target consumer toward the 'ad' message. It is more appropriate to say that during post testing observe the cause and effect relationship between advertising message and consumers purchasing decision.

## METHODS OF POST TESTING 'ADS'

- Aided recalls or Recognition-readership– In this method respondents are shown 'ad' message and asked about their previous exposure about the 'ads'
- Unaided recalls– Without showing the 'ad' messages, respondents are asked, whether they know about particular 'ad' messages.
- Attitude Test– Direct questions, semantic differential tests are conducted to explore the liking of respondents. In-depth and unstructured interviews are taken to measure changes in respondent's attitude after the exposure of 'ad' message.
- Inquiry Tests– Additional information about product, product samples, or premiums is given to audience of ads to judge the effectiveness of message.
- Sales Test– Sale before the campaign and sale after the advertising campaign is measured. Consumer purchase test measures retail sale and store inventory measure retailers stocks before and after campaign.

Various advertising research approaches and testing methods are available. Each advertising research method has its advantages and limitations. So advertising research requires formal planned design and quality standards for data collection to ensure the reliability and accuracy and to increase the usability. Advertising research requires rigorous explanation of problem because most of the advertising research has immediate applications and entire message is created because of research.

To determine the reliability, a careful selection of research design is necessary. Sampling techniques, question formation, data collection techniques and data analysis methods must be chosen carefully as advertisers use research for testing. Advertising research, especially pre-testing, helps to detect and eliminate the weak spots before launching the advertisement message in media. Before production, audience analysis and market and product analysis is important to analyze the behavior of consumers and help in creative strategy. After the campaign, post testing helps to evaluate the actual impact of advertisement campaign.

However, advertising effectiveness can not be measured by only one method. Accordingly different techniques are used. New trends in advertising are emerging and scope of research is increasing day by day. Profound changes in the technology in the last decde have changed the applications of advertising research. New form of internet advertisements, globalization, free market concept has puffed up the dimensions of advertising research. Integrated marketing concept and enlarged field of media and entertainment industry multiplied the stipulation of advertising research. Therefore, market researchers promote innovative approaches and procedures to determine information about the consumers to set their market strategies. Finally, future research will examine more closely the cognitive processes involved in consumers' behavior. Cognitive response measures as well as experimental manipulations should be employed to provide further evidence for the cognitive mechanism to reduce the perceived distance between the advertising message and the consumers.

# 3

# The Impact of Intermedia and Newspaper Competition on Advertising

A truism of the media industry is that newspapers face increasingly complex and competitive markets for advertising. The growth of other media during the past few decades has been remarkable. The number of radio stations in the United States almost doubled between 1970 and 1996, and the number of television stations increased from 872 in 19703 to 1,576 in 1998. Daily newspapers' share of total advertising revenues declined from 26.4 per cent in 1986 to 22.5 per cent only ten years later.

As the number of media outlets increases, there is a potential for advertising in a greater number of outlets and a greater diversity of media. However, the degree and nature of intermedia advertising competition's impact on newspapers remain unclear. On the one hand, newspaper managers argue they face an extremely competitive advertising market where they fight with other media to survive. Media economics scholars, on the other hand, maintain that the print and electronic media are not good substitutes for all types of advertising.

The nature of intermedia competition with newspapers has gained importance as the newspaper industry becomes more concentrated. The 1990s has seen an increase in groups buying independent newspapers and other groups. One force behind this concentration process is the practice of clustering, a business strategy in which a group buys several newspapers in close proximity. Clustering allows a group to share printing and distribution costs and to provide regional advertising. Although clustering makes good business sense, there is some evidence that it can reduce competition for readers, which in turn can affect newsrooms budgets" and news coverage.

However, the potential impact of group clustering on regional competition has led to little action by the Justice Department with one exception. Observers have suggested that the lack of antitrust activity reflects the recognition that newspapers compete with a variety of media for advertising. However, this assumption has received little empirical testing. This study examines this assumption and the nature and degree of intermedia competition for newspapers by using a convenience sample of forty daily newspapers. More specifically, it explores the connection between the availability of other media outlets in a county and number of advertising lines in the daily newspapers.

Competition occurs among products when buyers are willing to substitute these products for each other. A standard way of defining the degree of substitutability is price cross-elasticity of demand, which is the change in demand for a product when the price of a substitute changes. The greater the change (elasticity), the better substitutes the products are for each other. Of course, demand also can be elastic with respect to other variables, such as quality. The degree of substitutability reflects the similarity of products. In perfect competition markets, products are homogeneous and, therefore, perfect substitutes. However, in monopolistic competitive markets, products are heterogeneous to varying degrees and substitutability varies.

Monopolistic competition was developed as a reaction to the limitations of monopoly and perfect competition theories because most markets do not fit the assumptions of these types of theories.

Chamberlin's theory states that in monopolistic competitive markets, products compete through advertising and the nature of the products, as well as price, which is the primary variable affecting demand in perfectly competitive markets. Chamberlin concludes that in markets with heterogeneous products, firms tend to develop market segments through advertising and product characteristics in which they have monopoly power. This allows firms to increase prices above perfectly competitive levels. However, these segments are not perfectly monopolistic either because higher prices will push people toward imperfect but acceptable substitutes, or higher prices can induce other marginally competitive firms to produce products more like the one that dominates a market segment.

Lacy and Simon state that advertising markets, when defined as all media, are monopolisticly competitive rather than perfectly competitive because print and broadcast by their nature result in a degree of product differentiation. Although broadcast and print advertising can be substituted for one another, the degree of substitutability varies with the function and nature of the advertising. According to Picard, different media are not completely interchangeable for advertisers because they provide different types of access to audiences. Their audiences vary in how they use the medium and in the nature of the audiences delivered to the advertisers.

Busterna goes even further, saying,"To some degree, broadcast stations also compete with daily newspapers for advertising dollars. In practice, however, most advertisers do not see the different media types as good substitutes for each other." Niche theory has been applied to media competition for advertising. This theory, however, has not been used to compare pairs of media in local markets.

In summary, theory about newspaper competition does not support a strong assumption that other media are always good substitutes for newspaper advertising in all markets. Theory suggests that the degree of substitutability of television and radio for newspapers varies by type of advertising and possibly by market. However, theory should be tested empirically.

If broadcast advertising is an acceptable substitute for newspaper advertising, all other factors being equal, theory suggests two results:

- The amount of advertising in a newspaper would be lower as the number of media outlets in a market increases, and
- Newspaper advertising prices would be lower with more non-newspaper media in the market, but they would not be as low as with more direct newspaper competition.

The first occurs because acceptable substitutes will siphon off some advertising revenue from newspapers, reducing linage, and the second occurs because, if newspapers do not lower ad prices, advertisers will move some advertising dollars to lowercost-per-thousand broadcasting.

Previous research into competition and advertising has concentrated on advertising price as the dependent variable while ignoring the impact of competition on linage. The former is more problematic because the price a newspaper charges for ad space represents a variety of variables besides demand. Production costs, the skills of sales personnel, and managers' perceptions of demand, as well as competition, can play a role in advertising prices. Prices are decisions made by managers that reflect perceptions of the marketplace, whereas linage purchases represent direct decisions by advertisers. This implies that level of newspaper linage is a good measure for studying advertising competition in local markets.

Theory suggests that non-print forms of advertising are imperfect substitutes for newspapers advertising. However, being an acceptable substitute for another product is a matter of degree. Imperfect substitutes can result in competition if enough buyers accept them as substitutes. The nature of newspaper and intermedia advertising competition has been examined empirically in a variety of ways.

## NEWSPAPER COMPETITION AND ADVERTISING

A series of studies during the 1960s and 1970s examined intracity daily newspaper and intermedia advertising competition with mixed results. The studies differed in their dependent variables (line rate versus cost-per-thousand), and the independent variable for competition was often a dummy variable, which may be an inadequate measure for competition. Overall, studies that used the costper-thousand rate as the dependent variable found increased competition was related to price decreases.

A similar pattern for use of open-line and cost-per-thousand rates was uncovered with weekly competition. Blankenburg concluded that competition had no relationship with the open line rate in Wisconsin weeklies.

Lacy and Dravis replicated and extended the study with Michigan weeklies and found that when cost-per-thousand was used as the dependent variable, a relationship was discovered. Matthews found that some ad prices in competitive markets were lower than those in monopoly markets. In a further test, she noted that the results were the same regardless of whether the open line rate or average line rate was used.

## BROADCAST COMPETITION AND ADVERTISING

Just as with intracity newspaper advertising competition, most studies of intermedia competition have looked at the impact on advertising rates. A series of studies examining the relationship between newspaper and television joint ownership found that when cost-per-thousand was used, joint ownership resulted in higher rates. Ferguson examined 815 newspapers and found markets with more radio and television stations had lower national and run-of-the-paper (ROP) cost-per-thousand. He also concluded that cross-ownership of radio and newspapers did not affect the cost-per-thousand rate, but cross-ownership between television and newspapers did.

Busterna, however, examined the elasticity of demand for daily national advertising from 1971 to 1981 and reported no significant relationship between ad prices and other media. He did not use the cost-per-thousand rate.

Looking at intermedia competition for advertising in six small daily markets, Smith concluded that advertisers were largely uninformed about the advertising conditions in their particular markets, but that the majority of advertisers believed the small dailies competed with other media for advertising dollars. However, many advertisers were unable to say which media choices were best for which purposes or the relative cost-per-thousand rate for the available and competing media. This is consistent with Sentman's study that found heavy newspaper advertisers in three metropolitan markets did not know the duplication in consumers among media, particularly for newspapers, nor were they certain which of the media they used was best for reaching their own target audiences in the most cost efficient manner.

The study also found that given a change in availability of newspaper outlets in a metropolitan market, the majority of advertisers would switch the allocation for advertising to other print media (suburban or a surviving daily). Fewer than 20 per cent of those surveyed stated they would move the money to radio, television, or direct mail.

## ADVERTISERS' PERCEPTIONS AND COMPETITION

A few studies have examined factors affecting advertiser satisfaction. Otnes and Faber examined 200 retailers across five business categories to discern reasons for media choices among local advertising options. They concluded that both product category and advertising budget were significant predictors in this type of decision. A study by Frederick-Collins extended the

Otnes and Faber work by asking about the service component and quality of the relationship with sales representatives. She found that a relationship with the sales representative was a factor in making decisions. Perhaps more importantly, this study considered value a factor in the relationship between price and effectiveness and stated that the advertiser is interested in achieving goals in a cost-effective method. This suggests that advertisers are more interested in the cost-per-thousand rate than absolute rates.

A similar result was found by Cameron, Nowak, and Krugman, who looked at two mid-sized cities and concluded that the ability to reach target audiences and cost effectiveness were important factors in placing advertising. Shaver, in a study of advertiser perceptions in a metropolitan area, found that advertisers ranked cost effectiveness above actual cost as a means of making advertising choices among available media. Advertisers defined this effectiveness as a combination of actual cost and perceived efficiency in reaching the desired target audience.

Smith studied advertisers in six smaller cities and concluded:"The vast majority of local decision makers are not sophisticated when it comes to advertising. They select media based on a diverse number of factors, with return (italics in original) being the factor cited most frequently in this study." The Shaver and Smith studies taken together suggest that advertisers vary greatly as to the factors that affect their buying decision.

## HYPOTHESES

Theory and research suggest that electronic media are at least imperfect substitutes for daily newspapers in some markets, but that competition will not have as great an impact as competition among newspapers themselves. The strength of the relationship between competition and advertiser behaviors can vary from market to market, and advertisers may lack knowledge as to the relative price and effectiveness of advertising in the various media.

Missing from the literature is evidence that intermedia competition affects the distribution of advertising space and time among media outlets in local markets. If advertisers substitute broadcast media for newspapers, it would seem that an increase in the number of broadcast outlets would increase the likelihood that advertisers would reallocate their advertising dollars away from newspapers toward these increased broadcast outlets. Economic theory predicts that increased sellers of advertising space and time will result in lower prices, and lower prices result in lower cost-per-thousand.

Chamberlin said lower prices can result in movement of dollars from higher price sellers to lower price sellers when buyers perceive the two products as being acceptable substitutes.

On the basis of this reasoning, this study tests the following hypotheses:

- *Hl:* As the number of TV stations per 1,000 households in a daily's market increases, total ad lines will decrease.

- *H2:* As the number of TV stations per 1,000 households in a daily's market increases, run-of-the-paper ad lines will decrease.
  If television is considered a substitute for dailies by a sufficient number of advertisers, an increase in the number of outlets in a market would likely result in the movement of advertising dollars from newspapers to television.
- *H3:* As the number of radio stations per 1,000 households in a daily's market increases, the daily's total ad lines will decrease.
- *H4:* As the number of radio stations per 1,000 households in a daily's market increases, the daily's run-of-the-paper ad lines will decrease.
  The same logic underlying Hl and H2 applies here. Increases in substitutable outlets should lead to a decline in ad linage at newspapers.
- *H5:* As the penetration of other dailies in a daily's market increases, the daily's total ad lines will decrease.
- *H6:* As the penetration of other dailies in a daily's market increases, the daily's run-of-the-paper ad lines will decrease.
  As other dailies in a market gain penetration, they will become better substitutes for a competing newspaper. This reflects the role of penetration as a measure of advertising quality at a newspaper.
- *H7:* As the penetration of weeklies in a daily's market increases, the daily's total ad lines will decrease.
- *H8:* As the penetration of weeklies in a daily's market increases, the daily's run-of-the-paper lines will decrease.

Theory and research suggest that one daily is the best substitute for another daily from an advertiser's perspective. However, one study found a negative relationship exists between weekly and daily penetration within a county. This indicates that these two forms of newspapers are substitutes for readers in some markets, so the relationship in the advertising market should be tested. Although the hypotheses are written as bivariate relationships, each assumes that the relationship will hold even after controlling for other independent variables. Multiple regression is used to provide this control.

## METHOD

Lack of access to advertising linage data has always created problems in studying the impact of competition on ad lines. Most newspapers do not make this information available, which explains the lack of published research using this dependent variable. However, the compilation of linage given voluntarily to Editor & Publisher, the source of data for this study, is available.

Data were taken from 40 newspapers that reported their advertising linage in Editor & Publisher during 1994. They represent a wide range of geographic distribution, ownership patterns, and circulation size. This year was chosen because it was the latest year for which all the other desired market statistics were available. The number of run-of-the-paper (ROP) ad lines was selected as one dependent variable because local retail ads make up more than half of a newspaper's advertising. Total ad lines were selected as a dependent variable because that figure represents the newspaper's overall success at selling advertising. Other forms of advertising lines, inserts and classified ad lines, were not studied separately (but they were part of total ads) because these data were missing for many cases.

This study controlled for advertising price by using the open-line, cost-per-thousand rate. The cost-per-thousand was calculated using ABC circulation figures and open line rate reported in the Editor & Publisher International Year Book. It may appear that using the open rate as a price control for total ad lines is problematic because inserts and classified advertising have different prices. The researchers could think of no way to create a combined price for all forms of advertising.

However, using the open rate for all hypotheses was acceptable because the Pearson's product moment correlation between the open line rate and classified rates equaled. and the Pearson's r between the open line rate and insert rates equaled. These high correlations suggest that the measurement error created by using the open line rate would not be large enough to alter the conclusions. Measures for radio and television competition were based on the number of stations per 1,000 households. Such a measure was used because of the strong correlation between market population and number of radio and television stations. Weekly and daily newspaper competition was measured by using the penetration of all other dailies and all weeklies in the county in which a daily was located. Penetration levels came from Circulation.

The penetration of competing newspapers as a competition measure rests on the assumption that an increase in a competitors' penetration makes them better substitutes for the daily being studied. Newspapers vary in their geographic markets, and no one political boundary will describe all accurately. However, most dailies aim to circulate widely in their county, and the county has been used in previous studies as a geographic basis for defining the market. Using the county also allowed the collection of data from a variety of sources for the same geographic area. Classical economic theory states that income plays a role in demand. The appropriate measure of income would be the advertising budgets for all firms in a daily's market that advertise.

However, because these data are proprietary and unavailable, this study used the effective buying income (EBI) of the county. The assumption is that business (advertiser) revenue is related to the income of consumers in a market, and that advertising expenditures are related to business revenues.

The total local ROP lines and all advertising total lines for 1994 were used to measure the dependent variable, in twelve months from 19 March 1994 to 18 February 1995. These editions yielded 50 newspapers.

However, because of missing data, the actual number of papers used in the total linage regression was 40, and the number used in the ROP analysis was 31. These dailies are not a random sample. Therefore, no sampling error is present and statistical significance was not used to interpret the regression analysis. The test for hypothesis support was a part correlation squared of.04 or higher. This indicates that 4% of the variance in the dependent variable is shared with an independent variable. This cut-off point for degree of relationship is arbitrary, but it was selected because it represents a part correlation of.16 or higher rather than the.09 associated with a part correlation squared of.03.

A higher standard would increase the chance of type II error, which should be avoided at this stage of research because this is an under-researched topic. Hierarchical multiple regression was used, and the hypotheses were evaluated using beta weights, change in R-square and regression coefficients. The data were tested to see if they fit the assumptions of regression analysis. One or two outliers (defined as plus or minus three standard deviations from the mean) were found with cost-per-thousand, EBI, radio stations per 1,000 households, total ROP lines, and TV stations per 1,000 households. The outliers were reassigned the value of three standard deviations from the mean, which reduces the extreme impact of the outlier and retains the case.

The standardized residuals were plotted against the standardized predicted values to see if the linearity assumption was violated. The distribution of the cases was random, which indicates the assumption of linearity was appropriate. Residuals were examined for violation of homoscedasticity. Only minor violations of normality were found, which most likely reflect the small size of the sample. Also, no evidence of multicollinearity was found. The variable to case ratio for the total ad linage was 1 to 6.66 and 1 to 5 for ROP linage. While this is below the optimal ratio, the ratio here is acceptable in exploratory studies such as this.

## RESULTS

The most notable observation about the data, and therefore the 40 markets, is the great variability. The standard deviations for all variables are high relative to the means. For three variables--penetration of dailies in the county, television stations per 1,000 households, and effective buying income--the standard deviations are actually larger than the means. This large variation reflects two characteristics of the data. First, the markets vary greatly in size; and second, the sample is not large enough to reduce the impact of this large range.

H1 states that as the number of TV stations per 1,000 households increases, the total ad lines will decrease. It is supported. The regression estimated that for every additional television station per thousand households the daily loses 279,810 ad lines a year. This variable had a part correlation squared of.087, which exceeded the.04 cut-off point. Similarly, the daily loses 454,257 ad lines for each radio station per 1,000 households. This variable had a part correlation squared of.064, which indicates H3 is supported.

H5 states that as the penetration of other dailies increases, the total ad lines will decrease. This hypothesis is supported. For each increase of 1% penetration by other dailies, a daily loses 22,241 ad lines per year. The part correlation squared for this relationship is.214, which exceeds the.04 cut-off point. H7, which states that daily ad lines are negatively related to the penetration of weeklies, was not supported. The part correlation squared was.003, and the daily loses only 5,893 lines a year for each percentage point increase in weekly penetration.

An interesting phenomenon is the wide variation among the cases in all four measures of competition. The standard error of the television regression coefficient is 7.8 times larger than the regression coefficient, while the standard error of the radio coefficient is 1.68 times the regression coefficient. The standard error of the weekly penetration coefficient is almost three times the coefficient, and the standard error of the daily penetration coefficient is only slightly smaller than the coefficient itself.

The wide variation in the impact of weekly penetration on daily ad lines may explain why H7 was not supported. Had the standard error been much smaller for weekly penetration, the relationship identified by the equation would have been stronger. The great variation in cases, which represents the small sample and the great variation among cases, resulted in small beta weights because standardization involves dividing values by the standard error; large standard error, relative to a coefficient, results in small beta weights. This is why the part correlation squared was used to evaluate the hypotheses. The two control variables, cost-per-thousand households and effective buying income, accounted for 18.9% of the variation in total ad lines. Total variance accounted for by all variables equaled 55.8%.

Data address the even numbered hypotheses, which concern the relationship of competition with lines of run-of-the-paper advertising. The total variance accounted for in the regression equation is higher than that accounted for by the regression equation, but at least part of this reflects the decreased number of cases. The adjusted R-squared is.717, compared to the reported R-squared of.774. H2 states that as the number of TV stations per 1,000 households increases, the number of ROP lines will decrease. This hypothesis is supported. The part correlation squared for this variable equals.224, which indicates 22.4% of variance in ROP lines is associated with TV stations per 1,000 households. For each increase of one TV station per 1,000 households, the daily lost 46,000 ROP lines. H4 states that as the number of radio stations per 1,000 households increases, the number of ROP lines will decrease. The part correlation squared equals.158, which exceeds the cut-off point. The equation indicates that for each increase in one radio station per

1,000, the daily lost 165,070 ROP lines. H6 states that an increase in the penetration of other dailies will be negatively related to the number of ROP lines. This hypothesis is supported. The part correlation squared of.058 exceeds the cut off. For each increase of one percentage point of penetration of other dailies, the daily lost 4,972 ROP lines.

H8 states that as the penetration of weeklies increases, the ROP lines will decrease. This hypothesis was not supported. Even though the relationship was negative, the part correlation squared only equaled.011, which did not exceed the cut-off point. The same wide ranging variation among the independent variables found with total ad lines also was present for ROP lines. The standard error of coefficients was much greater than the coefficient for TV stations per 1,000 households, radio stations per 1,000 households, and weeklies' penetration. The standard error of the coefficient for dailies' penetration was only slightly less than the coefficient itself.

Effective buying power explained a large amount of the variation in ROP advertising, accounting for 32.7% of the variation. This is even higher than the percentage for total ad lines. The purpose of this study was to test whether radio and television are acceptable substitutes for people and organizations seeking to advertise in newspapers. The data in this limited sample reveal a notable negative relationship between number of broadcast outlets and lines of newspaper advertising. Because this is consistent with economic theory and because other potential explanatory variables have been controlled for, a logical inference is that at least some advertisers are substituting advertisements on television and radio for ROP newspaper advertising in at least some markets. However, other dailies continue to be much better substitutes for total ad lines.

This probably reflects the inclusion of classified and inserts advertising in these figures. Television and radio currently are not good substitutes for these types of advertising. These results are consistent with traditional economic theory and with statements by Picards and Lacy and Simon. In addition, they are consistent with research by Ferguson that radio and TV competition are negatively related to the ROP cost-per-thousand rate. It appears the intermedia advertising market is monopolistic competitive with some media being better at some types of advertising than others. The markets used here also tend to vary greatly in the level of substitution. This variation is consistent with the existing body of literature that shows advertisers tend to be uninformed about advertising conditions in their markets and the importance of sales representatives in selling advertising. The conclusions must be tempered by the limitations of this study. The sample was small and not representative of anything other than the dailies examined. In addition, the mean level of penetration by competing dailies and weeklies was low on average. A sample with more extensive penetration by dailies and weeklies might show a stronger impact on print competition on ROP lines. It may be that TV and radio become attractive ROP substitutes when no other newspaper has enough household penetration in the county to act as an acceptable substitute. However, the consistency of these results with theory and research and the strength of the relationships suggest that these findings should be pursued with replications. Furthermore, the use of ad lines instead of price to study competition looks promising because it sidesteps the argument about whether to measure the dependent variable price as a set rate or as the cost-per-thousand rate. Future studies should include larger samples, and the role of noneconomic variables, such as advertisers' knowledge of the advertising market and the role of sales representative, should be incorporated into studies of advertising competition. The development of online advertising also needs inclusion in the future. Electronic classified advertising and online merchandising could offer better substitutes for some forms of newspaper advertising than currently exist.

This study holds policy implications as well. There is some justification for assuming daily newspapers compete with other media for advertising, but that level of competition varies by type of advertising and from market to market. Because one justification for lack of antitrust actions in recent newspaper group acquisitions is that newspapers compete with other media, these results have interesting implications. The variations in television's and radio's impact on daily linage found here suggest the Justice Department cannot assume that intermedia competition in every market reduces a daily's monopoly power in all advertising submarkets. This finding should be pursued as newspaper companies increasingly reduce competition through clustering. The Justice Department should expect adequate evidence from ownership that acquisition of newspapers to promote clustering will not have anticompetitive effects in the advertising market as well as in the circulation market. The need to study the impact of clustering is urgent because the pace of newspaper groups acquiring other groups and single newspapers is expected to continue if not increase61 and the recreating of competition after it disappears is extremely difficult.

# 4

# Effects of Online Advertising on Readers' Perceptions

Individuals' growing reliance on Web-based information exchange leaves little doubt as to the importance of the Internet as a source of news information. However, online news sources have been criticized for their commercialization. Given the increase in advertising on the Web, how might the combined presentation of news and advertising affect people's perceptions? In research and commentary on the impact of advertising on perceptions of news, the greatest amount of critical attention has been directed toward television.

For example, Postman argued that the banality of advertising embedded in television news programs undermines the perceived credibility and importance of serious social and political news stories being reported. In other words, commercials may make serious matters appear trivial. Additionally, other researchers have suggested that advertising may intensify the perceived importance of trivial or soft news.

Specifically, Biocca et al. conducted an experiment to examine Postman's assertions, and while the inclusion of advertising in news programming had little effect on perceived importance in general, the inclusion of humorous or silly advertising did result in increased perceived importance of soft news stories. One interpretation of Biocca et al.'s failure to find an advertising effect on perceived importance of news in general or hard news specifically may simply be that television viewers have become adept at ignoring or discounting advertising interruptions while viewing television news. From this perspective, greater exposure to television news should lead to enhanced skills in this regard and should lead to diminished effects of advertising on news perceptions. On the other hand, an alternative interpretation may relate to the fact that news content is typically presented separately from commercial messages, thereby creating a temporal and perhaps psychological distance between news content and advertising. In contrast, other media such as the Internet tend to present advertising and news simultaneously, with advertisements intermingled with, obscuring, and sometimes even blocking the viewing of news content. As a result, the adverse effects of advertising on viewers' news perceptions may be enhanced. The purpose of this study is to examine the effects of advertising on viewers' perceptions of news stories in the context of an online news site.

## CONTEXTUAL RELEVANCE AND COGNITIVE INTERFERENCE

Research exploring the reciprocal influences of news and advertising has centered primarily on the effects of media context (i.e., the programming or editorial environment in which an advertisement is embedded) on processing or evaluations of advertising.

In general, this research suggests that ads surrounded by media content that has irrelevant or inconsistent tones and manners can evoke less favorable perceptions or attitudes than can ads surrounded by media content that is relevant. In fact, research has generally found that irrelevant information results in less favorable attitudes than does relevant information, and that consumers' ability to integrate relevant information with ease can result in favorable attitude and behavioral changes.

However, as Stewart and Ward point out, it is conceivable to expect that context effects, in addition to affecting viewers' perceptions or attitudes about advertising, also play a similar role in affecting viewers' perceptions or attitudes about media content that surrounds the ads. That is, in the context of an online news page, a news story surrounded by advertising that is irrelevant or inconsistent in terms of tone and manner should be perceived less favorably than a news story surrounded by advertising that is relevant or that is not associated with advertising at all. For example, exposure to a humorous or silly ad while reading a hard news story dealing with a serious topic may harm perceived news value or credibility of the news.

What cognitive mechanisms are involved in the effects (on news perceptions) of contextual irrelevance between news stories and advertisements? Some researchers have suggested that news processing may be interfered with by ads that prime inappropriate cognitive strategies, moods, and schemas. For example, Chaudhuri and Buck explored how different advertising strategies evoke different cognitive responses, and reported that product information strategies generate analytic cognition (e.g., thinking of differences between the brands and its competitors) and discourage affective cognition (e.g., feeling happy or sad), whereas mood arousal strategies generate affective cognition and discourage analytic cognition.

Gunther also pointed out that viewers who possess or use the wrong schema for processing news, or are not familiar with the appropriate schema, fail to understand information, allocate less attention, and remember less news information. It might be reasonable to expect that if advertising primes cognitive strategies, moods, or schemas that are inappropriate for news processing, perceptions of the news content itself may be adversely affected.

For example, if serious news stories, such as one about a deadly fire that has killed children, are being reported in an online news page where silly and jovial advertisements are being advertised, perceived newsworthiness or quality of the stories may be negatively affected by those ads, because moods or schemas to process those serious news stories may be interrupted by moods and schemas introduced by the funny ads.

With these perceptual mechanisms in mind, it is also important to consider how advertising is presented in different media. In television, commercials are presented sequentially, not simultaneously, with essentially no overlap between advertising and news content. In newspapers, advertising is often presented on the same page (or nearby pages) as news content, but ads are rarely embedded within the news stories themselves.

Consequently, when watching television or reading a newspaper, news users could more easily (and intentionally) ignore ads and pay attention to news stories because advertisements are typically easily distinguishable from and separated from news stories. However, in typical online news sites, the physical distance between news stories and ads is more intermingled. That is, on the Internet, one can hardly expect to read news stories without being interrupted by ads because there are no areas of Websites that are predictably devoid of advertising content.

In addition, online advertisements are often more distracting than in traditional media, employing colour, animation, and pop-up techniques. As a consequence, effects of advertising on news perceptions may be particularly likely in an online context. The purpose of the present study is to explore the effects of advertising on perceptions of hard news (i.e., evaluation of newsworthiness or credibility of hard news stories). Specifically, based on prior research findings concerning contextual relevance and the processing of news information, the following hypothesis was examined:

*H*1: Online news readers exposed to silly ads will tend to evaluate hard news stories more negatively than will online news readers exposed to no ads or to serious ads. If we assume that exposure to a humorous or silly ad in the context of a hard news story may harm perceived news value or perceived credibility of the news, what can we assume with regard to soft news stories? We sought to replicate Biocca et al.'s finding that humorous or silly ads can also impact perceptions of soft news stories, leading to perceptions of increased importance. Thus:

*H*2: Online news readers exposed to silly ads will tend to evaluate soft news stories more positively than will online news readers exposed to no ads or to serious ads. Internet User Experience. When we consider the characteristics of the Web, user experience is clearly an important factor. For example, Benway and Lane suggested that expert users have a tendency to avoid banner ads when they browse the Internet. Similarly, Dreze and Hussherr employed an eye-tracking device to examine users' attention levels, finding that expert users paid significantly less attention to banner ads and remembered fewer brands displayed in banners than did novices. These studies are consistent with additional research reporting a negative relationship between user experience and inclination to click on banner ads.

In sum, research generally suggests that experienced Internet users are more adept than are light users at avoiding online advertising, and may consequently be less likely to be influenced. Therefore, we may tentatively assume that effects of online advertising on news perceptions may be more pronounced among light than among heavy Internet users:

*H*3: Ad inclusion will have more salient effects on online news perceptions among light Internet users than among heavy Internet users. Perceptions of Online Advertising. News and advertising likely have reciprocal effects as many previous studies have shown. That is, the perceptions of online ads could vary as a function not only of factors such as the seriousness of ads and Internet use, but also as a function of story type (hard news versus soft news). Therefore, this study examined the following research question:

*RQ*1: How do ad perceptions vary as a function of ad type, Internet use, and story type?

*Method*: Participants. Two hundred and sixty-three undergraduate students taking communication courses at a large Northeastern university participated in the study. All participants were juniors or seniors with a median age of 21. Participants were awarded a nominal amount of extra credit in exchange for their participation. Responses from three participants were discarded due to incomplete answers. As a result, responses from 260 participants were analysed.

Experimental Design and Procedure. A 2 (Story Type: Hard News, Soft News) × 3 (Seriousness of Ad: No Advertisement, Silly Advertisement, Serious Advertisement) x 2 (Internet Use) between-subjects experiment design was employed in which Internet Use was measured and all other factors were manipulated.

In addition to Story Type, Seriousness of Ad, and Internet Use, this study also considered another factor, Ad Format (banner versus pop-up). Among conditions with ads present, Seriousness of Ad (silly versus serious) and Ad Format (banner versus pop-up) were counterbalanced.

All stimulus presentation and data collection was conducted via the Web, with a JavaScript employed to randomly assign participants to experimental conditions.13 To maximize external validity, all procedures were conducted outside of the laboratory. Participants were allowed to participate in the study at any time and in any location during the course of a one-week time period. During the week, participants were sent an e-mail explaining the study and providing them with a URL that directed them to the study site where further instructions were provided, the news stories were presented, and questionnaire data were collected.

Each participant was presented with three news articles to read, each on consecutive pages. Each news story was accompanied by a silly advertisement (either pop-up or banner), a serious advertisement (either pop-up or banner), or no advertisement.

Among the conditions with ads present, participants were exposed to just one ad; the same ad was shown during all three stories. For example, a participant assigned to the hard news with pop-up, serious ad condition was exposed to an identical pop-up, serious ad three times while reading three different hard news stories. Subsequently, participants proceeded to the questionnaire page where they reported their overall perceptions of the three news stories, their perceptions of the advertisements, and their typical Internet use. Participants were divided into groups of heavy or light Internet use on the basis of two measures: years of using the Internet and daily Internet use hours. Standardized scores for each of these two measures were first calculated, and the average of these two z-scores was then computed. Respondents with mean z-scores of more than or equal to 0 were coded as heavy Internet users, with others coded as light Internet users. Independent-sample t-tests revealed that there were significant differences between light and heavy Internet users both in the average years of using the Internet.

## STIMULUS MATERIALS

A pretest was conducted to determine which news articles to use for this study. Twelve news articles from various online news sites were used in the pretest. Forty-seven undergraduate students rated the news articles using a 7-point scale anchored between 1 (Consider as soft news) and 7 (Consider as hard news). To control for the effects of differing articles in each story type condition, three soft and three hard news stories were used for this experiment. In the hard news condition, topics included a deadly fire, an international child pornography case, and Gulf War veterans' complaints of dizziness; in the soft news condition, topics included an annual international whistlers convention, professional Etch-a-Sketch artists, and a dog casting call by a theater. A paired t-test of the average score across the three soft news and the three hard news stories selected in the pretest revealed that participants perceived significant differences between soft news stories and hard news stories. To control for order effects, the order of the news stories was varied within each condition. Thus, three different orders of the soft news stories and three different orders of the hard news stories were created such that equivalent numbers of participants read each order.

To determine which ads to use for this study, 20 banner ads from various online news sites were also pretested using two semantic differential scales anchored between 1 (Silly) and 7 (Serious) and between 1 (Boring) and 7 (Interesting). Based on the mean scores, two ads were selected to represent"silly advertisements," and two ads were selected to represent"serious advertisements," in such a way that the two ad types maximized differences in perceived seriousness, but minimized differences in perceived interest.

Two different ads were used to represent silly and serious advertisements to reduce problems associated with idiosyncratic effects due to a specific ad. The brands used in the silly ad condition were an online game company and an online sweepstake company, and the brands used in the serious ad condition were an e-service company and an online health (fitness) service company. All ads selected for this study used animated GIF images with multiple image frames. The overall tone of the silly ads was light and bouncy. For example, in the ad for the online sweepstake company, frames displayed texts such as"Have fun" and"Win Prizes," and the font was designed so that it looked like handwriting. In contrast, the overall tone of the serious ads was straightforward and nonhumorous. For example, in the ad for the online health (fitness) service company, frames displayed texts such as "Are you overweight?" and"Try our body mass calculator" by turns. Paired t-tests between the average seriousness scores of the two silly ads selected versus the two serious ads selected revealed that the silly ads were perceived as significantly less serious than the serious ads. Importantly, there was no significant difference in Boring/Interesting ratings between silly ads and serious ads, suggesting that any differences obtained between the two ad types reflect differences in seriousness rather than in interest.

The stimulus Website was designed to look like a typical online news site. To rule out possible confounds, a bogus masthead was created, and dates and reporter names were not included in the stories. At the bottom of each online news story, a link would take participants to the next news article. Pop-up ads were developed, which were identical to banner ads selected by the pretest. The size of all the ads was 300 x 250 pixels. For conditions with pop-up ads present, each Web page was designed in such a way that a pop-up ad appeared over the text of a news story, and participants could close the pop-up ad window by clicking on the"close" (×) button at the top right of the pop-up ad window to start reading the news article of the Web page. For conditions with banner ads present, a banner ad appeared within the frame where the text of the news article was presented.

## DEPENDENT MEASURES

Twelve news perception items were employed in this study: Important, Newsworthy, Serious, Valuable, Trustworthy, Credible, Believable, Accurate, Objective, Lively, Entertaining, and Interesting. These items were extracted from Sundar's news evaluation items and modified to fit the purposes of the present study.

## NEWS PERCEPTIONS

News perception items were subjected to an exploratory principal components analysis with varimax rotation. An examination of factor loadings, eigenvalues greater than one, and the scree plot suggested three factors: news value, news credibility, and news entertainment. News value was composed of four items (important, news worthy, serious, and valuable; Cronbach's alpha =.91); news credibility was composed of five items (trustworthy, credible, believable, accurate, and objective; alpha =.77); and news entertainment was composed of three items (lively, entertaining, and interesting; alpha =.82). Scales for each of three factors were computed by averaging the scores of the items that loaded highly on a given factor. Consequently, scores could range from 1 to 7.

To examine how the seriousness of advertising (silly versus serious) affected perceptions of the news stories, a 2 (Story Type) × 3 (Seriousness of Ad) × 2 (Internet Use) general linear multivariate analysis of variance (MANOVA) was employed. This analysis revealed a significant multivariate main effect for story type. An examination of the univariate results showed significant main effects of story type on each of the three perception measures. Participants rated the hard news stories higher on news value and credibility than the soft news stories, but rated the soft news stories higher on entertainment value than the hard news stories.

Among these participants, the inclusion of silly ads resulted in the lowest news value scores, with no ads or serious ads receiving equal ratings. Similar patterns were observed for ratings of credibility, though no pairwise differences in means were detected.

To examine how the presence of advertising per se affected perceptions of the news stories, regardless of the seriousness (silly or serious), a 2 (Story Type) × 2 (Presence of Ad) × 2 (Internet Use) general linear multivariate analysis of variance (MANOVA) was employed, with both the silly ad condition and the serious ad condition being collapsed. As with the previous analysis focusing on Seriousness of Ad, this analysis also revealed a significant multivariate Story Type × Presence of Ad × Internet Use interaction, with Wilks'.

An examination of the univariate results revealed significant interactions for both ratings of news value and credibility: for news value, and for credibility. The effect of Presence of Ad on perceived news value was evident only for the hard news condition among light Internet users. Specifically, among light Internet users, the presence of ads resulted in lower news value scores than no ads. Similar patterns were observed for ratings of credibility, though no pairwise differences in means were detected.

To summarize, H1 that explored the effects of silly ads on lower newsworthiness and quality evaluations of hard news stories obtained partial support, with the expected effects obtained for light Internet users only, whereas H2 that predicted the effects of silly ads on heightened newsworthiness and quality evaluations of soft news stories received no support in this study. Alternately, H3 that examined the effects of Internet experience on news perceptions obtained partial support, with the expected effects obtained only for hard news stories among light Internet users.

## AD PERCEPTIONS

Ad perception items were subjected to an exploratory principal components analysis with varimax rotation that yielded two factors: professionalism and inappropriateness. Professionalism was composed of three items, and inappropriateness was composed of three items.

This analysis revealed significant multivariate main effects for story type, seriousness of ad, and ad format. Among these participants, silly ads presented with soft news were rated as significantly more professional as were silly ads presented with hard news.

Do perceptions of online news stories vary as a function of the presence or seriousness of online advertising? Do the effects of online advertising on perceptions of news stories vary as a function of Internet use (light versus heavy)? Given the differences in both viewer experience and presentation styles between television news and online news, this study tried to explore Postman's arguments and to extend Biocca et al.'s research to the context of online news.

Although Biocca et al. failed to show unambiguous effects of television commercials on news perceptions, this study provided evidence for Postman's arguments in the context of online news. Advertising interruptions can have a negative impact on perceptions of news, though only for some users. Specifically, light Internet users exposed to ads (and particularly silly ads) tended to perceive hard news stories as less newsworthy.

Additionally, among light Internet users, advertisements embedded in hard news stories were perceived as significantly less professional as were advertisements embedded in soft news stories.

The findings have practical implications for both news providers and advertisers. Insofar as advertising may lead to inappropriate characterizations of serious or hard news content, online newspapers may be well advised to place advertisements in separate sections than those that feature important and serious news content. Similarly, insofar as silly ads are perceived as particularly inappropriate when paired with serious news, advertisers of products that depend on humorous strategies may opt to have their advertisements placed in news sections that feature soft news or other content that is of a less serious tone.

In addition, findings of this study may also raise concerns over how news stories are selected and covered in news organizations. If advertisers begin to recognize that silly or trivial ads are perceived more negatively when paired with serious or important news, greater pressure may be exerted on news agencies to include more soft news or human interest stories that are more amenable to advertisers' interests. As Gunter pointed out, although online news providers must produce attractive sites that will appeal as much to advertisers as to readers, this business strategy may lead to concern for the quality of online journalism.

The difference between light and heavy Internet users in avoiding advertising raises another concern. The fact that inexperienced Internet users are less adept at avoiding online advertising and more influenced by advertising in their perceptions of news stories than are experienced users may affect the future of the Internet as a news medium. That is, novice users' inability to ignore Internet advertising or their aggravation with commercialization may lead them to avoid the Internet for news information.

More important, though, the combination of advertising and news content on the Internet may have implications that go beyond just perceptions of news stories themselves. One concern is that the combination of online news and advertising may ultimately have effects on viewers' perceptions of issues. For example, if viewers perceive news stories as lacking news value when paired with silly online advertising, this may imply that the issues themselves are less important. Commercialization of the Internet may make the medium another culprit in trivializing important and serious information and discourse in society.

Despite general support for the hypothesized effects of advertising on news perceptions, there are several limitations that deserve consideration. First, this study did not consider source effects; i.e., the same fictitious Web news company and masthead were employed across experimental conditions. However, source-related variables (e.g., source credibility, source reputation, etc.) are obviously critical factors in message perceptions.

For example, research has shown that messages from high-credibility sources are generally more readily accepted by consumers and encourage greater attitude change than do messages from low-credibility sources. Consequently, future research that examines the effects of advertising on news perceptions could incorporate different sources as another variable.

Second, although the current study intended to explore perceived credibility of news stories as a function of the presence or seriousness of online advertising, it should be noted that perceived credibility of source may also vary as a function of online ads. For example, news readers exposed to unwanted, bothersome ads in a news site may evaluate the news site or news organization more negatively than do news readers who are not distracted by advertising. As such, future research might want to explore how various online ads affect the perceived credibility of the online news sites or organizations per se, in addition to perceived credibility of the stories themselves.

Third, this study employed college students as online news readers, separating them into high- and low-experience groups. However, college students likely have more expertise in Internet use than does the general population. Consequently, the low-experience group may differ from low-experience groups in the population of Internet users. Future research that employs noncollege samples may find more pronounced effects than those obtained here.

Finally, while the procedures used in the data-collection process maximized natural Internet-use settings by allowing users to participate in the setting and the time of their choosing, such a procedure clearly involves loss of some experimental control. That is, because researchers were not present with the participants during their viewing of the stimulus materials and their completion of the questionnaire, there is no way to discern the types of distractions that may or may not have been present.

Of course, although there are no a priori reasons to suspect that such distractions or other variations differed systematically between experimental conditions, such variations do introduce"noise" or additional error variance. Consequently, future research that examines similar effects in a more controlled environment may find stronger effects than those obtained here, though sacrificing the extent to which such effects can be generalized to more natural Internet-use situations.

In spite of these limitations, this study suggests that people's perception of online advertisements and news stories can have mutual impact on each other. Considering the rapid development in online advertising techniques, the reciprocal effects between advertising and news could open a new research avenue for both advertising and journalism. In particular, the time is ripe for journalism researchers to think seriously about the role of the Internet as a news medium, as we witness more and more that, in cyberspace, news information runs the risk of giving way to commercial messages and being packaged as entertainment.

# 5

# Audience Valuation and Minority Media

All advertiser-supported media Organizations operate in what is best described as a dual product marketplace. That is, media organizations produce one product--media content--that is either given away or sold in an effort to attract the second product--audiences. The attention of these audiences is then sold to advertisers seeking consumer exposure to commercial messages. The audience and content markets are tightly inter-related.

Success or failure in the"content market" is dependent upon success or failure in the"audience market" and vice versa. For this reason, policymaking involving the preservation and enhancement of competition and diversity of sources and content within the media industries has been--and continues to be--guided by research on how various market and institutional factors affect what media organizations are able to charge for their audiences.

One recent manifestation of this general concern with source and content diversity involves the viability of minority-owned media outlets. Per the directive of Congress, the Federal Communications Commission initiated an investigation into the barriers affecting minority-owned media outlets and the associated availability of minority-targeted programming. One of the barriers that may face minority-owned and -targeted media outlets is the possibility that minority audiences are valued at a much lower level by advertisers than majority audiences.

If this is the case, then minority-targeted media outlets face a substantial hurdle to remaining viable, as their ability to monetize their audience is compromised by lower advertiser valuations of their target audience. Lower audience values lead to lower revenues, lower levels of investment in programming, and an overall diminished ability for such outlets to compete and remain viable. In this way, the nature of the content market (in terms of the diversity of available sources and content offerings) is affected by the dynamics of the audience market. This study investigates the possibility of lower valuations of minority audiences through a quantitative analysis of the determinants of the value of commercial radio station audiences.

## MINORITY MEDIA AND DIVERSITY POLICY

The general policy imperative that drives concerns about the viability of minority-targeted media outlets stems from policymakers' long-standing commitment to diversity in the sources of information and the content that these sources provide. The diversity principle extends, in part, from the traditional democratic theory notion of a well-functioning"marketplace of ideas," in which citizens' abilities to participate effectively in the democratic process are contingent upon their abilities to consider a wide array of ideas and viewpoints from a wide array of sources. Diversity concerns have economic motivations, as well, since policymakers have sought to maximize the choices available to media consumers, thereby increasing their overall satisfaction.

The availability of content targeting minority interests has long been perceived as an important means of providing such content diversity. As the FCC (1948) noted as far back as 1948,"It has long been an established policy of... the Commission that the American system of broadcasting must serve significant minorities among our population". Research has demonstrated that minority audiences focus much of their media consumption on minority-targeted programming and outlets--and even increase their media consumption--when such services are available. This suggests that such content is highly valued by its target audience. It is important to emphasize that such diversity is seen as benefiting not only those who are targeted by minority-appeal content, but those whose tastes are"majoritarian" as well. For the"marketplace of ideas" to enhance citizen knowledge and the consideration of diverse viewpoints, citizens must be exposed to diverse points of view. It has been argued that this exposure diversity is particularly vital within the context of minority media so that greater cultural understanding and social cohesion can be achieved.

In an effort to identify the potential barriers facing minority-targeted media content, the FCC commissioned a study of the value of minority audiences to advertisers. The results of this study raised the possibility that advertisers may place significantly lower values on minority audiences and that these lower valuations may arise, in part, from advertiser misconceptions about minority spending patterns and product purchasing decisions. A recent NTIA survey raised similar concerns about the challenges associated with selling minority audiences to advertisers. The NTIA survey found that minority broadcast station owners cited obtaining advertising as their most common difficulty.

Lower advertiser valuations of minority audiences have significant implications for the viability of minority-targeted media outlets since the provision of minority-targeted content potentially involve financial challenges not faced if more mainstream content options are pursued. In such a situation, the diversity of content long valued by policymakers can be undermined by the valuations placed upon different segments of the media audience by advertisers.

## AUDIENCE VALUATION

Those minority audiences may be valued at a lower level than majority audiences may be a reflection of the basic economics of the audience marketplace. Advertisers typically value various audience segments differently, based upon their demographic characteristics. These demographic characteristics are presumed to correlate with purchasing power and purchasing behaviour. Thus, for instance, younger audience members generally are valued more highly than older audience members (i.e., 50+) due to factors such as their presumed greater inclination to switch brands, their higher levels of disposable income, and their lower levels of availability in the media audience.

Income is another important factor that guides advertiser valuations of media audiences. Some products and services are likely only to be purchased by consumers of certain income levels. For this reason, advertisers frequently will use income as a variable by which to screen out certain media outlets.

There are a number of possible reasons why ethnicity may factor into audience valuations as well. To a certain degree, ethnicity correlates with income. The median family income for Whites is almost $46,000, compared with approximately $30,000 for African Americans and $33,000 for Hispanics. Thus, advertisers seeking higher-income consumers may avoid minority-targeted media outlets.

It is also the case that African Americans and Hispanics consume significantly more television and radio on a weekly basis than Whites. The associated greater ease with which minorities can be reached by advertising messages may reduce their value to advertisers. Finally, some within the minority media community argue that advertisers form their valuations of minority audiences on the basis of severe misconceptions about minority product preferences and purchasing habits, which leads to a devaluing of minority audiences.

Regardless of the reason, there is a growing body of evidence that such"minority discounts" do exist. Ofori's analysis of commercial radio stations found that stations with formats that targeted minority audiences earned less for their audiences than stations with general interest formats. However, because this analysis focused only on formats, and not on audience composition, no strong conclusions regarding the relationship between audience composition and audience valuation could be drawn. An earlier analysis by Webster and Phalen found that greater proportions of non-Whites in a market had a significant negative relationship with the average cost of reaching 1,000 television viewers within a market. This analysis controlled for income variations across markets, suggesting that ethnicity was not simply a proxy for income.

The Webster and Phalen study focused on advertiser expenditures at the market level, leaving open the question of the existence of such effects at the outlet level. No research has, at this point, directly examined the relationship between actual demographic composition of media outlets' audiences and advertiser valuations of these audiences to see if there is a significant relationship between audience ethnicity and audience value. The study presented here attempts to fill this gap through an analysis of a sample of commercial radio stations.

It is important to emphasize that lower valuations of minority audiences may make economic sense from an advertiser's perspective. Regardless, such lower valuations may undermine the viability of minority-targeted media content. Such impediments to the economic viability of minority-targeted media could undermine the principles of source and content diversity that long have been objectives of electronic media regulation in the United States.

## METHODOLOGY

Given the nature of the policy issue, this analysis utilizes a dependent variable--the power ratio--that provides an indication of the extent to which an individual station is capable of monetizing its audience. Power ratios are computed by dividing a radio station's share of the total radio advertising expenditures in its market by its share of the total radio listening audience in that market. Thus, a power ratio greater than 1 suggests that a station is able to capture a share of advertising dollars that exceeds its share of the total audience. Such a station is"overselling" its audience.

A station with a power ratio of less than 1 is capturing a share of advertising dollars that is lower than its share of the listening audience. Such a station is"underselling" its audience. Because the power ratio controls for audience share, it provides a measure that is uniquely well suited to assessing the impact of audience composition on audience value.

Power ratio data were obtained from the 1999 Media Access Pro commercial database produced by BIA Research. For the regression analysis, the natural log of the power ratio was used as the dependent variable. This transformation was conducted in accordance with the conclusions of Bates' research into the various methods and models employed in the analysis of the value of broadcast audiences, which found models employing such a transformation to be both theoretically appropriate and to provide a better fit to the data than models without such a transformation.

An emphasis on audience composition has been maintained for the independent variables, as well. Station power ratios for 1999 are regressed against Fall 1999 Arbitron data on the demographic composition of individual stations' audiences. Thus, instead of incorporating each station's ratings or share points, or raw number of listeners for the different demographic groups listening to each station, this analysis employs per cent composition data.

Arbitron provides data on the percentage of each station's audience that is comprised of various demographic groups (according to age, gender, and ethnicity). Thus, for example, Station A's audience may be 40% African American, while Station B's audience may be 80% African American. Clearly, such figures provide no indication of which station has the larger number of African-American listeners. Station A may reach more African Americans than Station B if Station A's total audience is much larger.

The use of pure composition figures was deemed most appropriate given the nature of the dependent variable. Using raw numbers or rating/share points would not as effectively address the issue of the viability of minority-targeted media outlets, given that minority-targeted media outlets are not defined in terms of audience size, but in terms of the extent to which the composition of the outlets' audiences consists of minorities.

Arbitron breaks down each station's audience into men and women for seven age Categories. Arbitron provides data on the average quarter-hour percentage of each station's 6:00 a.m.-to-midnight audience that is comprised of each of these demographic categories. For the purposes of this analysis, these demographic categories were collapsed to produce two independent variables:

- The percentage of a station's audience comprised of men within the ages of 18 to 54,
- The percentage of a station's audience comprised of women within the ages of 18 to 54.

These two demographic categories roughly represent the audience groups with the highest demonstrated value to advertisers. Thus, it is presumed that there will be a positive relationship between MEN1854 and WOM1854 and station power ratios.

Broadcast band was included as a dummy variable to account for the likelihood that FM stations are able to charge more for their audiences than AM stations because of the better sound quality of FM signals. The station's average quarter-hour share (6:00 a.m. to midnight) of the listening audience (SHARE) also was included as an independent variable to account for the possibility of advertisers paying a premium for larger audiences, independent of the composition of those audiences.

Although this analysis focuses on the issue of audience composition, research has suggested that advertisers will pay more on a per audience member basis for larger audiences. Such patterns may be due to the efficiencies derived from engaging in fewer transactions in order to reach the desired number of consumers.

Or, this premium may be derived from the value advertisers associate with the likely greater reach of a single ad placement relative to two ad placements that achieve the same level of audience exposure. In the latter case, there is the possibility that some consumers appeared in both audiences (unless the advertisements are run simultaneously on different channels), thus the overall reach in the latter case is lower. To capture the ethnic composition of each station's audience, the two composition-based ethnicity variables provided by Arbitron were employed. The first of these is the percentage of a station's average quarter-hour audience that is African American (AQBLACK). The second is the percentage of a station's average quarter-hour audience that is Hispanic (AQHISP).

It is important to note that Arbitron does not report ethnic composition for stations in all of the markets that it measures, but only in those markets where there is a significant minority population; nor does the company provide data on ethnic groups other than African Americans and Hispanics in any of its markets.

A number of market-level variables were included as control variables to account for the possibility that station power ratios vary in accordance with market size and demographic fluctuations. Two ethnicity variables (per cent Hispanic in the station's market [HISPANIC]; per cent African American in the station's market [BLACK]) were included, as was per capita income in the station's market (PERCAP).

Market size was controlled using total radio advertising revenues in the market (MARKETREV). This variable was very highly correlated with other potential measures of market size, such as total population and number of radio stations in the market. The use of a market-size variable that most directly reflected market value was deemed most appropriate, given the nature of the issues being addressed.

The inclusion of these market-level independent variables addresses the possibility that variations in market size and demographics affect audience share and revenue share (the two components of the power ratio) disproportionately, independent of a station's audience composition.

Perhaps a more likely relationship involves possible interaction effects between audience ethnicity and market conditions. Thus, for instance, the extent to which African-American/Hispanic audience composition affects audience value may be different in markets with higher African-American/ Hispanic compositions than in markets with lower African-American/Hispanic compositions, given the different supply and demand dynamics for African-American/Hispanic audiences in markets that are heavily African American/ Hispanic versus those that are not.

Similarly, in larger or wealthier markets, advertiser demand for African-American/Hispanic audiences may be different than in smaller or less wealthy markets. For these reasons, six interaction terms were created. Two inter action terms were created for interactions between audience ethnic composition and market ethnic composition to address the possibility that the effect of audience ethnicity on audience value varies in accordance with market ethnic composition,

Two interaction terms also were created for interactions between audience ethnic composition and market size to account for the possibility that the effect of audience ethnic composition on audience value varies in accordance with market size. Finally, two interaction terms were created for interactions between audience ethnic composition and market per capita income to account for the possibility that the effect of audience ethnic composition on audience value varies in accordance with per capita income in a station's market.

Utilizing interaction terms typically raises problems of multicollinearity between the main effect independent variables and their associated interaction terms. The recommended procedure for reducing such multicollinearity problems is to"centre" each main effect independent variable used in the computation of the interaction terms.

Centering involves subtracting the independent variable mean from the independent variable value for each case. These centered independent variables were then used as the main effect variables in the multivariate analysis and to compute the interaction term used in the multivariate analysis.

Although it would have been desirable to also incorporate data on the average income levels of the audience members for each station studied, such data were not available via the data sources obtained for this analysis. As was noted above, station-level audience income delta are not part of Arbitron's syndicated reports (the reports obtained for this study) and are only available to Arbitron clients for an additional fee. This limited availability of audience income data even to advertisers likely limits the extent to which such data are employed in radio buying decisions. Regardless, such data would have made it possible to separate the effects of income from the effects of ethnicity. Given, as was noted above, that ethnicity is correlated with income, it is possible that advertisers are using ethnicity solely as a proxy for income.

Although previous research has provided evidence that contradicts this assumption, the analysis presented here cannot address this issue directly. However, as was noted above, even if lower valuations of minority audiences are largely a function of lower income levels, such lower valuations still could undermine the source and content diversity that policymakers traditionally have sought as well as the provision of content serving minority interests and concerns. Finally, it is important to address a number of limitations in the scope of the database. First, Arbitron does not measure all radio stations in the United States. Of the roughly 13,000 radio stations in the United States, only about 6,000 are in Arbitron-defined and measured radio markets. Moreover, as was noted above, Arbitron does not provide data on the ethnic composition of station audiences for all of the radio markets it measures.

Generally, Arbitron only provides such data in markets where there is a significant minority population. These factors limit the number of stations eligible for analysis and weight the stations included in this analysis toward those in markets with large African-American and Hispanic populations. The number of eligible stations was limited further by the fact that not all commercial radio stations report their revenues to BIA Research (BIA's reported response rate is roughly 80%). In cases where station revenues are not reported, it is impossible to compute the power ratio that serves as the dependent variable for this analysis.

Due to these limitations, within this data set there is a total of 810 stations with Hispanic audience composition (and revenue) data, 1430 with African-American composition (and revenue) data, and a total of 461 commercial radio stations with reported revenues and with both African-American and Hispanic audience composition data available. It is this latter set of stations that is the focus of this analysis as these stations represent the only context in which it is possible to investigate simultaneously the effects of both of the minority-audience characteristics at issue on audience value.

In sum, while previous research has explored the relationship between audience ethnicity and audience value via market-level demographic data, market-level CPMs, and differences in power ratios across programme formats, the approach outlined here moves beyond these approaches by directly examining the relationship between the audience composition of individual media outlets and their ability to successfully compete for available advertising dollars.

## RESULTS

The mean power ratio of stations that target minority audiences was first compared to the mean power ratio of stations that do not target minority audiences. For the purposes of this analysis, minority-targeted stations were defined as those stations for which the majority of the station's average quarter-hour audience (i.e., greater than 50%) is comprised of African-American and/or Hispanic listeners.

In this means comparison, stations with a minority audience of greater than 50% (n = 121) have an average power ratio of.82, compared with an average power ratio of 1.06 for other stations (n = 340). This difference is statistically significant at the.01 level. As these results suggest, minority-targeted stations tend to undersell their audiences, meaning that their share of the total radio audience is greater than their share of the total radio advertising revenues in their markets.

Of particular importance is the fact that correlations between the main effect variables and their associated interaction terms generally are modest. Before these variables were centered, some of the correlations between main effect and interaction terms were as high as.90, a level indicative of a potentially serious multicollinearity problem. There remain, however, a few strong correlations between some of the interaction terms.

There is a similarly strong correlation between the Hispanic versions of these interaction terms. However, tolerance statistics for all four of these independent variables are reasonably high (ranging from.39 to.52), alleviating concerns about multicollinearity in the multivariate analysis. Hierarchical regression was employed due to the inclusion of interaction terms. When working with interaction terms, hierarchical regression is necessary in order to determine whether the interaction terms provide significant explanatory power beyond that provided by the main effect variables.

Using hierarchical regression in this context also makes it possible to better examine the relative contribution of market-level versus station-level independent variables. (Given the nature of the dependent variable, it was presumed that station-level independent variables would provide greater explanatory power than market-level independent variables).

The first set of independent variables entered into the model was the market-level control variables. These variables alone explain none of the variance in station power ratios. All six station-level independent variables are significant in the expected direction. There is a negative relationship between modulation type and power ratios, with AM status having a negative effect on power ratios. Both the MEN1854 and WOM1854 demographic composition variables are positively related to power ratios, indicating that the greater the extent to which a station's audience is composed of men and women 18 to 54, the greater the station's power ratio. A station's overall audience share (SHARE) also is positively related to a station's power ratio, providing evidence that sellers of audiences are able to charge a premium on a per audience member basis for larger audiences.

Finally, in terms of ethnicity, both the AQHISP variables are negatively related to power ratios, suggesting that ethnic composition exerts a downward pressure on a radio station's ability to monetize its audience.

The magnitude of the beta coefficients indicates that the age/gender independent variables are the most important in terms of explanatory power, followed by the ethnicity variables. The AQBLACK and AQHISP coefficients are similar in size, though African-American audience composition seems to exert a slightly stronger downward pressure on audience value than Hispanic audience composition. In block 3, the six interaction terms were added to the equation. The addition of interaction terms explains only an additional 5% of the variance in the dependent variable; however, this improvement in explanatory power is significant at the.01 level. Only one of the six interaction terms is statistically significant.

The significant negative coefficient for the AQHISP*MARKREV interaction term indicates that the magnitude of the negative relationship between Hispanic audience composition and station power ratios decreases slightly as market size increases.

The analyses presented here represent the next step forward in determining the extent to which advertiser valuations of minority audiences affect the viability of minority-owned and minority-targeted media outlets.

The results conform to those of previous studies, which found that minority audiences are more difficult to monetize than non-minority audiences.

This study also has extended previous research by examining the value of minority audiences at the level of individual media outlets and by employing detailed data on the demographic composition of the audiences for those outlets. Future research should seek to better separate possible income effects from ethnicity effects.

From a media policy standpoint, however, whether lower valuations of minority audiences are purely a function of income or also are a function of other factors such as advertiser perceptions of minority spending and product usage patterns, the implications for diversity in the electronic media are the same--the viability of minority-targeted media content suffers.

It is important that these findings be placed within the broader context of the economics of minority media. Minority-targeted media content suffers from not only the potentially lower valuations of minority audiences but also the fact that, by definition, it appeals to a small audience. Smaller audiences mean smaller revenues, particularly when the audience is not highly valued by advertisers (if the small audience segment being targeted is highly valued by advertisers, then, of course, revenue potential increases).

Recall that this analysis also found that stations with larger audiences are able to charge more on a Per audience member basis than stations with smaller audiences, a finding that further illustrates the compounding negative consequences of being a niche programmer. These economic handicaps result in lower incentives to produce such programming and, consequently, lower levels of availability of such programming.

Moreover, lower levels of audience size and value both exert downward pressures on the production budgets of minority content, which further undermine the ability of such content to compete and remain viable. The smaller and less valuable the potential audience for a media product is, the smaller the likely investment in programming.

At the same time, research shows that audiences are drawn to content with higher production budgets over content with smaller production budgets. Together, these processes create a situation in which minority content loses some of its appeal--even to minority audiences--relative to majority content. The differential in production budgets may be enough for some minority audience members to find the majority content more appealing than the content targeted at their particular interests and concerns.

Such defections further undermine the viability of minority-targeted content and contribute to the availability of minority audiences in non-minority content that further discourages advertisers from advertising on minority-targeted media outlets. In the end, the lower valuations that advertisers place on minority audiences feed into an economic process that works against minority-targeted content being able to compete and remain viable in both the audience and content markets. The end result is lower levels of availability of minority-targeted content.

This Perspective suggests that policymakers seeking--at the general level--to preserve and promote diversity of sources and content in the electronic media, and seeking--at the specific level--to promote minority ownership of media outlets and the production of minority-targeted content, need to investigate new strategies and tactics. Previous policy initiatives, such as minority preferences in the license allocation process and minority tax certificates, have focused on increasing the likelihood of minorities becoming owners of media outlets.

The results presented here suggest that if policymakers want to preserve and promote minority-targeted media outlets, their efforts may need to address the barriers not only to establishing such media outlets but also to maintaining the financial viability of such outlets once they are established. Possible mechanisms might include subsidies for minority-targeted media outlets or education campaigns designed to counter any advertiser misconceptions about minority media audiences that may be driving down their value. Of course, such recommendations are premised upon the notion that existing levels of minority-targeted media content are not sufficient. Whether--and to what extent--this is the case is a question that is beyond the scope of this analysis. The analyses presented here suggest that the economic handicaps associated with targeting minority audiences may lead to a disconnect between the availability of minority audiences and the availability of minority-targeted media content. Future research should explore this issue in greater detail. However, in order to effectively address this issue, and the necessity of a policy response, policymakers need to work toward establishing more concrete objectives in terms of the desired levels of both ownership and content diversity in the electronic media marketplace.

# 6

# Trust in Different Advertising Media

Trust has long been considered an important element of human relations. Investigated from different behavioral and social scientific perspectives, trust has been defined in various ways, both conceptually and operationally, in the disciplines of psychology, sociology, communication, organizational behaviour, and business. In recent years, trust has been studied in advertising, though the research literature is not extensive. In contrast, credibility, a construct related to trust, has been the subject of many studies in advertising and other communication-related fields.

Trust is important to the study of advertising because there is a consistent tendency for consumers to distrust advertising. From a rational perspective, a primary communication function of advertising is to inform consumers about market offerings to help them weigh one purchase choice against another. Crucial to the fulfillment of this function is the belief that consumers must trust advertising for it to perform effectively as an information source.

Past research suggests three points about trust in the advertising context:

- Trust is an established antecedent of persuasion and has been long studied in attitude theory;
- Trust in mediated communication is a demonstrated correlate of information acceptance, liking, and other processing effects;
- Trust is fundamental to consumer/seller relationships.

In this chapter, we report a study conducted to examine consumer trust in different advertising media and the relationship of trust in advertising media to media credibility.

*The research was designed to*:

- Determine if consumer trust differs across advertising media;
- Identify which advertising media are most trusted;
- Examine how trust in advertising media differs across consumer demographic characteristics;
- Establish the association between an advertising medium's credibility and trust in that medium.

Both past and recent research indicates that trust and credibility are distinct constructs with different conceptual characteristics.

In advertising research specifically, a measurement validation study by Soh, Reid, and King found that the two constructs are distinct from one another and that the trust in advertising construct is mutltidimensional in nature." We adopted the validated measure, which Soh, Reid, and King named the ADTRUST Scale, to address four research questions.

Later, we discuss the conceptual differences between the two constructs and review the Soh, Reid, and King study in detail. In the following sections, we review existing research on trust and credibility in advertising.

Trust Research in Advertising. Studies of trust are not abundant in the advertising literature, though both academic and trade investigations have incorporated and measured the construct. In advertising research, trust has been commonly measured with single-item measures or ad hoc multiple-item scales, without empirical validation and testing.

Additionally, while most theorists describe trust as a multi-dimensional construct, there is no consistency in advertising research as to the number of items or dimensions of the trust construct, nor has the dimensionality of the construct been determined. Trust has been treated typically the same as"accuracy" or as an aspect of the integrity of advertising (i.e., falsity, deception, and manipulation). Of the advertising trust studies, two are particularly relevant to our study of advertising media.

In 2002, Menon and colleagues reported a study of the determinants of consumer trust in prescription drug information on the Internet and its influence on online information search. The study found trust in traditional media (i.e., TV ads, TV programs, newspaper ads, and newspaper articles) predicted trust in online drug information, indicating that consumer trust in traditional media transfers to the Internet.

Health status was the only predictive demographic of trust in online drug information; age, gender, race, and education were not significant predictors. The study also reported that two consumer subsets were most likely to engage in online information search for advertised drugs: whites and consumers who exhibited trust in online drug information were significantly more likely to engage in an Internet search.

Three years later, Huh, DeLorme, and Reid published a study modeled after Menon et al. The study used different variables, operationalizations, and measures, adding two demographic variables (income and media use) and expanded traditional media to include not only TV and newspaper advertising, but also magazine, radio, leaflets/brochures, and direct mail advertising. Like the earlier research, the study found that online drug information is not highly trusted, and that trust in the traditional advertising media is predictive of trust in Internet advertising; however, the study found that the relationship between traditional advertising media and online media is not uniform (i.e., varies by medium). None of the demographic or predispositional variables (age, education, gender, drug use, media use, income, race, or health status) was positively associated with trust in online drug information. The lack of association between health status and trust contradicts the finding of Menon and colleagues.

The study also found that consumers who trust online information are more likely to pursue information online for advertised drugs. Additionally, the study reported that trust in online drug information is directly associated with specific types of ad-promoted behaviour following exposure to DTC ads (communicating with doctors, talking with others, and seeking more information).

## CREDIBILITY RESEARCH IN ADVERTISING

It is not difficult to locate credibility studies in advertising research. In the literature, credibility has been conceptualized and measured in four forms: source credibility (i.e., trustworthiness, expertise, and attractiveness of endorsers and advertisers); advertising credibility (i.e., in general); ad content credibility (i.e., perceptions that ad-claims are truthful and believable); and media credibility.

### SOURCE CREDIBILITY

Two types of credibility involving the source of product information have been studied: endorser credibility and advertiser credibility. Research on source credibility has repeatedly found that trustworthiness, expertise, and attractiveness are the major dimensions of endorser and advertiser credibility.

### ADVERTISING CREDIBILITY

Advertising credibility has been conceived and studied as the perception of the truthfulness and believability of advertising in general, not simply of a particular source or ad. According to Lutz, advertising credibility is formed by a subsystem of three constructs (i.e., ad claim discrepancy, and advertiser and advertising credibility). Obermiller and Spangenberg approached the construct of advertising credibility from the opposite direction, which they called"advertising skepticism" (defined as"the tendency toward disbelief of advertising claims"). Even though they did not explicitly mention the relationship between advertising skepticism and advertising credibility, the conceptual and measurement similarities of the two constructs suggest that advertising skepticism is not different from advertising credibility, but the same construct which views advertising credibility from another perspective. The conceptualizations and measurements of advertising credibility suggest that the construct refers to consumers' evaluations of the integrity (i.e., truthfulness, honesty, etc.) of advertising.

### AD-CONTENT CREDIBILITY

Ad-content credibility has been considered the perception that ad-claims are truthful and believable. Beltramini and Evans developed a scale to measure believability of ad-conveyed performance claims. The scale was later used by O'Cass to measure political advertising believability in an Australian context.

## ADVERTISING MEDIA CREDIBILITY

The channels of ad delivery have been the focus of media credibility research. Three studies have examined the credibility perceptions of different advertising media. The studies report that credibility perceptions vary across different media and consumer demographics.

Becker, Martino, and Towers found that newspapers were perceived as the most credible advertising medium and that advertising credibility varied as a function of two audience demographics: age and media use. Younger consumers perceived few differences across ad media; older consumers perceived large differences. Media use was also positively associated with credibility perceptions, and consumers perceived credibility differences across advertising media depending on their primary source of local information.

Durand, Teel, and Bearden investigated racial differences in perceptions of ad media credibility. The study found that, with the exception of magazine advertising, blacks considered all ad media more credible than whites. Blacks perceived TV as the most credible ad medium; whites perceived magazine advertising as the most credible.

A study of older consumers' perceptions of media credibility for direct-to-consumer (DTC) prescription drug advertising was conducted by Huh, DeLorme, and Reid. The research found that credibility perceptions varied across the media of DTC advertising and with different consumer predispositional and demographic characteristics. Place-based media (leaflets and brochures) were perceived significantly more credible than any of the other media.

Credibility perceptions did not vary across the four traditional media of DTC advertising-newspapers, magazines, TV, and radio-though newspapers, magazine, and TV advertising were perceived as significantly more credible than Internet advertising.

Artitude-toward-DTC advertising was the most uniform predictor of ad media credibility (across seven media), followed by DTC ad-familiarity which was predictive of newspaper, magazine, TV, and radio credibility. Consumers who liked and were most familiar with DTC advertising perceived higher media credibility, regardless of their age, education, income, gender, race, rate of drug use, or perceived health.

## TRUST AND CREDIBILITY AS INDEPENDENT CONSTRUCTS

The preponderance of evidence from credibility research in advertising and elsewhere suggests that trust is a dimension of credibility (i.e., defined and measured as trustworthiness, truthfulness, believability, etc.). However, the relationship between credibility and trust is not universally agreed upon. Some literature suggests trustworthiness is one of the two basic underlying components of credibility; other literature suggests that trust has several factors not typically reflected in credibility, including confidence, competence, benevolence, and reliability; mutual emotional investment; and willingness to rely on.

Most of the behavioral and social science research indicates that trust should be treated as a separate and independent construct. Credibility in advertising refers mostly to generalized beliefs about advertising's integrity (i.e., trustworthiness, truthfulness, honesty).

Conceptualizations and measurements of credibility do not consistently deal with such things as the benevolent intent of advertising or consumer willingness to rely on advertising as an input for decision making. As a result, it is possible that credibility deals with only a part of trust in advertising; credibility may be associated with trust, but may not be sufficient in itself to indicate the nature and scope of trust in advertising.

A study by Soh, Reid, and King specifically examined the scope and nature of trust in advertising and the relative relationship of the construct to similar constructs, including advertising credibility. Drawing on interdisciplinary trust research, Soh, Reid, and King developed and validated a twenty-item trust scale for advertising research. The measure, which they named the ADTRUST Scale, was produced by a threestage, nine-step research design. The study followed prescribed measurement development procedures32 and the three stages were: identification, reliability, and validation.

In the identification stage, the domain of trust was specified by literature review (e.g., studies, dictionary, etc.), consumer interviews, and card-sorting tasks. The process yielded thirty-three items from an initial pool of 412.

In the reliability stage, the reliability and dimensionality of the thirty-three items (in Likert-format) were assessed by analyzing split-sample data: the first half of the data set was analysed using exploratory factor analysis (EFA) to explore factor structures and to identify appropriate items for construct measurement; the second half was analysed using confirmatory factor analysis (CFA) to verify and validate the structure of the measurement items specified in the first data set. Internal consistency tests were performed to determine the reliability of the identified factors in both factor analyses. A twenty-one-item, five-factor model emerged from the process.

In the validation stage, the reliability and dimensionality of the twenty-one-item scale was reassessed. Factor analyses were repeated and produced the twenty-item, four-factor ADTRUST Scale. The scale was then subjected to concurrent, convergent, discriminant, and nomological validity testing: concurrent validity was examined by comparing ADTRUST scores with those of a single-item measure; convergent and discriminant validity were explored using a multitrait-multimethod matrix (MTMM), CFA, and EFA to determine the relationships among trust in advertising, advertising credibility, and attitude-toward-advertising-in-general; and nomological validity was examined by testing hypothesized relationships between advertising trust and other theoretically related ad-responses (i.e., ad avoidance, use of ad-information, adinvolvement, trust in test ads; attitude-toward-test ads).

The study found that:

- The ADTRUST Scale exhibited sufficient reliability and concurrent, convergent, discriminant, and nomological validity;
- Trust in advertising is a multi-dimensional construct (i.e., cognitive, affective, and behavioral dimensions) with four distinct factors (Reliability, Usefulness, Affect, and Willingness to Rely On), which reflect a combination of
  - Consumer perception of reliability and usefulness of advertising,
  - Consumer affect toward advertising,
  - Consumer willingness to rely on advertising for decision making;
- Trust in advertising and advertising credibility are separate and independent constructs;
- Trust should be operationalized and measured as an independent, three-factor structure (i.e., Reliability and Usefulness = cognitive dimension; Affect = emotional dimension; and Willingness to Rely On = behavioral dimension) in advertising research. The last two findings are especially important to this investigation.

Research comparing attitudes toward advertising across different media generally indicates that consumers have different attitudes toward advertising depending on the advertising medium. For instance, print ads are perceived as more enjoyable and informative than broadcast ads; television and radio commercials are rated more offensive and annoying than print ads.

The differences in attitudes toward advertising and credibility perceptions across media suggest that there might be differences in consumer trust in advertising by specific advertising media. Thus, we suspect that trust differs for different advertising media, and that some media are more trusted than others. Perceptions of trust in different media might vary as a function of consumer demographic characteristics. The studies on advertising trust and ad media credibility suggest that consumer response is not uniform and may vary as a function of demographic differences. Thus, we suspect that consumer demographics are differentially associated with trust in different advertising media. If trust in advertising varies across different media, other ad-related factors affecting such differences are also of interest. Of the possible factors, media credibility is examined herein as a variable which may be associated with trust in advertising. Research has shown that audience credibility perceptions vary by medium, and that the more credible the particular medium, the more it is relied on as a primary information source. Flanagin and Metzger suggest that overall media credibility affects the credibility of information delivered by specific media.36 Based on these findings, we suspect consumer credibility and trust perceptions of advertising media are positively associated.

## METHOD

To answer the research questions, a sample of 600 adults was randomly drawn from the 6,700 staff of a large state university. The list from which the sample was drawn was obtained from the university's Office of Institutional Research and represented employees distributed across diverse regions of the state.

### SURVEY QUESTIONNAIRE

The questionnaire was pretested before it was field administered. Two hundred and sixty students completed an initial version of the questionnaire and provided comments and suggestions about problematic instructions, questions, and measures. No major problems were uncovered by the pretest; however, some minor wording changes were made.

The questionnaire contained 225 questions measuring ten variables and demographics, including generalized trust in advertising, trust in advertising media, advertising credibility, artirude-toward-adverrisingin-general, and ad media credibility Generalized Trust in Advertising. Generalized trust in advertising was measured by the ADTRUST Scale. Respondents were asked to indicate their level of agreement with the twenty 7-point items of the scale.

Trust in Different Ad-Media. Trust in five advertising media was also measured using the ADTRUST Scale: TV, radio, newspaper, magazine, and Internet. Items of the ADTRUST Scale were adjusted for each medium (e.g.,"information conveyed in national newspaper advertising is..." vs."information conveyed in national TV advertising is...":"willing to recommend... that I have seen in newspaper ads..." vs."willing to recommend... that I have seen in TV commercials..."). The respondent's ratings were limited to"two media only" to avoid task fatigue and boredom. The order of the pairs were counterbalanced to control for order and combination effects (i.e., ten media-pairs were rated). As a qualifier, respondents were instructed to evaluate a medium only if they had used that medium in the past six months.

### ADVERTISING CREDIBILITY

Advertising credibility was measured using a set of nine 7-point Likert-format statements adopted from Obermiller and Spangenberg.

### ATTITUDE-TOWARD-ADVERTISING-IN-GENERAL

Generalized attitude-toward-advertising was measured by a set of seven 7-point Likert-format statements adopted from Bauer and Greyser.

## MEDIA CREDIBILITY

Respondents were asked to rate the credibility of the information conveyed in the five media. Each medium was judged on four bi-polar semantic differential scales: extremely believable/not at all believable, extremely accurate/not at all accurate, extremely fair/not at all fair, and extremely in-depth/not at all in-depth. Respondents were asked to indicate if they had used each medium in the past six months before completing the measure to enhance response validity.

## DEMOGRAPHIC CHARACTERISTICS

Information on respondent age, gender, level of education, household income, and race was collected. Age was collected by an open-ended question. Closed-ended questions were used to collect gender, education, race, and household income information.

## DATA COLLECTION PROCEDURE

The questionnaire was mailed in two waves with three reminder e-mails. In the first wave, a survey packet was mailed to the 600 staff via the campus mail system."Thank you" notes and promised $3 incentive checks were mailed upon arrival of completed questionnaires. The mailings and reminders generated 261 returns (259 usable and 3 incomplete questionnaires), for a gross return rate of 43.5%. The adjusted return rate was 45%, excluding the 20 undeliverable returns from the 600 original mailings.

# RESULTS

Chi-square tests were conducted to examine differences between gender, age, and race of the respondents and the population. Information on education and income of the population could not be located, and thus was excluded from the sample/population comparisons.

The respondents were similar to the population by age, but significantly different from the population by gender and race. More females were in the sample than in the population, and whites were overrepresented; blacks were underrepresented. The household incomes of the respondents varied and they were well-educated, with 59% being college graduates, and 29% having attended college.

*RQ1 asked*: Does trust vary across different advertising media?

*RQ2 asked*: In which medium is advertising most trusted? Post hoc analysis using the Tukey HSD criterion for significance revealed that trust is significantly lower for Internet advertising than for the other media, radio, newspaper, and magazine advertising. Other than Internet advertising, there were no significant differences in advertising trust across TV, radio, newspaper, and magazine media. The results indicate Internet advertising is the least-trusted advertising medium.

For closer examination of the relationships between advertising trust and media type, two-way ANOVAs (including demographic variables of age, gender, education, and income) were conducted to address RQ3 (Does trust in different advertising media vary by consumer demographic characteristics?). Gender and age exhibited no direct or indirect associations with trust in specific advertising media. Education exhibited a direct association with trust in advertising media without indirect association. Post hoc analysis using the Tukey HSD criterion for significance revealed that trust in advertising media is significantly higher in the low-educated group (completed high school or less, than in the highly educated group.

Level of income exhibited two-way interactions with media-type. The plot shows that the pattern of advertising trust in media is different depending on level of income. Respondents in the lowincome group tended to exhibit more trust in TV and newspaper advertising than in radio and magazine advertising. On the other hand, respondents in the high-income group exhibited more trust in radio and magazine advertising than in TV and newspaper advertising. The Internet was evaluated as the least-trusted advertising medium by the high- and moderate-income groups; it was the third most-trusted medium by the low-income group, following TV and newspaper advertising.

To test the association between credibility and trust in specific advertising media, RQ4 asked: Are consumer perceptions of a medium's credibility associated with trust in that specific medium? Five hierarchical regression analyses were conducted for each of the five media. The dependent variable in each analysis was trust in advertising for a specific advertising medium.

The independent variables were entered in the following hierarchical blocks:

- Co-variates including age, gender, education, and income;
- Generalized trust in advertising, advertising credibility, and attitude-toward-advertising-in-general; and
- Medium credibility. Within each block the stepwise inclusion method was used.

For TV advertising, level of income, generalized trust in advertising, and perceived TV credibility were significant predictors, explaining 72.3% of the total variance. Generalized trust in advertising and radio credibility were significant predictors of trust in radio advertising with an adjusted R2 of 44.8%. Age, level of education, generalized trust, and newspaper credibility explained 69.9% of the total variance of trust in newspaper advertising.

For magazine advertising, generalized trust in advertising and magazine credibility was significant predictors, explaining 73.9% of the total variance. Generalized trust in advertising and Internet credibility were significant predictors of trust in Internet advertising, with an adjusted. Across all five media, media credibility consistently exhibited an independent contribution to the variance explained in trust for a specific advertising medium, when other possible covariates were taken into account in the model. The total explained variance for each of the five regression models increased when medium credibility was included in the models: the R2 changed after including TV credibility by 2%, radio credibility by 21%, newspaper credibility by 10%, magazine credibility by 5%, and Internet credibility by 28%. These results suggest that media credibility is directly associated with trust in specific advertising media. Media credibility provided separate explanatory power when other significant variables were taken into account.

## IMPLICATIONS AND RESEARCH DIRECTIONS

Consumer perceptions of trust in five different advertising media and the relationship of trust in those media to media credibility were investigated to advance research on trust in advertising. Four conclusions can be drawn from the study's findings. First, the major media of advertising are neither especially trusted nor distrusted by consumers. The mean ratings of all five media were lower than the neutral point of the 7-point measure, with magazine advertising rated the highest in trust and Internet advertising rated the least-trusted medium. Similar findings were reported by Menon et al. and Huh, DeLorme, and Reid.

Considered together, the evidence strongly indicates that consumers are not very trustful of advertising media. Consumer neutrality in the trustworthiness of ad media is not particularly surprising given the finding that people are skeptical of advertising messages, though they like advertising more than they dislike it, and that people find ads enjoyable, informative, and useful in purchasing deliberations.

Second, there is variation in consumer trust across different advertising media, though the difference is attributable to one medium. Trust in Internet advertising was significantly lower than trust in the other media. Consumers perceived Internet advertising as less trustworthy than the traditional media of advertising (i.e., TV, newspaper, radio, and magazine advertising); there were no significant differences among the four broadcast and print media.

Although the perceptions were not statistically significant, print advertising was rated higher than broadcast advertising. Magazine advertising was the highest-rated medium, followed by newspaper, television, and radio advertising. Third, trust in advertising media is differentially associated with the demographic characteristics of consumers.

Though consumer trust perceptions of different advertising media were consistent across age, gender, and race characteristics, education and income were differentially associated with specific media trust. Trust was significantly higher in the lower-educated group than in the higher-educated group; respondents in the higher-income group put more trust in radio and magazine advertising than in TV and newspaper advertising.

Also, respondents in the lower-income group tended to trust TV and newspaper advertising more than radio and magazine advertising. These findings are generally consistent with past research which indicates that low-income, less-educated consumers tend to hold more positive attitudes toward advertising than others and with the studies of media credibility (i.e., there were differences by age, media use, race, attitude-toward-advertising, and ad familiarity).

However, the findings are inconsistent with the studies of trust in DTC advertising which reported no differential associations between trust in advertising media by education and income. It should be pointed out that these inconsistencies are possibly attributable to the use of different measures of the two demographic variables across studies.

Fourth, consumer trust in advertising media and media credibility are associated constructs, though trust in advertising is distinct and separate from credibility. Across the five advertising media, media credibility was consistently associated with media-specific trust, indicating that the credibility of a medium and trust in that medium are directly related. These findings suggest trust and credibility may be necessary evaluative conditions of advertising media, but neither construct in itself is sufficient to indicate the other-they are related but separate indicators of consumer judgment.

## IMPLICATIONS AND RESEARCH DIRECTIONS

Research that periodically tracks consumer trust in advertising settings is important to both academic and practitioner researchers. As noted earlier, trust is a separate and independent construct, an established correlate of other adresponses, a crucial ingredient of the advertiser/consumer relationship, and a basic indicator of the effectiveness of rationally processed advertising.

For practitioners of advertising, the finding that Internet advertising is less trusted than the traditional media of advertising should be especially interesting and suggestive. Though no medium of advertising is particularly trusted, it would appear that consumers place significantly less trust in Internet advertising than in traditional advertising media. The implication?

When trust matters, managers and media planners should exercise caution in placing too much weight on Internet advertising in building media schedules, and possibly in other new media as well. Whether trust in Internet advertising will improve over time, and whether other new media are indeed less trusted than traditional media, are questions for future research.

For both academic and practitioner researchers, the findings suggest that the measurement of media trust should move beyond the use of single-item or ad hoc scales of past academic and industry studies of media trust. To reflect the true independent, multidimensional nature of the trust construct, application of validated measures, such as the ADTRUST Scale, should become a staple in research on forms of advertising trust, including trust in advertising media. The result of a move away from single-item and ad hoc trust scales? Greater confidence in the validity of studies of trust in advertising media as well as other aspects of advertising trust (e.g., ad content trust, institutional trust). For academic researchers, future investigations should extend these findings beyond trust in the media of advertising and media credibility by investigating the relationships between trust in advertising media and other ad-responses. Past trust research has found that trust is correlated to trust-related behaviors in different strengths. In the context of advertising media, trust-related behaviors might include consumer attentiveness to advertising or the use of ad-conveyed information.

It might be hypothesized that consumer beliefs about trust have direct effects on attention to specific advertising media (i.e., consumer engagement) or that trust-beliefs have indirect effects on the behaviors through trusting intent (i.e., willingness to rely on the information conveyed in different ad media). A profound understanding of the relationships among trust in different advertising media and other ad-responses may help with the development of a framework to model how trust in media is related to advertising persuasion. The theoretical foundation of earlier work on trust, attitude formation/change, and persuasive communication should be considered as the model for future investigations.

Other academic research should involve more than five advertising media. Investigators should replicate this research across other media (e.g., direct mail, out-of-home and/or intra-media types such as cable vs. network TV, daily vs. weekly newspapers, consumer vs. business magazines) to determine if these findings are generalizable to other media contexts.

*Additionally, investigations of trust should focus on*:

- Advertiser-type/media matches (e.g., local/retail advertising, businessto-business advertising, public service advertising, and public relations/corporate advertising);
- Media/advertised object matches (e.g., new products versus mature products; products types);
- Media/cultural orientation matches (e.g., domestic vs. global; English vs.

Spanish language) to develop a fuller understanding of advertising media trust. If trust is to be studied in advertising contexts, we would strongly argue for the adoption of our approach.

At the very least, it is our hope that these findings will do two things:

- Spark interest in studying trust in advertising, including more research in trust in advertising media, and
- Provide an empirical foundation for future investigations.

# 7

# Increasing Advertising Effectiveness

As the nation's demographics, lifestyles, and family life-cycle stages change, assumptions about the effectiveness of a specific advertising vehicle are being challenged. In particular, the challenge for the retailer is strong in the area of consumer media exposure habits. Today no longer can a large number of consumers be easily identified on a basis of once-powerful segmentation variables such as values, attitudes, opinions and motivation; nor can they be reached as easily as before using the same traditional media vehicles.

Although addressing the target audience is the primary concern of retailers, advertising cost is also an issue. Depending on their availability (the time and space the ad can be placed) and reach the number of people exposed to the ad), some media vehicles are more expensive than others. Obviously it is very important to the advertiser to select the appropriate media vehicles with the necessary weight given to cost effectiveness.

Thus the question raised: Can the urban daily newspapers, the advertising vehicle expensively used by retail businesses, remain cost effective in the light of these changes? This chapter will evaluate the effectiveness of urban newspapers as compared to suburban weeklies, and radio broadcasts as advertising vehicles for retail businesses.

## SELECTING ALTERNATIVE MEDIA VEHICLES

Most retail businesses usually commit a large portion of their advertising dollars to newspapers, with the balance allotted to radio and television spot advertisements. They rely on newspapers to bring the customer in and make the business visible in the minds of the consumer. Once the budget is determined, the only question left is how frequently to advertise.

Other important considerations include: the strength of the competition and the effect of the pricing policy adopted by the firm. The adoption of local newspapers as the primary advertising vehicle is seldom questioned. Newspapers have, naturally, asserted that repeated, consistent advertising in their papers brings consumers into the store and helps promote a positive image of a business.

Retailers say that the equation,"Retail business; therefore, newspaper advertising," is a false premise forced on them by traditional practice and by newspaper advertising departments. Nevertheless, many of these retailers continue to use local daily newspapers as the primary vehicle for advertisements. For example, supermarket-style liquor stores generally spend a high proportion of their media budget on newspaper advertisements. Their product offerings, discount specials and sales are thus mainly communicated via newspaper advertisements.

Supermarket-style liquor stores, or for that matter liquor stores in general, have shunned the use of television and radio because of the National Association of Broadcaster's Code and the fear of possible public outcry against such advertisements.

Consequently, their advertising budgets, which often range between one and two per cent of their sales revenues, are fully committed to print medium, specifically newspapers. Where newspapers are used, the advertisements of one store are practically indistinguishable from those of others. To be sure, the advertisements are sale-specific, with very little in either subject matter or form (since most use very little open space between the block-style displays) to distinguish one from another.

The implementation of the recent liquor industry policy that allows television and radio advertising of certain categories of distilled spirits, coupled with the dissolution of the National Association of Broadcasters' Radio and Television Codes, gives advertisers an additional choice that was not available in the past. Since the change, liquor retailers, as well as some national advertisers, have begun to use new and different media vehicles in an attempt to custom-build their advertisements to their clientele's changing demographics and psychographics.

In the wake of these changes, it is important to investigate whether or not supermarket-style liquor stores should develop a different media mix. This study was therefore designed to determine the effectiveness of the various media vehicles being used experimentally by a chain of supermarket-style liquor stores. The study is based on a telephone survey and a field experiment conducted in a large metropolitan area in New England.

## TELEPHONE SURVEY

In an effort to understand the target market a telephone survey was conducted among a stratified random sample of 2100 households, selected from telephone directories, representing the diverse communities in the metropolitan area. The listing was further improved and made more complete by including the unlisted telephone numbers (estimated at 7 per cent) using the add-a-digit dialing technique. In terms of specific subsamples, 1200 households were selected from the city proper and 900 households were selected from the communities within 15 miles radius of the city proper.

The major objective of the telephone survey was to complement the experimental study by providing demographics, psychographics, media awareness and exposure habits, and other purchase-related data on consumers and prospective consumers. To this end, members of the selected households were asked screening questions to determine whether they purchased beverages at any liquor stores, and then the qualifying households were asked to identify the person who normally made these purchases.

Telephone interviews were conducted only with those who made most of the liquor purchases within a household and were willing to participate in the study. The interviews were conducted over a period of four consecutive evenings. The total number of useable questionnaires obtained this way was 797, with 300 from urban and 497 from suburban areas. This will make the overall response rate approximately 40 per cent.

Specifically, the participants were asked questions which pertained to their shopping habits and demographics. Shopping habits questions were asked, on one hand, to determine who shopped where and when and what was purchased and, on the other hand, to assess the effects of advertisements on their purchase decisions. The demographic component was added to find out whether the suburban target market was significantly different from the urban target market.

## EXPERIMENT

The experiment involved the manipulation of three different media vehicles (i.e., radio, urban daily newspapers and suburban weeklies) in three different retail outlets and three separate markets. The impact and effectiveness of these vehicles were measured by comparing store traffic and sales revenues of the previous quarter with the quarter during which the experimental changes were instituted. Further, to assess the impact of uncontrollable changes in the external environment, the advertising and sales promotion activities of competitors were monitored both in the pre and post experimental periods.

The major objective of the experiment was to identify any shift in attitudes and purchase behaviour patterns resulting from the changes in media vehicles:

- From urban dailies to suburban weeklies,
- From urban dailies to radio broadcasts (urban and suburban areas).

By so doing, the effects of the independent variables (media vehicles) on the dependent variables (store traffic and sales volume) were investigated using a pre and post group design.

To determine the media exposure (i.e., newspaper reading and radio listening) habits of households in the central metropolitan area and its surrounding (suburbs), the responses were categorized, the percentages computed, and the appropriate statistical tests performed. Thus through the examination of consumer responses to the changes in media vehicles, the study attempts to address three specific issues. First, with respect to the type of newspapers regularly read by consumers, determine whether or not:

- Consumers use liquor store advertisements,
- Urban dailies and suburban weeklies are effective advertising vehicles.

Second, with respect to the types of radio stations regularly listened to by the target market, determine the reach of radio broadcast in the morning and evening drive time. Third, with respect to cost effectiveness and impact of media vehicles, compare the ability of newspapers and radio to draw the public into the store.

Beyond the issue of newspaper reading and radio listening habits of suburban and urban populations, is the question of the similarities and/or differences between the two target markets. To test the difference between the two target markets, the media exposure habits of the two markets shall therefore be compared with one another using a chi-square test.

## EXPECTATIONS

The expectations of management (and our tentative hypotheses are rational) were as follows:

- Since customers and prospective customers in the urban location have a low opportunity to see advertisements in the urban dailies, a change in the choice of media vehicles may generate an increase in sales. Because they result in less than optimal media exposure (20 per cent awareness), it was felt that the advertisements in urban dailies can be discontinued, and be replaced by radio broadcasts. Radio was expected to increase the urban population's opportunity to listen to the messages and therefore its exposure to the advertisements.
- Since the two target markets are different at least in some important aspects, initiating advertisements in suburban community weeklies may be an appropriate way to increase that target market's media exposure.

Some overlap in media exposure was expected in the reach of radio and weekly newspapers in suburban target markets, as suburban residents listen to many radio stations. Although this might confound the effect of weekly newspapers in the suburbs, we expect the crossover to have limited impact.

## RESULTS AND ANALYSIS

The findings indicate that in the central metropolitan area, 95 per cent of the households in the target market read the major daily newspapers with 20 per cent being aware of the regular appearance of advertisements for supermarket type liquor stores. Less than half of the target market (47 per cent) listened regularly to one or two of the six most popular radio stations with no one station holding a substantial rating edge. Roughly half of this group (48 per cent) was college students. In the suburban target market, 95.3 per cent read the urban dailies. Nevertheless, only 15.8 per cent were aware of the supermarket-type liquor store advertisements. In terms of radio listening habits, 65.4 per cent listened regularly to radio stations whose call letters they could identify. Some 12.6 per cent of the people in the suburbs habitually tune to one radio station.

The second most popular radio station was listened to by 1 1.7 per cent of the target population, while some 10.4 per cent listened to the third most popular station, and some 8.9 per cent listened to the fourth. Two radio stations tied for the fifth spot with a market share of 8.4 per cent. The remaining 34.6 per cent of the target market audience reported occasionally listening to another of the available 34 stations.

The results of the change to local community weeklies were quite dramatic. Compared with past sales revenue when urban newspapers were in use bench mark), the change away from urban daily newspapers resulted in an increase of 8 per cent in sales revenue in one store, and an increase of 3 per cent in another store.

Furthermore, the change from urban daily newspapers to suburban weeklies resulted in total savings from prior advertisement expenditures of about 50 per cent. Assuming an equal effectiveness in urban and suburban markets, the savings for the suburban market were roughly 25 per cent. The gain for the suburban market, however, is believed to be much higher than the reported 25 per cent, since the suburban target markets cannot be effectively reached through urban dailies.

The increase in store traffic after the change in media vehicle was substantial for one of the suburban locations. The urban target market where radio was used as a vehicle of communication, replacing the urban daily newspapers, showed a significant change both in store traffic and sales.

Measured during the quarter before and after the experiment, sales for the urban store registered an increase of 12 per cent. The increase in traffic counts (i.e, the number of people visiting the store) was 6.53 per cent. The change in media vehicles therefore appears to bring about a better fit between the target audience's media exposure habits and the new media vehicles.

## DISCUSSION

The results of this study suggest that the responsiveness of some target markets can be enhanced by changing the advertising vehicles. Clearly, the increase in sales revenue and store traffic would not have come without the prerequisite change in media vehicles. The increase in sales in the suburban store suggests that the new vehicles created a better opportunity for the message to be seen and heard by the target population than did urban daily newspapers.

However, it was also possible that the change in consumer purchase behaviour in the metro area resulted from the fact that the radio advertisements received greater attention because they were a new phenomenon. But do consumers pay that much attention to advertisements? Is a liquor ad, because it was inserted in a community weekly paper for the first time, likely to arouse the curiosity and interest of the public?

We do not discount the possibility that the change in advertising format plus the change in vehicles may have brought about a change in message awareness among the public. However, the fact that sales and store traffic remained steady for more than 90 days is an indicator that the change in the advertising vehicle was of tremendous value in creating a better fit with the lifestyles of the target market.

If the chosen radio station provides the public with a better opportunity to listen to an advertisement, it may subsequently fit better with the target market's psychographics. Based on this principle, an effort was made to increase the reach of radio broadcasts by fine-tuning the selection of stations. This strategy may have reinforced the awareness created by previous newspaper advertisements. For a multi-store operator with outlets in urban as well as suburban locations, the desire to use an urban paper is based on tradition and on lesser advertisement preparation costs. It is cheaper to prepare a message that is repeated time and again.

It may also seem to be cost effective in that both markets can be addressed in one vehicle. However, it may not generate the desired media exposure. In our field experiment, advertising exclusively in urban daily newspapers decreased the power of the media budget.

## LONG TERM MEDIA DECISIONS

Nevertheless, before the chain-store decides to change its media vehicles in the future, it should examine the similarities between the urban and suburban target markets. Such an investigation should give the advertiser the best opportunity to have his or her messages seen or heard by the target population. If, for example, the demographics are different, then the issue of media appropriateness and fit will become the central question. Following this reasoning, the demographics and media exposure habits of the urban and suburban target markets were compared.

Notably, the findings from the study indicated that there were mainly in the sex composition of the two target markets. There were also significant differences in the age composition and in the incomes of the urban and the suburban target markets. When the two target markets' exposures to radio commercials and newspaper advertisements were compared, there were also significant differences between the urban and suburban populations in exposure habits. These differences between the urban and suburban target populations raise the important question: Should the traditional advertising vehicle (i.e, urban daily newspapers) continue to be used, ignoring the apparent differences in both media exposure opportunities and actual media exposure habits in the target market? Should the vehicles be changed to fit the exposure habits of the population?

In this study, the retailer/advertiser felt that the changes in media vehicles promised some acceptable exposure levels. Therefore the adjustments made assumed two different forms: change in media vehicles, and/or change in message content, and the frequency of the message.

In a field experiment involving three retail outlets in three distinct markets, the effects of urban dailies, suburban weeklies and urban radio stations on store traffic and sales volume were investigated. Before and after changes in advertising vehicles were evaluated by comparing sales records and store traffic counts for the quarter before and the quarter during the experiment. Systematically changing the media vehicles used in store advertisements resulted in better responsiveness in terms of store traffic and sales volume. The savings to the advertiser were considerable. The suburban weeklies were found to be an excellent media vehicle in reaching the suburban target segment while radio appeared to create a better fit with the lifestyle of urban residents. Urban dailies, despite their popular use, were not as cost effective as the other media vehicles.

The study suggests that advertising in local, weekly community papers may be a better alternative than urban dailies for two reasons: first, because it is difficult to reach the suburban market using radio (the audience's listening tendencies are spread over several radio stations); second, because urban dailies, as an alternative media vehicle, offer lower advertisement exposure opportunity to suburban residents.

Radio presents a unique alternative. As judged from the media exposure habits of the target market, radio broadcasts appear to fit best with the psychographics of urban residents. The change to radio was thus viewed as desirable in creating synergy and in increasing the target market's opportunity to listen to the messages. This is further manifested by the improvements in store traffic and sales revenue for the store in the urban location.

Thus, whether it is a one-store or a multi-store operation, this field experiment suggests that, in spite of cost advantages promised by urban daily newspapers, it may be strategically unwise to exclusively use one medium in a major market with overlapping suburban-urban target markets. The emphasis should be on creating a fit with the target market's demographics and psychographics. What may be a good choice at one or two locations may be unwise at others.

This study is valuable in showing that the appropriate choices of media vehicles result in better media exposure and reach; however, it has some limitations. First, the findings may not be sufficient to generalize to other markets, retailers, or classes of trade. Second, the study could have been affected by the first time use of radio broadcasts. These shortcomings may be overcome by replicating this study in other regions of the country. It would therefore be of great research interest to analyse the differences in consumer responses as a result of the changes in advertising vehicles in other parts of the country.

Despite these limitations, this field experiment is of value to multi-store operators in showing that the absence of demographic differences between urban and suburban consumers does not mean that the same media vehicles can be used in all markets. The underlying differences among target markets have to be investigated.

# 8

# Journalistic Responsibility and Political Advertising

In modern political campaigns voters must rely on the mass media for most of their information about political candidates and issues. Candidates, of course, seek to maximize the advantages of this reliance for their own campaigns by providing voters with information the candidate can control directly, usually in the form of televised political advertising. As advertising has become more and more dominant in campaigns and as new media technologies have provided campaigns with new ways to manipulate media messages, journalists have recognized the importance of providing voters with independent information about such advertising messages. In fact, Washington Post columnist David Broder issued a call for journalists to improve their efforts to verify claims made in candidate spots. Political consultant Roger Aries characterized news coverage of candidate spots as follows:"... journalists, who had begun to feel ignored, decided to go on the offensive.

They vowed to protect the American people and formed, as Michael Oreskes of the New York Times termed it, a self-appointed journalistic `police force' to clean up campaign advertising".

Researchers noticed the increased attention given to political spots and began to investigate journalistic coverage of candidate advertising. However, most of the research focused on journalistic coverage of political advertising has been done on presidential campaign coverage on national television networks or prestige press print outlets, ignoring state and local elections and journalistic reporting for state and local newspaper and television media.

This neglect is particularly significant since survey evidence indicates that less than half (42%) of the American public regularly watch one of the network news broadcasts while 650/0 say they watch their local news. This study seeks to address this deficiency in existing literature by examining both print and local broadcast analysis at both the presidential and nonpresidential level during the 1996 campaign.

## JOURNALISTIC COVERAGE OF POLITICAL ADVERTISING

The media's role in this relationship is usually highlighted by its responsibility to provide citizens with information needed to make informed and rational decisions (often labeled the social responsibility theory of the press). Among the tenets articulated by the Commission on the Freedom of the Press in 1947, social responsibility theory of the press instructs that media should"represent all hues of the social spectrum," take responsibility for the quality of their programming, and"inject truth in advertising".

Although there may be many applications of these tenets to media coverage of political campaigns, the"truth in advertising" responsibility is particularly relevant here, especially since a regulatory agency for political advertisements does not exist. As Patterson and Wilkins in their popular textbook on media and ethics point out, this journalistic responsibility is a challenging one in modern campaigns because candidates now have so many capabilities for manipulation.

In the late 1980's journalists began to recognize how significant television advertising had become in the voter decision-making process and to see the need to provide another viewpoint or interpretive mode for this type of direct, unmediated form of candidate to voter communication. Journalists subsequently adopted a new strategy for covering campaigns, the"adwatch."

Adwatches can be defined as"media critiques of candidate ads designed to inform the public about truthful or misleading advertising claims". As described by West adwatches "review the content of prominent commercials and discuss their accuracy and effectiveness".

At the national level, at least, there has been a tremendous increase in recent years in news coverage of political television spots. Scholars have presented numerous possibilities that may explain media coverage of candidate ads, such as the drama of a close election campaign. Kaid et al. argued that candidate ads have received more attention in recent years because ads provide an easily transferable format for news reports, ads fit the horse-race nature of political reporting, and ads serve as a platform for campaign discourse.

Furthermore, Jamieson asserted that journalistic attention to candidate spots enables the spot to shape the news. Given the fact that the media may use spots as springboards or lead-ins to other campaign coverage, coverage of political advertising may not always be labeled as a formal"adwatch."

Content analyses of journalistic coverage of political advertising, despite focusing on presidential campaigns, show some important patterns. For example, the percentage of adwatches that address negative and issue ads is relatively stable across election years. More critically, research shows that print and televised adwatches are not always fair, neutral, or sufficiently critical. For example, as Tedesco et al. report, Perot ads were the dominant focus of

43% of network adwatches in 1992, whereas Bush and Clinton ads were much less likely to receive scrutiny (21% and 7%, respectively). Thus, despite the fact that the 19 short spots Perot produced and aired in 1992 were far fewer than the 39 spots aired by Clinton or the 32 shown by Bush, Perot's ads were far more likely to receive media attention.

In addition, content analyses show that presidential adwatches are given high priority in television news segments and in newspapers by appearing mostly within the first 10-minutes of the news broadcast or the first section of the newspaper. Researchers have concluded from the few studies that have been done on adwatches, either in print or broadcast media, that the journalists doing the adwatches have tended:

- To focus primly on television ads in presidential campaigns
- To analyse negative ads much more than positive ads from campaigns.

This approach may have left ads in state and local races less covered, ignoring positive ads in which candidates can make as many false and misleading claims as in negative advertising. Another disturbing trend in political ad coverage, particularly in the national network coverage of political spots, is the lack of in-depth interpretation and analysis of the ads. According to Jamieson, only 1.7% of the content of coverage about ads dealt with the accuracy of the ad claims. In her comparison of print and broadcast adwatches from 1992 and 1996, Bennett indicates that the percentages of advertising reports with in-depth analysis of spots dropped 68% for the networks and 20% for print sources from 1992 to 1996.

To address some of the criticisms of media adwatches, several scholars have offered suggestions for more systematic and effective results. For example, Jamieson developed a critique framework that incorporates previewing (setting up), distancing (setting off) disclaiming (labeling), displacing (interrupting), and recapping (summarizing) the ad under analysis. Furthermore, suggestions were made to extend the analysis of the ad claims to broader patterns and more concrete audiovisual and narrative frameworks.

Although Richardson acknowledges the constraints hindering analysis of long-term candidate policy stances and major argument premises, he argues that current practices of isolating specific claims,"rather than patterns of behaviour and record, moreover, may contribute to the alienation among voters that some scholars have attributed to adwatch journalism".

Yet adwatches can be an important tool in pointing up manipulative and deceptive ads. For instance, in the 1996 Virginia race for U.S. Senate, incumbent Senator John Warner ran a television ad in which the head of his opponent Mark Warner was substituted for the head of Virginia's other Senator, Chuck Robb, in a picture designed to show that Mark Warner was a liberal associating with other"known liberals" like President Clinton and former Virginia governor Wilder. If news reporters had not spotted the manipulation, voters might never have been informed about it. John Warner was forced to fire his advertising consultant and apologize for the deception, although he did go on to win re-election.

Indeed, how adwatches affect voter interpretations of ads is not completely clear. According to Cappella and Jamieson, how a reporter frames a political adwatch may affect voters' attitudes toward the ad itself, the perceived fairness of the ad, and the perceived importance of the ad. Cappella and Jamieson's research shows that well-constructed adwatches accomplish their goal and inform voters about the deceptive appeals made in candidate spots. However, such effects do not always have the effects journalists intend. In fact, because the advertisement appears in a credible news environment, it may actually benefit the political campaign. The majority of research shows that adwatches may produce a boomerang effect, further enhancing the ad itself. Likewise, Jamieson found that viewers in focus group, s recalled the ad itself better than the corrections made by the media commentator. These findings suggest that journalists must develop new and compelling ways to analyse spots or they risk failure in their attempts to provide voters with better decision-making tools.

This background on prior research on adwatches suggests that very little is known about how journalists cover advertising below the national level. The research reported here addresses this question by considering the following research questions about the 1996 campaign:

- How much coverage of political advertising do state and local media outlets give to presidential versus non-presidential races?
- When state and local media outlets cover political advertising, are there differences in the types of ads (negative versus positive) and in the party (Republican vs. Democrat), gender (male vs. female), or position (incumbent vs. challenger) of the candidate?
- Are there differences between television and print outlets in the nature of their coverage of political advertising?

## METHOD

The study relied on content analysis to determine the characteristics of adwatches in state and local media outlets. The sample of newspaper and television coverage came from a database of materials collected by the Political Communication Centre (PCC) at the University of Oklahoma during the 1996 campaign. As part of a larger study on the campaigns, the PCC coordinated an election study in cooperation with 16 locations around the United States, balanced for regional diversity. At these t6 sites, the researchers working with the PCC collected local newspapers and recorded local television newscasts for the eight weeks from Labour Day through election day in 1996. A list of the newspaper and television station sites is included at the end of this chapter. All television stations are, of course, generally local ones, although many have statewide reach in their areas. In addition to a mixture of large and small city daily newspapers, we also included USA Today in our newspaper sample because, while it is in some ways a national newspaper, it is also a paper that makes an attempt to cover major competitive races below the presidential level. In the case of newspapers, the first edition of the day, as distributed to subscribers, was chosen, and the television station recorded in each market was the one with the highest viewership ratings in the fall of 1996. The first step in the project involved going through all newspapers and all local television newscasts for these eight weeks and identifying the stories in which campaign spots were analysed.

Thus, each story identified in the newspapers or the local television news broadcasts was a unit of analysis. Since our goal was to identify and analyse all types of coverage given to political spot advertising, a story did not have to be identified as a formal"adwatch" or use that term specifically in order to fall into the sample of stories analysed. Indeed, most of the stories were a type of"adwatch," but media outlets, both print and broadcast, have many different ways of incorporating spot coverage into their stories, and we wanted to get a broad and comprehensive look at the treatment of television spots.

A series of categories were developed, derived from prior work on adwatches described above, and applied to each story or unit of analysis.

*This would include such standard categories as*:

- Story placement (quadrant location for newspapers, location in first, second, and third part of newscast for television stories),
- Length of story (in column inches for newspapers; in minutes and seconds for television,
- Type of story (campaign news report, advertising feature, candidate profile, issue report, etc.),
- Level of race covered,
- Type of ad analysed (negative ad/positive ad);
- Candidate and political party,
- How the ad is analysed (verbal content, visual content),
- Whether misleading verbal or visual techniques are identified,
- Reproduction of ad (for instance, is part of the ad played on television or shown in picture frames for newspapers?),
- Use of experts for criticism (are other analysts quoted or consulted in critiquing the ad?), and several additional categories.

Coders also determined if the advertising discussed in the story received in-depth analysis by marking if the ad received any specific commentary by the reporter, beyond mere description, about its content or campaign context. Coders specifically marked if the story attempted to label the ad as misleading, false, untrue, wrong, unfair, or some other evaluative characterization.

A written codesheet for these categories was developed, along with a written codebook defining each category. One graduate student and one undergraduate student were trained in the use of the codesheet and did the actual coding. Intercoder reliability was computed on a sample of the print and newspaper stories and averaged across the categories reported here. Individual category reliability was also high, ranging from a low of.88 for how video content was analysed to a high of 1.00 for several categories such as identification of party and level of race covered.

The sample described above yielded a total of 190 adwatches; 143 of these were in newspapers and 47 were on local television stations. This differential between newspapers and television is partly accounted for by the larger number of adwatches undertaken by the larger dailies in the sample. For instance, of the 143 newspaper adwatches, 28 (20%) were done by the New York Times. The Washington Post and USA Today printed 18 (13%) adwatches each, and the Boston Globe contributed 17 (12%) to the newspaper sample. Thus, well over half of the newspaper stories were done by these three large dailies. Of the less well-known papers, The Oregonian did 15 adwatches, the St. Louis Post-Dispatch printed 10, and the Sacramento Bee provided 9. Only one newspaper in our sample, The Indianapolis Star, failed to write any adwatch stories during the time frame of the sample.

In the television sample (n = 47), the distribution among outlets was more even. No local station carried the national obligations of the large city dailies. The largest number of adwatches on television came from KVAL in Eugene, Oregon, and WTVD in Raleigh, North Carolina (7 each; 15% each of the total sample), followed by KARE in Minneapolis and WCJB in Gainesville, Florida (6 each; 13% of the total sample). Several stations undertook no adwatches at all.

## COMPARISON OF PRESIDENTIAL AND NON-PRESIDENTIAL COVERAGE

An important reason for looking at ad coverage from more local sources is to determine, as our first research question suggested, the amount of coverage that advertising receives for races below the presidential level. In the newspaper sample of 143 adwatches, 80% of the candidates covered in the ads were presidential candidates. Of course, as in the overall numbers of adwatches, the largest numbers of these adwatches for presidential candidates came from the prestige dailies.

Of the 114 (80%) newspaper adwatches covering presidential candidates, 20 presidential adwatches came from the New York Times, 18 came from USA Today, and the Washington Post was the source of another 16. However, it is clear that many smaller dailies also gave their attention to the presidential race. Even the television stations, which were all local stations, focused their attention on presidential races; 36% of the local television adwatch stories were on presidential candidates. While we have no way of knowing if, in fact, all Congressional candidates aired political spots, with the growth of political advertising on state and local levels, we feel safe in our assumption that spot ads were featured in these races yet ignored by state and local media. In the 16 states represented by our various newspapers and television news stations, nine of the states (or 56.25%) featured a U. S. Senate race, and three states (18.75%) had gubernatorial races.

## TYPES OF CANDIDATES AND ADS COVERED

Our second research question concerned the types of candidates and ads that received coverage. The first thing to notice is that party affiliation of the candidate does make a difference; Republican candidates receive the most adwatch scrutiny. Both newspapers and television give Republican candidates three times as much advertising coverage as they give Democrats.

An interesting finding, however, is the large amount of coverage received in 1996 by Independent and Reform Party candidates in television adwatches. One reason for this attention was the fact that Reform Party candidate Ross Perot chose television ads as a way to highlight his exclusion from the presidential debates, and many television stations chose to use analysis of these ads as a way of airing this issue.

For example, the local news in Gainesville, FL (WCJB), after reporting that Republican nominee Bob Dole narrowly trailed Bill Clinton in Florida polls, next noted that Ross Perot's support was low in that state and that he had been excluded from the upcoming presidential debate. This campaign news report then went on to highlight Sunday morning interviews in which Perot blamed Bob Dole for excluding him from the debates,"he [Dole] has been rude and arrogant... I guess he's desperate."

Next, a Perot ad was featured which claimed Perot"won the debates" in 1992, that"76% of voters" wanted Perot in the 1996 debates, and concluded with"let Ross speak, the truth never hurt anyone." The news report in no way attempted to analyse the claims made by the Perot ad, but rather was an analysis of campaign strategy. The ad received flee media exposure because it conveniently helped to tell the story of Perot vs. Dole and Perot's debate plight.

Another ad sponsored by an independent candidate that garnered considerable media attention was that of Taxpayer Party candidate Chad Koppie who was seeking the U. S. Senate seat in Illinois. Koppie's ad, which deals with the abortion issue, opens with a choir of young children singing the words,"How long must the killing go on? How long must the blood be on our hands?" The ad then fades from the chorus of children to show an adult hand holding the remains of a bloody fetus.

The local TV news programme that reported on the ad began their segment by showing the candidate in their studio viewing his own ad. The news report then featured a few seconds of the actual ad but blurred the screen when the fetus appeared. Finally, the candidate was allowed to comment on his ad.

The use of candidate commentary was noted often in our analysis of television news' reporting of local races and candidate ads. Frequently, when a station would highlight a local candidate's ad, and often these ads would be of some controversial nature, the station would then invite the candidate him or herself to explain or justify their own ad. Thus, not only would the ad receive free media exposure through its airing on the local news broadcast, but the candidate would also receive exposure on the local news to further comment on what they were saying in the paid advertising messages.

The controversial Koppie ad described above also received national attention when the New York Times reported that Koppie was a little-known candidate in Illinois until he began running his controversial abortion advertisement featuring the remains of dead fetuses. The Times article did not examine the actual ad, but rather focused on the dilemma faced by the two Chicago TV stations from which Koppie had purchased time to run his ads.

The stations had received many complaints and requests to stop broadcasting the"graphic" spot as many viewers were"horrified... that young children [were] watching." The article reported that the TV stations, due to a recent Federal court ruling, had"no choice but to broadcast it, and to do so when children are likely to be watching, because the commercial advocates the election of a candidate for the United States Senate."

As Kahn has shown, female candidates often do not receive their fair share of news coverage, and clearly this extends to coverage of their ads. In 1996 in this sample no woman candidate received individual coverage of her ads in newspapers or on television. In fact, 90% of newspaper adwatches and 70% of television ones focused on male candidates. Even when featured with male candidates, women candidates could not hope for much coverage. The lack of coverage for female candidates' spots may actually be a feature of the type of ads covered by the media. As discussed in the previous section, advertising in U. S. Congressional races was among the most neglected, the very campaigns that most often featured female candidates.

In fact, of the 16 states represented by our media sample, all but one state (Oklahoma) featured female candidates vying for U. S. Congressional seats. While there were no female Senate candidates in the nine Senate races from our 16 states, two of the three states from our 16-state sample with an active race for Governor (Indiana and Missouri) did feature female Gubernatorial candidates. Again, Gubernatorial campaigns received the least amount of coverage in both print and broadcast media.

In considering the disparity of whose ads receive attention by the news media, one may question the advantages and disadvantages of having one's spot ads the focus of media analysis and commentary. Clearly, existing evidence suggests that lack of attention to one's ads, even as part of news critique and commentary, places a candidate in a disadvantageous position.

First, as the current study has found, most often the attention paid to ads in state and local media is devoid of critical assessment and, particularly in television coverage, provides a free airing of at least a portion of an ad, and furthermore, may often serve as an opportunity for the candidate to provide their own analysis of their ad message. Also, as discussed in our review of literature, a growing body of adwatch research has shown that the credible environment of news reporting may actually enhance an ad's effectiveness.

One of the very few female-candidate sponsored ads that received news attention was that of Connie McBurney, Democratic challenger for a congressional seat in Iowa. McBurney first aired a spot dealing with the issue of abortion, which was followed by a response ad from her opponent, the incumbent Republican member of Congress, Greg Ganske. The two ads were the focus of a report by the local Des Moines, IA (KCCI) evening news programme.

The news anchor announced that both candidates had just"unveiled new TV ads about abortion," and clips from both candidates' ads were then shown, set off in a TV screen and clearly labeled"advertisement." The challenger, Connie McBurney, who supports abortion rights, revealed in her ad that"We were excited about having a baby, but something went wrong and she died only six days old. I thought I would have more children, but I didn't. Now Greg Ganske says I want to kill children. That's indecent." Next, a segment from the Ganske ad was shown which featured a head-shot of the candidate stating,"and we can only have compassion for the loss of Connie McBurney's new born baby, but I have never accused Connie McBurney of wanting to kill children." The TV report then featured an interview with candidate Ganske who called McBurney's ad a"media ploy," and he concluded the news report by stating"I really think that probably the McBurney campaign feels that they need to try to do something dramatic in the last few days to try to turn this campaign around." Interesting in this news segment is the fact that while both candidates' ads were featured, only the male incumbent Ganske was interviewed and allowed to comment on his opponent's ad.

Another finding that stands out is that challengers are much more likely to receive adwatch attention than are incumbents. On both television and in newspapers, 2 out of every 5 adwatch stories (38%) were on challenger ads, double the amount for incumbents in newspapers and triple the coverage for incumbents on television. As with previous research on adwatches at the national level, this study shows that negative ads are the most likely type of ad to be analysed in an adwatch. Negative ads were the dominant focus of 50% of the newspaper stories and 60% of the television stories.

## COMPARISON OF PRINT AND BROADCAST COVERAGE CHARACTERISTICS

In addition to looking at what types of candidates and ads were the focus of adwatches, our third research question focused on the characteristics of the adwatches themselves in print and broadcast outlets. Here there were some clear differences between newspapers and local television stations. The ads themselves were the main focus of the newspaper adwatches (88% of the time for newspapers but only 36% of the time for television stations). This finding may substantiate the fact that television stations often use ads and analyse them as a supplement to other stories and as a way of providing video or dramatic visuals for general campaign news stories.

**Table: Characteristics of Adwatches in Newspapers and on Local Television**

| | Newspaper n = 143 | Local TV n = 47 |
|---|---|---|
| Advertising main Focus | 88% | 36% |
| Use of Experts | | |
| Independent consultant | 3 | 4 |
| Campaign consultant | 8 | 0 |
| Campaign official | 42 | 11 |
| Candidate | 27 | 19 |
| Media | 11 | 38 |
| Academic expert | 10 | 2 |
| Picture or Video Shown | 32 | 98 |

Often, the story that ads help local television stations tell is of a negative campaign with"nasty" attack ads that only succeed in alienating voters. For example, the Minneapolis, Minnesota station led with a story on the Paul Wellstone/Rudy Boschwitz U. S. Senate race that blamed candidate ads for turning voters off. The anchors began this story by proclaiming,"Nasty sums up the advertising war between Paul Wellstone and Rudy Boschwitz... what the negative ads have done are anger the voting public."

The local correspondent introduced the report by noting,"If you're like many Minnesotans, you've seen a lot of this..." which was followed by clips of three uninterrupted ads, labeled"adwatch."

Following the three ad clips, the correspondent concluded,"And if you're like many Minnesotans, you're not happy about it." Next, a citizen on the street is interviewed, and offers his assessment:"I think they suck... it's all kinda `B.S.' You know, they're not looking at issues, they're just sniping at each other." More segments from ads are shown, and the news story ends with yet another citizen proclaiming,"It makes me not want to really vote, or not have too much faith in either one of the candidates."

A similar story of negative ads and voter alienation appeared on the Des Moines, Iowa (KCCI/Channel 8) news, as its lead segment was introduced with the following question,"They're getting a lot of air play these days, but are the politicians getting all the mileage they want from all those commercials you've been seeing running just these days before the election?" The second anchor picks up the introduction with"Election day will be a day of ending-an ending to some political careers and to all political campaign commercials... we want to go ahead and show you just how tired people have been getting of all the political campaign commercials here in Central Iowa."

The local news correspondent first revealed that 71 paid political campaign ads would be aired on their station that day alone, and the report then goes to a local shopping mall to find a citizen who laments,"That's all that's on television." Next, this story features uninterrupted clips from three different ads, labeled"advertisement", with each of the three ads focusing on the abortion issue. Following the three ads, it's back to the shopping mall where one citizen proclaims,"Oh, I'm pretty well burned out on them. You learn to filter them out." As these examples illustrate, quite often when local television stations do feature candidate ads as part of their campaign reporting, they do so not to analyse the content of ads, but rather to use ads as convenient material to help them tell their story of a negative campaign. While the ads' claims and counter claims go unanalysed by the local journalists, citizens are provided with frequent reminders of just how nasty the campaigns have become.

Further reinforcement of the importance the television stations place on the visuals is provided by the fact that 98% of all television adwatches use a video clip of one or more spots in their stories.

On the other hand, although it would be quite easy to reproduce a picture or still frame image from a spot in print, newspapers use pictures of ads to support their analyses only one-third as often as television stations do. It is also clear that newspapers often rely more on experts to assist in the analysis of spots. While local television stations find their own or other media experts, or as noted earlier, use the candidates themselves, to be the best source of opinions on spots, newspaper are more ready to consult other experts, frequently tapping into campaign consultants and officials and even academic experts.

Even more significant than the simple content characteristics of ad coverage may be the approach that is taken to analysis of the ad. As mentioned in the introduction, other research, particularly on national television networks and large daily newspaper adwatches, has suggested that the media are often not sufficiently analytical in their scrutiny of ads and perhaps do not provide voters with sufficient information to judge the flaws in political spots.

This study suggests that these earlier findings provide continuing cause for concern. Local television stations in particular are not providing much in-depth analysis of the spots they analyse.

Fewer than one-third (28%) of television adwatch stories attempt any in-depth analysis of the spots they examine. Based on our category definitions this means that the media outlet coverage was basically descriptive and did not make any attempt to analyse the ads being covered, to evaluate them or characterize them in any way that would provide voters with a cue as to the truthfulness or fairness of the claims in the ad.

The failure to provide in-depth analysis may leave voters confused by competing, and often contradictory, claims that go unexplained or clarified. Such journalistic coverage of ads was most apparent in local television newscasts, as campaign reporting would often feature candidates' response ads as a convenient way to develop the narrative of a negative or nasty campaign, while ignoring the actual claims made in the ads.

An example of unexamined competing claims is illustrated in a lead segment of the local news programme of WISH (Channel 8-Indianapolis) on the Indiana gubernatorial campaign. The 1996 Indiana governor's race featured Democrat Frank O'Bannon and Republican Steve Goldsmith. This local newscast began with one of the anchors announcing"We start with the race for Governor today as the negative tone of the campaign is growing harsher." The second anchor concluded the introduction with"This time Frank O'Bannon has a new attack ad on the air."

The anchors then go to their correspondent who introduces the story by noting,"Steve Goldsmith launched a television volley on Friday, and today Frank O'Bannon answered." The report next features an uninterrupted portion of the O'Bannon ad, labeled"counterattack," that stated"How low can Frank O'Bannon go? He knows Steve Goldsmith never raised a tax-never!"

The journalist continues to tell the story of candidate attack and counterattack by informing viewers that"The latest ad war surrounds Frank O'Bannon's claim that taxes in Indianapolis have gone up under Steve Goldsmith. A Goldsmith ad refutes this claim and Republicans on the city/ county council today called the O'Bannon ad `quote' false." Next, a Goldsmith campaign representative is interviewed, stating"The taxes went down, they did not go up. Very simply, Steve Goldsmith has not increased taxes... and we demand that he [O'Bannon] take the ads off the air." The local journalist continues the story of dueling ads and competing claims,"But not only is O'Bannon refusing to apologize, his campaign unveiled a new ad today that repeats the claim while attacking Goldsmith."

Viewers are then shown an uninterrupted portion of the ad that states"Steve Goldsmith has resorted to negative attacks the press calls sleazy, deceptive, not true." The ad clip is followed by an O'Bannon campaign spokesperson who comments"anyone who's got property tax bills for'95 and'96 can see that their property taxes went up."

As this news story is constructed, its primary focus is to demonstrate to voters that their gubernatorial candidates were attacking one another over the issue of taxes in their most recent ads, yet the reporting does nothing to examine the competing claims made by the candidates and their ads. In fact, the correspondent leaves the voters to figure things out for themselves when he concludes the report with,"Democrats points to higher property tax assessments, while Republicans point to a lower rate. It's become a game of he said/he said."

While fewer than one-half of newspaper stories also performed in-depth analysis (43%) in their ad watches, newspapers sometimes were more substantive than television in giving voters independent information needed to evaluate competing candidate claims. For instance, The Oregonian, in a series of adwatches called"Analyzing the ADS," often engaged the actual content of ads and pointed up correct and incorrect information.

The paper did exactly that in a September 24 story assessing one of Perot's ads complaining about his exclusion from the presidential debates. In the spot, Perot claims that support"seventy per cent of Americans want Ross Perot in the debates." The adwatch report tells voters that this is a bit misleading since that figure was from an early September poll, and that now the percentage who want Perot included has dropped to only 52%. Other statistics are evaluated as well, and thus, the newspaper provides the reader with more information to evaluate the claims made in the ad.

While newspapers analyse the audio content of spots in 89% of their stories, television stations actually engage and analyse the audio content in only 40% of their adwatch stories. Neither television nor newspapers give as much consideration as may be justified to the video content of spots. Only just over half of all newspaper stories (55%) address the video content of an ad, and only 13% of television analyses do so.

In addition, most stories about spots are"neutral" in their focus, providing neither a negative nor a positive focus most of the time. Only 13% of newspaper stories and 4% of television stories actually critique ads as misleading, and fewer provide sufficient judgmental information to suggest that any ad is false or untruthful. Only about one in seven stories (13% for newspapers and 15% for television) make any mention in their analyses of suspect technological maneuvers in the spots.

That is, the analysis do not call to the attention of the voter any use of special effects, video editing, digital alterations, colour or shaded video, altered sound effects or any other technique that might be designed to mislead or create false impressions for viewers.

While statistics for ads in the same races covered here are not available, recent research on presidential elections suggests that 42-43% of television spots from the 1992 and 1996 campaigns had identifiable distortions, far more than the percentages identified by the media coverage. Some political observers have feared that showing political spots on television without setting them off in some way or labeling them may actually serve to reinforce the effect of the ad, rather than to point up its faults. This study shows that most television news stories now take note of this concern.

When candidate spots are shown as part of an analysis, 83% of television stories label the ad or set it off in some way, and 87% provide a journalist or other voice-over that further serves to interrupt and break-up the ad's flow. Only 21% of the stories analysed in this study allowed political spots to run"full screen" in original form without offsetting or labeling. The conclusions from this study begin to provide a clearer picture of the media coverage of candidate advertising below the presidential level. First, as our analysis reveals, congressional and state-wide races are often ignored even by local media. Quite often, and particularly with local TV news programs, the local media will feature analysis of the presidential candidates' ads provided by their network affiliates.

With such"news" material easily available to the local stations, it appears that these news organizations may not be willing to invest the time and resources needed to analyse the advertisements that are featured by their local and state-wide candidates. With more and more candidates at all levels increasingly turning to advertising as their primary way to communicate with voters, local media must begin to devote the resources needed to help readers and viewers understand the messages of their local and state-wide candidates.

Another troubling conclusion that can be drawn from this study is the lack of in-depth analysis provided by local media. Here, local TV, as opposed to print media, is even more negligent in analyzing the actual content of candidate advertising. As illustrated above, often an ad is featured in a broadcast news report to help tell a larger campaign story; and the story told is most often that of campaign strategy-particularly how candidates are engaged in attacking one another.

In reporting candidate attacks made through their advertising spots, very rarely would the reporter/journalist analyse the often competing claims made in the ads, providing voters with an assessment of those ads and claims that might be misleading, false, or unfair. While the current study provides a more in-depth picture of ad coverage at the state and local level than previously available, our findings point to several additional questions for future analysis. For example, why would Republican candidates receive three times as much advertising coverage as Democrats? Is this level of coverage in any way equivalent to the proportion of Republican vs. Democratic ads that appear? National trends have shown that Republican candidates are often better funded than their Democratic counterparts.

Perhaps a greater number of Republican ads appear at the state and local level and thus receive greater media coverage. While it is much easier to determine the numbers of ads produced and broadcast by presidential candidates, one might also be able to monitor ads that appear on local stations and then compare the frequency of these ads to the coverage and analysis of ads provided by local news media.

While newspaper coverage and analysis of advertising is most often based on televised ads, with the exception of a small number of print ads, the coverage of televised ads by local news organizations raises several interesting questions. For example, in terms of the actual ads that are selected for analysis or commentary in local news broadcasts, what relationship, if any, is there between the advertising that appears on (and generates revenue for) a local station, and that which is given critical assessment by the local news operation?

The influence of money in political campaigns, and advertising in particular, has emerged as a major concern in the electoral process. A more complete understanding of the role of money, political advertising at the state and local level, and critical assessment of such ad messages by media organizations require a closer look at the candidate ads that are broadcast by local stations and that receive analysis by these same stations.

Our analysis describes the differing amounts of ad coverage based on level of race, party and status of candidate, as well as candidate gender, with those races that most often feature female candidates receiving the least amount of attention. In addition to these factors, other features of a campaign may also influence the coverage afforded particular ads and candidates.

For example, do more ad watches appear in highly contested races? Does the coverage of ads, and particularly the type of critical analysis or commentary of ads, differ for successful vs. unsuccessful candidates? Such questions would require monitoring the development and outcome of particular races combined with the type of content analytic analysis provided by the current study. In failing to provide in-depth analysis or to point up potential ethical abuses, journalists may be failing in their responsibilities to provide voters with the information they need to make good voting decisions. As interpreters of the candidates and their campaign messages, journalists must realise the extent to which voters rely on them to help us make sense of the many and often conflicting messages. As political communication scholars, it is imperative that we continue to investigate how the media establishment is fulfilling, or abdicating, this"watchdog" role.

# 9

# Empirical Analysis of Advertising

Women are starting businesses at over twice the rate of men and could well own and operate 50 per cent of all businesses by the year 2011. The majority of research on women-owned businesses is a relatively recent phenomenon focusing on a wide range of issues.

An early study by Schwartz examined the characteristics and attitudes of women business owners. He found that female entrepreneurs tended to closely control their business operations and also experienced barriers to the acquisition of initial capital. Several studies found that women entrepreneurs were generally married and between the ages of 30 and 45, typically had backgrounds in the liberal arts, and had previous work experience in a variety of areas, such as teaching, retail sales, and office administration. Birley, Moss, and Saunders examined the differences between female and male entrepreneurs and found that both women's and men's past experience helped in providing managerial skills in the start-up stage.

There was little difference between their levels of education and their financing process. Many studies have determined that women business owners are more similar to than different from men across psychological and demographic dimensions, such as motivations for starting their businesses (independence, achievement, and job satisfaction). The most frequently cited problems of women-owned businesses are the lack of experience in management, accounting, advertising, and finance (financial planning, obtaining lines of credit, collateral position, and lending processes). The biggest obstacles for women are the financial aspects of venture start-up and management.

Despite the tremendous growth in the number of women-owned enterprises and the increasing impact on society and the economy, there are few studies discussing the relationship between women entrepreneurs and advertising. Some research has been reported regarding entrepreneurs and advertising. A study by Van Auken, Doran, and Rittenburg examined advertising media strategies among entrepreneurs. Jackson and Parasuraman indicated that the disadvantages of advertising for small firms are their relatively limited financial and professional resources.

Their results support the traditional assumption that the yellow pages are a well-used advertising medium. Brunning and Adams examined the effectiveness of promotional tools for small industrial businesses and found that trade shows can be an effective means of competing on an equal level with larger firms and can deliver a qualified audience to the small industrial firm at a relatively low cost.

While women business owners may be more similar to men than different, the nature of differences might affect advertising strategy. There is evidence that men and women's communication styles differ. Tannen characterizes male-female conversation as cross-cultural communication:"...women speak and hear a language of connection and intimacy, while men speak and hear a language of status and independence...."

While women may use communication to establish connection with others, avoiding confrontation or conflict, men may tend to view others more competitively and use conflict as a way of negotiating status. A number of studies provide evidence that women tend to place more emphasis on relationships.

Konner argues that biological differences cause men to be more aggressive in nature, and that this aggression is further learned and reinforced socially; on the other hand, women tend to evolve behaviour patterns that emphasize sensitivity, communication skills, community, inclusion, and relationships. Jelinek and Adler report that women may have an advantage of good interpersonal skills, meaning that women and men may talk more easily about a wider range of topics with women.

All of these findings seem to support the notion that women have a nurturing nature, that they strive for community and try to build relationships, and that these characteristics are reflected in their communication styles. Since advertising may be the primary tool most companies use to communicate with potential customers, differences in communication style are relevant in examining the types of advertising strategies selected.

In addition to differences in communication style, women tend to be primarily concerned with the method used to accomplish a task, while men are more concerned with the result of the task. This difference also may contribute to differences in strategy development by men and women. With respect to advertising strategy, this might indicate a greater focus on the part of women on the advertising methods used, while men might be postulated to be more concerned with the results of that advertising.

Corporations are changing. As Kanter states, a growing number of companies are empowering more of their work force, both male and female. Nonetheless, the"glass ceiling" keeping women, out of the highest positions has not yet been penetrated to any great extent. One alternative for women facing the glass ceiling is to start their own businesses. So, even though androgyny, an approach which blends behaviors previously deemed to belong exclusively to men or women, may be the new management mode, it is unclear to what extent managerial behaviour has become androgynous, either in large corporations or small businesses. It might be speculated that,

particularly for women bumping up against the glass ceiling, creating their own businesses allows them to succeed using the style of decision-making and communication most comfortable for them. If this were true, differences might be detected in the advertising strategies selected by female entrepreneurs as compared to male entrepreneurs (who currently represent the vast majority of entrepreneurs).

## PURPOSE OF THE RESEARCH

The purpose of this study is to extend prior research regarding the selection of advertising media, building on findings regarding the use and effectiveness of advertising media by entrepreneurs reported by Van Auken, Doran, and Rittenburg. The current study focuses on advertising media decisions made by women entrepreneurs. Vaccaro and Kassaye noted that little is known about the effectiveness of alternative advertising media.

The difficulty of measuring the effectiveness of advertising media also has been noted by Belch and Belch. This chapter uses stepwise multiple regression analysis to analyse and better understand the determinants of perceived effectiveness of the various advertising media. It uses a nationwide survey of women entrepreneurs which collected information concerning their use of advertising media during their first and most current year of operation.

In a study sampling 375 small businesses in the Midwest, Van Auken, Doran, and Rittenburg found that the advertising media that was ranked as one of the three most effective during the first year in operation was the most important factor in determining which advertising media were used during the most current year in operation. Rather than changing the advertising mix over time, these findings suggest that small businesses do not change their assessment of the relative effectiveness of alternative advertising media as they become more established.

This study employs Van Auken, Doran, and Rittenburg's methodology to determine:

- The usage and perceived effectiveness of alternative advertising media used by women entrepreneurs;
- The relationship between firm demographics, business-related problems and previous usage of alternative advertising media, and the perceived effectiveness rankings of advertising media;
- Whether a national sample of women entrepreneurs exhibit a tendency to continue with the same advertising media strategy over time;
- Whether women entrepreneurs report similar media usage and effectiveness ratings as a general population of entrepreneurs.

An examination of these issues will provide a better understanding of patterns of advertising media and their relative perceived effectiveness by women entrepreneurs. An analysis of usage patterns, perceived effectiveness and what factors affect perceived effectiveness can provide a better understanding of women as business owners and of important operational aspects of their businesses.

The research expands our understanding of how smaller firms use advertising, which is an important operational consideration for smaller firms that has received very little attention in the literature. These results can be beneficial to potential and new women entrepreneurs in providing insight into developing advertising strategies for their businesses.

## SAMPLING METHODOLOGY

An initial sample of 400 women-owned businesses was selected from the Directory of Women Entrepreneurs. To ensure geographical representation, the U.S. was divided into four quadrants, and a random sample of 100 businesses was drawn from each quadrant. Questionnaires were sent to women-owned businesses in 45 states and the District of Columbia. A questionnaire was developed and pretested in April 1991, and all mailings occurred during May 1991. A total of 121 usable questionnaires were returned from 36 states, resulting in a 30.75 per cent response rate.

The survey collected information on the use and perceived effectiveness of alternative advertising media by the women entrepreneurs. Respondents were asked to indicate which of various alternative advertising media were used during the first and current years of operation and to rank those advertising media in order of perceived effectiveness. Advertising media not used by the women entrepreneurs were not ranked for effectiveness.

For example, if five of the alternative advertising media had been used, then the respondent was asked to rank those advertising media in order of perceived effectiveness (1 = most effective and 5 = least effective). If three of the alternatives had been used, respondents were asked to rank those advertising media in order of perceived effectiveness (1 = most effective and 3 = least effective).

The advertising media examined include: television, newspapers, radio, telephone directories, fliers, word-of-mouth/referrals, participation in community events, and direct mail. Information on the relative use of the advertising media provided a better understanding of the methods used by women entrepreneurs. Information on the perceived ranking of advertising media will provide insight into how women perceived the effectiveness of these alternatives. This aspect of the study will also address the lack of knowledge of the effectiveness of alternative advertising media as noted by Vaccaro and Kassaye. The respondents also were asked to rank the three most difficult problems they experienced during their first year and during their most current year of operation (establishing market identity, advertising, bookkeeping, personnel, inventory management, accounts receivable, supplier relations, short term debt, long term debt, cash flow, and balancing family needs with the demands of the business).

In addition, the survey gathered information on women-owned businesses' demographics such as: type of business (service, retail, and other), years in operation, type of ownership structure (sole proprietorship, partnership, and corporation), size of market served (local, regional, national, and international), initial capital, and size of the local community.

This type of information is likely related to the use and perceived effectiveness of the alternative advertising media. For example, the type of business, size of market served, size of community, or years in business may have a significant impact on the methods of advertising used and relative effectiveness of the alternative advertising media.

Female entrepreneurs experience varying business problems which directly depend on the type of business; however, similar women-owned businesses would be expected to have common problems. For example, the selection of the most effective advertising media would be expected to be a common problem among women entrepreneurs. It is also expected that the types of advertising media used will change over time in response to changing problems, markets, capital resources, cash flows, relationships with media agents, etc. The sample was initially subdivided into three groups (service, retail, and other). The percentage of each group using each type of advertising media was tabulated for the first and current year of operation. The percentage of firms ranking each advertising medium as one of the top three most effective methods also was tabulated for the first and current year of operation.

A series of stepwise regressions were used to analyse factors affecting the effectiveness of the various advertising media during the first and current year of operation. A total of eight regressions were used for both the first and current year of operation. The dependent variable in each regression was the effectiveness of various advertising media for the first and current year of operation. The independent variables in each regression consisted of the firm's demographics and the most common problems that women-owned businesses experienced in the operation of their businesses.

The small size and limited resources of women-owned small firms found by Van Auken, Gaskill, and Kao and Hisrich may place operational constraints, resulting in a variety of business problems, and limit available alternative advertising possibilities.

Limitations on the use of alternative advertising media may also be related to the demographic characteristics of the firm, such as type, location, market served, community size, etc., of the firm. The purpose of the regression analysis was to investigate and explain differences between the respondents' rankings of the effectiveness of the alternative advertising media.

Summary information of selected characteristics of the women-owned businesses in the sample indicated that:

- Approximately 49.6 per cent of the firms in the sample were service businesses, and 16.3 per cent of the firms were retail businesses. The remaining firms (34.1 per cent) were in other business categories such as manufacturing, finance, construction, wholesale, and professional. These results are similar to the findings in several other studies, which found that a great majority of the women-owned businesses were service-oriented. The high percentage of nontraditional women-owned businesses in such fields as manufacturing, construction, insurance, and finance is consistent with Hisrich and Brush.
- More than one-half (56.9 per cent) of the women-owned enterprises in the sample operated as sole proprietorships, while 32.5 per cent were corporations, and about 10.6 per cent were partnerships. This finding is consistent with other studies, which have found that women most often choose sole proprietorships as the preferred form of a business structure and is comparable to findings for male-owned businesses.
- The market that women-owned businesses in the sample served was almost equally divided into local, regional, and national (26.8 per cent, 29.3 per cent, and 26.0 per cent, respectively), while 17.9 per cent focused on international markets. In previous studies, most of the women-owned enterprises served only local markets. For example, the results of Hisrich and Brush indicated that almost one-half of the business served only local markets.
- The majority of the respondents (71.3 per cent) had an initial capitalization of less than $20,000. Of the remaining firms, 18 per cent required $20,000 to $50,000; 8.2 per cent required $50,000 to $100,000; and only 2.4 per cent required more than $100,000 to begin operations. The required initial capitalization in this study is somewhat higher than Hisrich and Brush, who reported that 53 per cent started their businesses with less than $5,000.

Referrals are the most commonly used method of advertising by all categories of firms for both the first and current year. In addition, community events, telephone directories, and direct mail were frequently used during the first year, while referrals, telephone directories, community events, and fliers were used more during the current year in operation.

Radio and television advertising by all categories of the firms was generally the least utilized of the media examined (less than 8 per cent) for both time periods. A likely explanation is that using television advertising is too expensive for most smaller firms, including those owned by women. Across all 121 firms, the percentage of firms utilizing referrals, community events, direct mail, telephone directory, and television advertising media did not change markedly from the first to the current year. However, approximately 50 per cent more of the sample firms were using fliers in the current year relative to the first period of operations. Similarly, approximately 50 per cent fewer firms were using newspapers and radio in the current year relative to the first period of operations.

An examination of usage patterns by type of firm indicates the following:

- *Service firms*: Less usage of all advertising media from the first year to the current year. The exception is that the use of fliers increased substantially.
- *Retail firms*: The use of advertising media generally increased from the first year to the current year, with the exception that radio and television usage declined.
- *Other firms*: The change in usage is mixed with some media increasing (referrals, telephone directories, and fliers) and other categories decreasing (community events, direct mail, newspapers, and radio).

Referrals are ranked as the most effective in terms of increasing sales by the highest percentage of firms. This is reasonable because referrals would be expected to have the advantage of greater source credibility and would not be viewed by consumers as advertising. The more believable the source of the referrals, the more likely the message will be perceived as credible. Crane has called credibility the most important source characteristic in marketing communication. The advertising media that was most often ranked as the second most effective varied. by the type of firm. The second most frequently ranked advertising medium by all firms and service firms is community events during the first and current year. Community events are inexpensive and have high message credibility. This combination of attributes suggests a powerful promotional force that might be attractive to most organizations, institutions, and individuals. Telephone directories and community events are ranked second by retail firms and other firms, respectively, during their first year.

Radio and television advertising were least often ranked as one of the most effective advertising media for all types of firms. Although television is an expensive advertising medium, the percentage of firms ranking it as effective increased from the first to the current year. Radio, which was used by less than 5 per cent, was generally not ranked as one of the most effective advertising media by the respondents for all types of firms. Retail firms, however, had a higher percentage ranking for both television and radio in terms of effectiveness than did service and other firms. These effectiveness rankings indicate the changes in how women-owned businesses perceive advertising after being in operation for several years.

*The shifts in the effectiveness rankings of various media are*:

- *All firms:* A large increase in the effectiveness of fliers, while direct mail and newspapers declined in effectiveness;

- *Service firms:* A large rise in the effectiveness rankings for fliers from 8.2 per cent to 27.9 per cent and a slight increase in television, while all other advertising methods declined;
- *Retail firms:* A large decrease in the rankings for telephone directories and newspapers, and a large increase in the rankings for community events; and
- *Other firms:* A large increase in the rankings for telephone directories and a large decline in the rankings for direct mail.

According to Govoni, Eng, and Galper's observations, direct mail advertising actively seeks out a designated reader and creates its own opportunities rather than passively waiting to be noticed at an opportune moment. However, this advertising method has become prejudged by recipients as"junk mail." This may explain the large decline in the percentage of firms that rank direct mail as an effective advertising medium.

This might be true if mailings have not been effectively targeted, which may be likely among small businesses that may not have the resources for efficient mailing list management. In addition, the effectiveness of direct mail is measured and evaluated more easily than other forms of advertising, which might account for the ability of entrepreneurs to assess its effectiveness or lack thereof. A series of ordinary least squares (OLS) stepwise multiple regressions were conducted to identify significant explanators of the perceived effectiveness of each of the eight alternative advertising media examined. The general formulation of the regression models examined and definitions of the variables utilized are presented.

Since the dependent variables are binary rather than continuous (1 if the advertising media being examined is ranked by firm management as one of the three most effective, 0 otherwise), weighted least squares and/or logistic rather than OLS regression techniques may result in more efficient coefficient estimates. However, OLS is utilized in the current study since the OLS estimated regression coefficients are readily interpretable as the change in probability that the advertising media will be ranked as one of the three most effective per unit change in the independent variable.

During the first year of operation, the effectiveness of the advertising media utilized is expected to be related to various characteristics of the business and market served. Differences in the effectiveness rankings, in the first year of operations, of television, newspapers/magazines, radio, telephone directories, fliers, word-of-mouth/referrals, participation in community events, and direct mail were found to be significantly related to certain of the independent variables.

However, the particular independent variables that are significant determinants of the ranking of any particular advertising media differ markedly across the eight advertising media examined. Specifically, the regression results indicate the following for the first year of operations. The probabilities for television and radio being ranked as one of the three most effective media utilized, in the first year of operations, are positively associated with the firm's initial capitalization (a 2 per cent increase in probability for each unit change in initial capitalization).

Given that these two advertising media are relatively costly compared to the others examined in this study, it should come as no surprise that the likelihood of a particular firm using this media and also ranking it as one of the three most effective utilized is positively related to the amount of initial capital available. Additionally, the likelihood that telephone directories will be ranked as one of the most effective advertising media utilized is positively associated with the firm being a retailer (a 24 per cent increase in probability).

Similarly, service firms, compared to other types of firms, are less likely (a 22 per cent decrease in probability) to rank fliers as being one to the most effective advertising media utilized. The likelihood of word-of-mouth/referrals being ranked as one of the most effective media is negatively associated with the firm's initial capitalization (4 per cent decrease in probability per unit change), and whether or not the firm is organized as a partnership (a 25 per cent decrease in probability).

The effectiveness ranking of participation in community events is negatively correlated with the size of the market (a 10 per cent decrease in probability per unit change), and positively correlated with the size of the community (a 5 per cent increase in probability per unit change). Finally, the effectiveness ranking of direct mail is positively associated with the firm being organized as a corporation (a 22 per cent increase in probability per unit change). The most pervasive finding of these regressions is that, for seven of the eight media examined, the most important determinant of the media's effectiveness ranking in the current year is whether or not it was ranked as one of the three most effective media in the first year of operation. In all cases, except for radio, the current year's effectiveness ranking is found to be positively associated with the first year's ranking (ranging from in excess of a 50 per cent increase in probability for word-of-mouth referrals, and telephone directories to 31 per cent for direct mail).

It was originally believed that women-owned firms would change their advertising mix over time. Instead, the regression evidence indicates that the forms of advertising deemed most effective and used currently were generally ranked as one of the most effective forms of advertising in the first year of operations as well.

This result suggests that women-owned businesses do not change their assessment of the relative effectiveness of alternative advertising media as they become more experienced and established. This finding is consistent with Van Auken, Doran, and Rittenburg's findings from a previous study of small business firms. Fiske and Taylor observed that once a cognitive structure is formed (an idea accepted), it may become more and more resistant to change over time. Similarly, once the manager of a female-owned business has formed an initial opinion about the effectiveness of particular advertising media, this opinion is likely to be quite enduring, unless strong contrary evidence emerges.

It is difficult for managers to estimate the effectiveness of advertising media. Therefore, it is quite reasonable that managers would like to hold to their early evaluations and continue to use what they are familiar with rather than take risks on media with which they have less experience.

While the pattern of advertising activity among women entrepreneurs is consistent with that of the broader sample (consisting of both men and women) reported by Van Auken, Doran, and Rittenburg in terms of current-year media selection being determined primarily by the entrepreneur's perception of media effectiveness in the first year, a sharp contrast can be seen in media usage reported by women entrepreneurs.

The questions asked were identical in the two studies, but Van Auken, Doran, and Rittenburg's list of media captured any direct mail under"fliers." The current study added"direct mail" in order to differentiate this from nonmailed fliers. Therefore comparisons cannot be made for the direct mail category.

Most dramatic are the percentages for referrals: more than 90 per cent of women-owned firms reported using them compared to about 30 per cent of all firms. Likewise, about half of women-owned firms reported using community events, compared to 13-14 per cent of all firms. About half the women-owned firms reported using the telephone directory, compared to about 20 per cent of all firms. Women-owned firms' use of newspaper advertising was higher in the first year than all firms' use (39 per cent vs. 26 per cent), but approximately the same in the current year.

Use of fliers was a great deal higher for women-owned firms, and increased from 32 to 48 per cent in the current year, while all firms reported a slight decrease from 12 to 11 per cent. Women-owned firms reported less use of radio, perhaps attributable to the smaller proportion of retail firms in the sample. Television usage was slightly higher for women-owned firms in the first year but about the same in the current year, around 4 to 5 per cent.

These findings would seem to suggest that female entrepreneurs either use different media or perceive their media usage differently from male entrepreneurs. Without another data source, perhaps provided by the media rather than a self-reported measure, it is impossible to determine whether female entrepreneurs actually use different media.

Some differences might be attributed to the high proportion of service firms in the sample of women-owned firms and lower proportion of retail firms, but even these differences would not seem to explain such dramatic differences in use of referrals, community events, telephone directory, and fliers. Another possible explanation is that women tend to communicate differently from men, and this difference is reflected not just in personal communication, but in business communication as well. Women's emphasis on relationships is consistent with the findings reported here. Differences in communication style might explain why women would favour personal communication with prospective customers through referrals, community events, or response to an ad in the telephone directory as opposed to the impersonal radio or television ad.

Capital resources for advertising might explain low usage of expensive media, but these media are used by a small percentage of all small businesses.

The greater reported use of personal communication methods by women-owned firms cannot be accounted for simply by considering capital resources.

Whether women actually use referrals and other personal communication methods more often cannot be evaluated, but clearly women perceive these forms of communication as important tools in promoting their businesses. An alternative explanation might be a greater awareness on the part of women entrepreneurs of the communication methods employed, and the value placed on such personal connections and relationships with others. Such an explanation is consistent with the findings of Baird, Rotter and Portugal, and Sargent regarding women's focus on methods used to accomplish a task.

## CONCLUSIONS AND IMPLICATIONS

The purpose of this study was to report the results of a survey of the advertising methods used by 121 women-owned businesses. The perceived effectiveness of advertising methods utilized by women entrepreneurs during the first year in operation and the current year were discussed and contrasted.

Determinants of the women-owned businesses' methods of current advertising were identified. These findings provide evidence that referrals were found to be perceived as both the most utilized and most effective advertising medium by the largest percentage of women-owned businesses.

During the firm's first year in operation, referrals, community events, direct mail, and telephone directories were commonly used by all firms. The pattern is similar for the current year of operation.

The results appear to be inconsistent with Vaccaro and Kassaye, who state that most small firms continue to place their advertising dollars primarily in newspaper ads, with occasional budgets allocated to radio and television advertisements.

The telephone directories are a well-used medium, which is consistent with the findings of Jackson and Parasuraman (1988). Trade shows (which would have appeared as"other-please specify" in the questionnaire) were seldom mentioned by the women business owners as a type of advertising. Trade show activity has increased dramatically in recent years, and it has shown to be a cost-effective advertising method for small businesses. Respondents in this study did not indicate increased trade show use, however. Referrals were ranked the highest in effectiveness of the various media by all categories of firms during the first year in operation. All firms except retailers ranked community events as being second most effective, while retail firms ranked telephone directories in second place during the first year.

The results indicate that women-owned businesses change their perceptions of effectiveness after being in operation for several years. Some rankings are consistent, while others change significantly between the first year in operation and the most current year. The changes in rankings of the different advertising media varied by category of firm.

One of the most significant findings in this study is that women-owned businesses tend to continue the method of advertising used during the first year in operation. This is consistent with findings by Van Auken, Doran, and Rittenburg. The result can be explained by assuming that female entrepreneurs may not be any more skilled at selecting appropriate advertising media than male entrepreneurs. Alternatively, they may have a limited advertising budget, as suggested by Seglund.

Another possibility is related to the personality traits of many women entrepreneurs, such as risk taking, autonomy, cognitive structure, innovation, creativity, competence, and leadership. Varadarajan suggested that most small business owners tend to be preoccupied with day-to-day operations and seem not to use formalized planning procedures in guiding the destiny of their businesses.

Therefore, they may conveniently continue to use the advertising media initially selected. It is very difficult to measure the effectiveness of advertising, and the additional cost associated with its measurement may be perceived as prohibitive by many women entrepreneurs. This difficulty forces them to rely on their own judgment and experience and the"biased" assistance provided by the advertising agencies.

A particularly interesting finding of this study is the difference in reported use of the various media between women-owned firms and all firms, the latter reported by Van Auken, Doran, and Rittenburg. Women entrepreneurs report greater use of referrals, community events, telephone directory, and fliers than a general sample of small business owners.

The difference, whether it is in actual usage of these media or perceived usage, might be attributable to differences in women's communication styles and the value women place on personal forms of communication. This finding would seem to have implications for relationship marketing and the strengths women might have in building rapport with potential customers. Some managerial implications for women entrepreneurs might be to build on this strength in developing effective communication strategies. Male entrepreneurs may need to examine their awareness of advertising strategies employed and the effectiveness of those strategies. All entrepreneurs might consider the value of a more androgynous approach. Academic training might include a greater emphasis on how the individual characteristics or communication style of an entrepreneur influences advertising strategy and its effectiveness. Such an approach might aid budding entrepreneurs in self-awareness and in selecting appropriate advertising strategies. This implication also applies to government agencies facilitating small business development.

While the findings of this study suggest a pattern, they are far from conclusive and represent an area ripe for further investigation. Despite the limitations, these findings serve as an excellent basis for hypothesis development in future research into the advertising methods of women-owned businesses. Data collected from women-owned businesses throughout the world would provide a more comprehensive understanding of how to select advertising methods and would allow many types of cross-sectional studies, especially geographic and multi-cultural comparisons.

Further research should focus on providing in-depth insights into other variables expected to be related to women-owned businesses' advertising, such as adeptness at media selection and level of preoccupation with operations. The contribution of this study may provide some insight toward the understanding of female entrepreneurs' business practices, increase the awareness of selecting effective advertising media, and improve the potential for success of women-owned businesses.

# 10

# Demand-side View of Media Substitutability

Competition among media for audiences and advertisers is fierce and unrelenting. In both local and national markets, with weapons ranging from prepackaged contests and promotions to drastic overhauls of talent and management, media wage war with one another to attract audiences to sell to advertisers. Often underlying these intermedia battles is a simple, if unproven, assumption: that mass media are interchangeable, competing in the same market for the same advertising dollars.

In this chapter, we report results of a two-stage study conducted to explore the media interchangeability assumption as it relates to national advertising. The study specifically addressed the question: What are toplevel advertising managers' judgments about the degree to which cable TV, broadcast TV, radio, newspapers, magazines, billboards, and place-based media are substitutable for one another in national media schedules?

Advertiser opinions were collected in two stages. In the first stage, we mailed questionnaires to a sample of 402 chief advertising managers with the leading 100 national advertisers. In the second stage, we personally interviewed another sample of 34 national advertising managers to validate and extend the survey results. As detailed in the following paragraphs, both practical and empirical observations about media substitutability and national advertising guided our research approach.

According to Picard, media substitutability may be more evident in the market for advertising than any other media demand area. However, there are both practical and empirical reasons to suspect that media will not be seen as completely interchangeable by advertising managers. Based on these reasons, we predict that:

*HI*: For national advertising campaigns, advertising managers perceive little, if any, substitutability among traditional media options.

## PRACTICAL CONSIDERATIONS

As any advertiser well knows, different media provide different access to different kinds of audiences, which in advertising terms are defined as target markets. Media for all advertising are typically selected based on a host of factors, including product consumption patterns, media usage patterns and habits, market size and location, vehicle cost efficiencies, specific media qualities (i.e., time and space availabilities, mechanical characteristics, delivery patterns, support services, etc.), and audience characteristics (i.e, demographics, lifestyles, psychographics).

Advertisers and their representatives, agencies, independent buying services, and in-house media planners, take these factors into consideration when planning advertising, seeking the media mix that best serves particular communication needs before specific media buys are negotiated and finalized. Therefore, for practical reasons, we predict that traditional media options will not be seen as completely interchangeable for national media schedules by advertising managers.

## EMPIRICAL CONSIDERATIONS

A few researchers have empirically examined the question of advertising media substitutability. For the most part, these studies have been confined to local advertising and to the newspaper medium relative to local media options. One study found that print media are the most likely replacements for newspapers; others suggest that other media are also considered by local advertisers. Sentman found that when a local newspaper goes out of business in a market where more than one newspaper is available, local advertisers are more likely to substitute the other newspaper in their media schedules than another medium. In two related studies, Smith found that the majority of local advertisers believe small dailies compete with other media, not just other newspapers, for local advertising dollars.

According to the Smith studies, more than three-fourths of the surveyed ROP advertisers said they would look to another medium if newspaper ad rates increased by 20 per cent; about 40 per cent said they would substitute another form of print media for newspapers, while more than one-third said they would use a broadcast medium as a replacement; and insert advertisers indicated that direct mail and a combination of other print would be appropriate substitutes for small dailies.

A study by Cameron, Nowak, and Krugman found that direct mail is seen by local advertisers as the primary substitute for advertiser dollars, although cable TV and yellow pages could be considered. Ferguson, in a study of newspaper advertising rates and competition for advertising dollars in a market, found that an increase in the number broadcast stations is associated with lower newspaper advertising rates, but that presence of a competing daily newspaper was not significantly related to newspaper advertising rates.

Work by Dimmick and Albarran adapted niche theory from the field of ecology to examine the displacement of existing media by newer media forms. Neither study specifically asked advertising experts about substitutability among media options. Nevertheless, the work is relevant to our study because the results are suggestive of patterns of substitutability in advertising media planning. Niche theory suggests that the more similar two media are perceived by advertisers and consumers, the more likely they are considered replacement options for one another. In one study, Albarran and Dimmick combined niche theory with a uses and gratifications approach to explore how niche breadth, overlap, and competitive superiority apply to the video entertainment industries. The study found a great deal of overlap among types of video media. In a later study, Dimmick suggests that the approach helps explain the"video revolution."

According to Dimmick, advertisers are proficient observers of changes in consumer media and audience compositions. As new media emerge that meet the same needs as already existing media, the two media overlap or compete. Advertisers react to media overlap by altering their ad placement patterns. The medium that is considered superior on the gratification dimension is the one that attracts more advertising dollars.

The study most relevant to our investigation was conducted by Busterna. Although there are arguably methodological grounds to question the absolute validity of Busterna's findings, his conclusions are suggestive, if not conclusive, and predicative of our hypothesis. Spurred by definition disputes and conceptual inadequacies in the published research literature, Busterna used secondary industry data to determine which media are in the same market with newspapers for national advertising. Specifically, he tested the concept of cross-elasticity of demand, using price sensitivity to define market boundaries:"In simple terms the cross-elasticity of demand measures the relative change in quantity demanded of a given product or service in response to a change in price of another good or service. If two products or services exist as reasonable substitutes, then an increase in the price of one will result in an increase in the quantity demanded of the other."

Demand functions for five media were tested: television (network and spot), consumer magazines, newspaper supplements, radio (network and spot), and outdoor. Regression analyses revealed that"cross-elasticity of demand between newspapers and other media is consistently nil across all media," meaning that none of the tested media resides in the same market for national advertising dollars. From the results, Busterna drew two conclusions:

First, it is clear that advertisers do not possess significant price sensitivity between newspapers and other media to consider newspapers a viable alternative for advertising that was intended to be placed in other media. Second, claims of significant competition between newspapers and other media often come from those who have a newspaper industry (seller) perspective rather than an advertiser (buyer) perspective.

## FOCUS OF THE STUDY

Our study goes beyond Busterna's examination of newspapers as a substitute for other advertising media, as well as the previous studies of media substitutability in local advertising. As described more fully in the following methodology section, we asked two samples of top-level managers of national advertising programs to evaluate the interchangeability of seven media options against one another, not just newspapers against other media.

The study was designed and executed to accomplish three objectives:

- To provide more evidence on the question of media substitutability in national advertising;
- To re-examine Busterna's finding about the substitutability of newspapers in particular;
- To augment Busterna's price-sensitivity-based"buyer perspective" with perceptual data like that reported by Dimmick and Rothenbuhler and Lacy.

## RESEARCH METHODS

*Stage* 1: Survey of Advertising Managers. To test the study's hypothesis, we first conducted a mail survey of top-level advertising managers, the individuals with large American companies who are responsible for spending national advertising dollars. Following Busterna's suggestion, we wanted to avoid the sampling error of studies conducted by Dimmick and Rothenbuhler and Lacy.

In their studies, the researchers sampled executives with media organizations (i.e., supply-side representatives) on the assumption that media are active agents in deciding what advertising will be scheduled. However, as pointed out by Busterna, the active agent in advertising media planning is the advertising executive, not the media executive. Therefore, we sought buyer judgment of media substitutability rather than seller judgment since it is the buyer of advertising, not the seller, that fuels intermedia competition.

### SAMPLE AND MAILING PROCEDURE

Advertising Age's list of "100 Leading National Advertisers" and the Standard Director of Advertisers were used as the sampling frame. Four hundred-two individuals listed as the chief advertising officer (i.e., brand manager, advertising director, vice president of marketing, marketing communications, or advertising) for each of the 100 advertisers' corporate, division, and/or subsidiary organizations were selected as survey participants.

A notification postcard was sent to each of the 402 advertising officers one week prior to the mailing of questionnaires. The postcard informed the individuals of the nature of the study, requested their participation, and informed them that questionnaires would be arriving in seven to ten days. One week following the notification, the questionnaires were mailed. Each questionnaire was accompanied by a cover letter and a postage-paid return envelope.

Three weeks after the initial mailing, a second mailing was sent to nonrespondents. Four weeks later, a third mailing was executed. The third mailing was followed two weeks later by a reminder letter. A copy of the questionnaire was not included in the fourth mailing.

Of the mailing of 402, a total of 91 completed, usable questionnaires were returned: 43 from the first mailing, 16 from the second mailing, from the third mailing, and 10 from the reminder mailing. Eleven questionnaires were returned incomplete and/or unusable, 42 were"returned to sender," and 19 were returned with notes of refusal, for an adjusted individual response rate of 28%. The 91 usable questionnaires were completed by individuals with 50 of the 100 national advertisers, for an advertiser response rate of 50%. The individual response rate is consistent with other surveys of advertising managers. A sampling of studies published in the Journal of Advertising, journal of Current Issues and Research in Advertising, and Journal of Advertising Research between 1981 and 1996 found that reported response rates ranged from 21% to 33%, with an average of 32%.

## QUESTIONNAIRE CONSTRUCTION AND PRETEST

An eight-page questionnaire was used to collect the survey data. The questionnaire was modified from one used in a past survey of agency media specialists. That questionnaire was stringently pretested with five advertising specialists located in New York, Chicago, Cincinnati, and Atlanta and produced a return rate of 54%.

The questionnaire contained seven sections, three of which are relevant to the focus of this study. The other four sections asked questions about media selection criteria and media-provided advertiser services.

## NATIONAL ADVERTISING DEFINITION

Included in the survey instructions was the following definition:"National ad accounts are accounts for brands/services that are distributed or available in most or all of the U.S. The advertising for these accounts need not be national. Coverage may be regional."

The definition was developed from interview information collected in the aforementioned advertising media survey and a search of basic advertising texts. The definition was provided to frame the construct for the respondents in an effort to reduce potential response variance.

## RESPONDENT QUALIFICATION

The first section asked one question:"Do you feel qualified to voice opinions about the appropriateness of media (i.e., TV and magazines) for national advertising campaigns?" The question had two closed-end options, yes and no, and was included to screen out respondents who felt unqualified to answer questions about national advertising and media substitutability.

## MEDIA SUBSTITUTES

The fifth section contained seven traditional advertising media options, cable TV, broadcast TV, radio, newspapers, magazines, billboards, and place-based, formatted in a matrix with"media to be replaced" listed ina vertical column and"appropriate media substitutes" listed in corresponding horizontal rows. The respondents were asked about media substitutability in the following manner:

Sometimes because of factors beyond advertiser control, one media type must be substituted for another in national campaign planning. The list in the left-hand column below contains several media options. For each medium in this list, please indicate those media that you believe are appropriate and reasonable replacements from the list of substitute media provided. Please indicate your belief by circling each medium you consider to be an appropriate substitute.

The final section of the questionnaire contained six questions designed to collect background information from the respondents about their age, gender, education, present title/position, and years of advertising experience. Education information was collected on a categorical basis. Open-ended questions were used to gather the other background information.

## QUESTIONNAIRE PRETEST

Although a version of the questionnaire had been pretested previously, we pretested the modified version because it contained three additional items: the respondent qualification question, the media substitutability measure, and several additional respondent background questions. Three advertising managers with Chicago- and Atlanta-based advertisers agreed to participate in the pretest.

The pretest was conducted using both mail and personal interviewing techniques. First, agreement to participate was secured by telephone contact. Pretest questionnaires were then mailed and returned completions were followed up by phone calls to discuss any identified problem areas.

No serious problems were uncovered. However, the format of the media substitutability measure was slightly modified to facilitate the response task (i.e., spacing was changed to enhance readability). Before final printing, the format change was cross-checked with the three pretest participants.

*Stage* 2: Personal Interviews with Advertising Managers. Using the same directory sources as the survey stage of the study, 50 additional advertising managers with large national advertisers were identified and contacted by telephone. Thirty-eight officers agreed to be interviewed; however, interviews could be arranged with only 34 of the 38.

Ten days prior to the scheduled interview, each participant was mailed a copy of the data analysis, with instructions asking them to consider and explain what the results indicate relative to their professional experiences.

All interviews were conducted by the same procedure and protocol: the study's purpose was reiterated and the participant was asked to interpret patterns in the survey data and to explain what the patterns suggest about the question of media substitutability for national advertising accounts. The interviews were conducted in fourteen metropolitan locations in the offices of the participants: Atlanta, Boston, Charlotte, Chicago, Dallas, Greenville, Indianapolis, Jacksonville, New York, Phoenix, Richmond, San Francisco, Seattle, and Tampa.

Following are profiles of the two sets of respondents and the results of both the survey and interview stages of the study. Wherever appropriate, the survey and interview results are integrated.

## RESPONDENT PROFILES

The majority of advertising managers who participated in the survey were male (73.6% male vs. 26.4% female) and under the age of 45 (57.3% under 45 vs. 42.7% over 45). Nearly all were college graduates (96.7%), with 56% having a graduate degree. Almost half had more than 15 years of professional advertising experience (48.4%io), either on the agency or client side of the advertising business. Just over one-fourth of the respondents had more than 20 years of professional advertising experience.

The profile of the 34 interviewed managers mirrored the characteristics of the survey respondents. Male managers outnumbered females (76.5% male vs. 23.5% female). The majority were under the age of 45 (55.9% under 45 vs. 44.1% over 45) and nearly all were college graduates (97.1%), with half having a master's degree. Fifty per cent of the interviewees had more than 15 years in advertising, and almost one-quarter had more than 20 years of advertising experience.

## QUESTION OF MEDIA SUBSTITUTABILITY

Not surprisingly, all 125 ad managers considered themselves competent to consider the issue of media substitutability and national advertising. The 91 respondents who returned useable questionnaires answered yes to the qualifying question about ability to judge media for national advertising campaigns. The 34 interviewees responded yes when asked about their abilities to consider the question during the opening phase of the interview session.

Each medium was perceived an acceptable substitute for another in national advertising planning. Analysis of the response frequencies and mean ratings revealed interesting patterns in the ad managers' judgments.

Consistent with the frequencies, substitutability among the six media is suggested by the means: every medium, on average, had at least one substitute mentioned and all but placebased were identified as a substitute for at least two other media. Cable TV had the highest mean number of mentions as a replacement (2.44) and placebased had the lowest (.83).

The mean number of mentions of cable TV as a substitute was significantly higher than those of the other five media, whereas the mean mentions of radio as a replacement was significantly higher than the means of three media: magazines, broadcast TV, and place-based media. The broadcast TV mean was significantly higher than the mean mentions of place-based media.

The interview results were consistent with the survey results. The consensus among the interviewed managers is that media are replaceable in national advertising schedules.

All of the managers told us that they considered both media and audience characteristics when trying to determine national media schedules. They acknowledged that there are clearly times when one medium will do a better of job of communicating a message than another medium. However, in many cases, availabilities in geographic markets, timing considerations, media costs, and other conditions force managers and their representatives to consider substitutes. *As two managers put it*: Though we prefer not to substitute, there are circumstances which dictate a change of direction in media planning. If you can't afford ABC, CBS, then you consider what we can do with a combination of magazines and USA, TBS, ESPN, or whatever other cable options are out there.

The key is trying to deliver a message to a certain audience at a certain place and time, with effective exposure in a cost efficient manner. Media are interchangeable, not in that they are all the same, but in the fact that it's audience delivery, message exposure, and cost which drive the typical national ad schedule. Yeah, there are options; there is an option for every medium because it's not media per se. It's what is being delivered by the medium that counts, and that what is the right audience.

Media is a negotiated process. The ideal often differs from what is planned for and what results. The issue of replacement comes down to a simple point-audience delivery. If you can't get it with a television schedule, then you back up and look at other combinations. It's difficult to talk about it, but when you get down to it, media provide access to audiences-some deliver a specific audience better than others. From my experience, while not preferable, there are always acceptable substitutes in some combination. Sure national media are replaceable... or substitutable for each other. Every competitor can't be in TV at the same time. You've got to look for other media to break through TV clutter, to out smart the competitor in another medium.

Costs, audience, and message impact... they are the factors that determine national media schedules, not media types.

One interesting factor mentioned by several of the ad managers was value-added opportunities, promotional incentives offered by media as inducements for media space and time sales. As suggested by two managers, these inducements sometimes persuade planners to took beyond time and cost when comparing media options.

We work with media to service our needs in ways beyond running our ads. Merchandising, joint-marketing efforts are important to us in stretching our promotional dollars. If a magazine comes to me and says I'll feature your product in a special section on house repair or gardening, and I'm considering buying TV spots, I'll try to do a cost analysis. The extra offered by the magazine might offset a higher actual cost between different media. Like in any situation, cost is a relative thing.

In today's planning environment, media extras are important. If a newspaper group comes to me and says they can get us premium space with a large retail chain in X number of cities, then I'm gonna listen. The same is true of media that offer to tiein our line with contests and special programs, for example, radio. Rates are important, yes. But, unless there's a tremendous difference in total schedule cost, sometimes the"extras" offset money differences. The whole process is more complex than comparing CPMs, and media incentives play a big part. Same is true with consumer incentive programs; advertisers are the consumers targeted by media sellers.

From the frequencies, it is apparent that not all substitutes are perceived alike; there are patterns in the responses which suggest that certain media fall into specific categories of substitutability. There is substantial agreement among the managers about the substitutability of both forms of television advertising. Cable and broadcast TV are considered highly appropriate substitutes for each other, with nearly 8 of 10 managers having judged one medium an appropriate and reasonable replacement for the other. Other combinations were identified as acceptable at the 40% to 50% range. Five of 10 managers judged newspapers and magazines acceptable substitutes of each other (52.8%/56.2%).

Radio was seen as a reasonable replacement for newspapers (53.9%), and cable TV an acceptable substitute for both radio (56.2%) and magazines (49.7%). Four of 10 thought billboards and place-based media were acceptable substitutes for each other (41.6%/39.3%). The same per cent judged newspapers an acceptable substitute for radio (42.7".io), and radio a reasonable replacement for both cable TV (41.6%) and billboards (41.6%).

Thirty of the 34 interviewed managers agreed with the survey respondents-that is, media fall into specific replacement groupings. The most interesting and common explanation offered for categorization is the belief that creative decisions drive media decisions.

You have to understand once a creative approach is decided upon, then media are planned around that approach. Media are considered, but they are secondary in my view. Look at it in terms of give and take. Once creative is determined, there is no replacement. Sure media differ in how they deliver and impact messages, but they can be interchanged to some degree. Creative can't. TV for TV, print for print. What's surprising about that? A point of fact is creative and media work hand-in-hand - they are like hand and glove. In my experience, creative drives the process, and when it comes to media... If you can't get network broadcast spots, you're going to look at cable. Same is true in print, and in reminder type ads - billboards.

We often prefer to buy network TV spots because of coverage and message delivery impact... allows us to demonstrate our brands at a pretty cost effective level. But if we have to we go with cable advertising in markets where we can't get the numbers with network... Or because the spots aren't available... We look to cable. Cable is relatively cheap, you can buy lots of spots at different times, on different networks. I certainly understand and agree that television is substitutable for TV. I see the same situation with print and out-of-home reminder media, like outdoor in store, or whatever.

A similar observation about magazines and newspapers was made by 9 managers. Said one manager: Look, when you are trying to run a print ad there's a reason-- you want to deliver a specific type of message to a particular type of audience. Suppose you want those people to spend sometime with what you are saying... to control exposure.

For whatever, if I can't get a magazine in a particular market-let's say a business mag-I'm not going to TV? A whole different ballgame there. No, instead, I'm going to look at newspaper options, particularly the business pages. Another example that comes to mind is a business magazine like Business Week or Fortune...

The ability of cable TV, newspapers, and radio to transcend media form was attributed to the fact these media are sometimes looked upon as secondary options in national advertising planning.

Radio is a great medium, especially for local advertisers. I think what you see is this... radio is generally regarded as filling gaps in a national schedule... building audience coverage, increasing total impressions when time can't be purchased in TV. It's a secondary medium for most national advertisers, a fall back option.

*Other managers explained it this way*: We use radio and newspapers to fill in holes in our schedule. We like magazines because of their specialization and extras. If we buy radio or newspapers, we are supplementing. I suspect that the same is true of users of cable TV. Cable is used to supplement network schedules and spot buys Why is radio a reasonable replacement for cable TV and billboards?

Simple. Radio is not a primary option for most national advertisers. If you can't schedule enough TV or print to meet your market-by-market objectives, you fill in with radio if creative allows it. Radio is secondary in national ad planning, not primary.

Contrary to our hypothesis, these results suggest that there is a degree of"perceived substitutability" among traditional media options for national advertising planning. The results also call into question the absoluteness of Busterna's finding that newspapers do not reside in the market for national advertising dollars with television, magazines, radio, and outdoor. It appears from our data that national advertising managers put traditional media in certain boxes, at least perceptually, when considering schedule substitutes. These findings are not particularly surprising if it is true advertising experts place media into national and retail boxes as well.

As for newspapers in particular, our findings suggest that newspapers compete directly with magazines and radio for national advertising expenditures. Though we would agree with Busterna that newspapers do not compete with every medium, the medium is not perceived by national advertisers in isolation, separate and distinct from other media options. Considering the evidence provided in our depth interviews, we would argue that the issue of substitutability in national advertising comes down not to the issue of media type per se, but to other considerations such as audience delivery, communication effectiveness, and value-added opportunities.

As suggested in the interviews, media are replaceable in national advertising because of similarities in form and function, that is, the physical and qualitative properties of each medium. Apparently in national advertising planning, when the first option is not available or too costly, then, the second option is considered on the same principle as the medium of choice-the ability to deliver the largest percentage of the targeted audience at the right time with the most frequency and the greatest communication impact.

In his economic analysis, Busterna focused on one factor of media selection-space and time costs. Our findings indicate that cost is not the only factor that plays a role in the decision to select a medium, including the decision to replace one medium with another. For a variety of competitive and creative reasons, a medium may be used in a national media schedule even though it is more expensive on an overall cost basis.

Actual media costs are important; however, unique communication qualities of a medium, delivery of a target audience (which would make a medium more cost efficient even though it is more expensive), value-added opportunities, as well as other factors certainly affect the relative cost of a medium as much as time and space cost. In fact, surveys of how advertising specialists choose media for both national and retail campaigns convincingly demonstrate that, while media costs are essential to the media selection process, selection decisions are driven by a medium's ability to effectively reach a specific audience.

Even cost-per-thousand data, a better measure than overall cost data adjusted for inflation (constant dollars) in determining the value of a medium because the measure considers the relationship between cost and audience delivered, overlook the effects of such factors as added-value opportunities, creative considerations, and audience characteristics.

All things considered, we suggest that differences between the newspaper-specific findings of the two studies are attributable to the temporal nature of Busterna's media data. From his analysis, Busterna concluded that leaving the large rate differential between national and retail ad rates in newspapers makes sense from a managerial view because advertiser demand for newspaper space is somewhat inelastic. Hence, he advised newspaper executives not to expect to get increased advertising business from advertisers in other media with national rate reductions.

The problem with Busterna's recommendation is that during the time period of his data, 1971-1985, national newspaper advertising made up a small percentage of total U.S. advertising spending; it declined steadily from 4.96% to 3.53%. There was very little variability in the amount of national advertising in newspapers. It is possible that the slope of the demand curve for newspapers would have been flatter (i.e., a sign of more inelastic demand), with more variation in 1971-1985 data, if national newspaper ad rates had been lowered significantly during the period. However, it is quite possible that trade-offs between media options already existed as the result of relative cost considerations; perhaps national advertisers were using newspapers less than magazines and radio on the basis of relative cost versus actual cost, for example.

Those advertisers who were consistent users of newspapers during the 1971-1985 period might have found them an effective and efficient way to reach their target audience, despite the national/retail rate differential. If our findings accurately reflect advertising manager perceptions, we suggest that a reduction in the national/retail rate differential may have attracted national advertisers from magazines and radio to newspapers during 1971-85.

There is also reason to suspect the relative price variation between newspapers and magazines may have been more dramatic than reflected in Busterna's data as the result of differences in another non-cost factor, valueadded opportunities. During the period, magazines became much more specialized and the number of magazine options offering specialized audiences increased dramatically. According to the MPA Handbook, the number of domestic consumer magazines which accepted national and broad regional advertising increased from 874 in 1970 to 1,492 in 1985. By 1995, the number of domestic consumer magazines increased to 2,454. As these magazines became more specialized, they also increased the number of value-added opportunities to national advertisers. Newspapers were much slower to jump on the value-added bandwagon. In addition to rate reductions, it is possible that newspapers may have attracted more national advertising dollars if the medium had countered magazines with its own value-added opportunities during the 1971-85 period.

## PRACTICAL AND RESEARCH IMPLICATIONS

The implication of our findings for the practice of advertising is that media should be sold against other media, but not in the straightforward, one-for-one manner of selling one medium against every other medium. Rather it is suggested by these findings that sales representatives pitch their time and space directly against.media perceived as acceptable substitutes among national advertisers. For example, national ad sales pitches for newspapers would be more productive by focusing on magazines and radio as the competition, not on television.

Pitches for billboards would work best against other out-of-home options, not against print or electronic options. Sales programs for radio would be more effective if positioned against newspapers, cable TV, and billboards, whereas sales efforts for cable TV would be more productive targeting broadcast TV, radio, and magazines. In each case, sales efforts should not concentrate exclusively on"absolute" cost differentials to sell media options.

National advertisers are interested in relative cost as much as absolute cost, and media must compete on non-cost competitive factors such as impact of message delivery, creative fit, and value-added opportunities. For researchers, the implication of our results is that questions of substitutability and other comparative inquiries must be asked of buyers, not just sellers of media. As with any one-shot survey, our study needs to be replicated among another sample of media buyers. While the acheived response rate was in line with other relevant industry studies, the rate was less than desired. Replication would confirm and enhance interpretive validity. Other studies on agency buyers, media sellers, and perhaps marketby-market comparisons are needed to flesh out our findings.

To extend our findings beyond the seven studied media options (e.g., syndicated TV, spot TV, network TV, internet), localized and specific market comparisons are needed to"tease" out differences and to expand the scope of the findings from general media options to specific market-based options. Others studies are needed to examine, among other things, (1) the relationship between what national advertisers try to accomplish with their advertising and how media substitutability is affected by different creative approaches, and (2) the effects of over-time variation in factors such as actual media cost, valueadded opportunities, and new media introductions on patterns of media usage and substitution. It would also be worth studying additional forms of advertising media, including new media options such as Internet advertising and direct mail advertising, and other categories of advertisers such as localized or retail advertising to compare and contrast opinions of media substitutability among national advertisers.

In the final analysis, these findings add to what is known about national advertiser opinions of substitutability among seven traditional media options. However, many other questions about advertising media substitutability need exploration, from many methodological viewpoints. Until those studies are conducted, we suggest that media, including newspapers, are substitutable to a certain degree and compete with each other in specific patterns for national advertising dollars.

# 11

# Advertisers' Media Selection in Small Newspaper Markets

As the market becomes continually more competitive for advertising dollars, newspapers need to develop more sophisticated sales strategies. Yet, due to personnel limitations and other economic considerations, smaller newspapers may find compiling data and developing sales strategies to be daunting tasks. Some relief is granted by the typical advertisers in small communities -- local merchants. They may not demand data that is as sophisticated as that required in larger markets because the vast majority of advertisers in smaller markets are not very knowledgeable about market conditions.

This does not absolve newspaper sales personnel from knowing their advertisers. In writing about the relationship between national advertisers and a sample comprised mostly of larger dailies, Daniel Stout concluded that when a salesperson comes to understand the factors that influence the advertiser,"the skills of that person are enhanced." The same could be said about the relation ship between advertising representatives at smaller newspapers and their clients. Even in those markets, as salespeople develop better skills, they may increase the ad revenues that will help fund an improved news product.

This study examines the factors that influence the selection of media by advertisers in smaller markets. The purpose is to identify some of the factors that affect media choice in an effort to help sales representatives at smaller newspapers do a more effective job of understanding and serving their clients.

In strict legal terms, some confusion exists as to whether newspapers actually compete for advertising with other media. The answer appears to hinge on whether newspapers and other media can be considered good substitutes for one another. Various court cases have determined that they are not good substitutes, that advertisers know the purpose for which each medium is best suited and use them accordingly. One Federal Communications Commission ruling determined that dailies and television, at least, are good substitutes and should be considered competitors for advertising. If different media do not compete - i.e., if they are not good substitutes for each other - then selecting the best media should not be a difficult task for advertisers. They could simply identify the media that are most appropriate for their purposes and then decide which among those are most cost effective.

However, most people working in the industry would argue that a number of media compete with newspapers for advertising, including radio, television, magazines, billboards, and direct mail. They believe that all advertising revenues are contested, that no medium is guaranteed a certain slice of the advertising pie, simply because it is the most appropriate medium for a specific advertising purpose.

To some degree this disparity may be explained by the sophistication of the advertiser. When advertisers are not aware of the purposes for which different media are best suited, it no longer becomes an important consideration, and they may choose advertising media based on other factors. Thus, an unsophisticated advertiser may choose radio even though newspapers are most appropriate for a certain campaign.

In those cases, the advertiser's dollars are up for grabs among many media. They all compete, and the one that gets the sale is not necessarily the one that is most appropriate, but instead the one that best meets the criteria established by the advertiser.

Studies of competition for advertising among newspapers and other media offer evidence of differences resulting from the sophistication of the advertiser. A study of national advertising that involved more sophisticated advertisers found that newspapers did not compete with other media.

Advertisers were aware of the differences among media and chose the ones that were most suitable for their purposes. Conversely, a study of local markets that involved less sophisticated advertisers found that newspapers did compete with other media. Unlike the sophisticated advertisers involved in national advertising, the local advertisers were not as aware of the differences among media.

Economic theory supports the contention that the manner in which a market functions is affected by the sophistication of the buyers. It assumes that when buyers are sophisticated, they will base their purchasing decisions primarily on objective and real differences between products. Douglas Greer defined sophisticated buyers as those who have accurately analysed their needs, know all the products available to them and the cost of each, can appraise product quality objectively, and can accurately calculate the advantages of choosing one product over another.

Using these criteria, sophisticated buyers would be defined as those who had accurately assessed what their advertising should achieve, were aware of all media available to them and which were best suited for a particular purpose, and knew the comparative costs of the advertising outlets.

Subjective considerations would not play much of a role in their purchasing behaviour. But while sophisticated buyers select media based on an objective and predictable set of criteria, unsophisticated buyers may base their purchasing decisions on any number of factors, many of which are unrelated to choosing those media that will best serve their purposes or that offer the best comparative cost.

The implication is that the media selection process may vary based on the characteristics of the advertiser. Smaller advertisers and those in local markets tend to be less sophisticated. As a result, Cele Otnes and Ronald Faber speculated that the selection of media by local advertisers may be based,"on what they can afford, and their perceptions of which media will be most useful for them."

A reason for this lack of sophistication on the part of local advertisers was addressed by Jana Frederick-Collins who wrote,"They are not necessarily likely to have formal education or special training in advertising. They often have limited time to spend on advertising-related tasks due to other management responsibilities such as accounting, sales management, finance, purchasing, inventory, personnel management, and customer services."

The importance of advertiser sophistication is not lost on sales strategists. As Charles Warner indicated, the intelligence of the advertiser plays an especially important role in sales. For intelligent advertisers, more objective and rational factors such as the needs of their businesses and the benefits of the product play a primary role. For less intelligent advertisers, subjective and emotional factors such as their personal needs or their relationship with the salesperson are more important.

This study examines the decision-making process of advertisers in the communities of smaller daily newspapers, markets that are more likely to contain a greater percentage of unsophisticated advertisers than larger markets. By definition, sophisticated advertisers use primarily objective and rational criteria in selecting media, criteria that are germane to the maximization of their businesses' self interest. This study examines whether unsophisticated advertisers also use rational and relevant criteria. Or, as sales strategists assume, do they tend to use subjective criteria including those that are based more on perceptions than on objective data. The study also examines the effect that different markets have on advertising decisions since, as Mary Alice Sentman found, when advertisers had to select alternative media after a local newspaper closed, the decision-making process varied by market.

- What are the factors that unsophisticated advertisers in the markets of smaller dailies use in selecting media? Are these factors objective and relevant to the best interests of the advertisers, or are they more subjective in nature?
- Do the criteria used to select media by unsophisticated advertisers in the markets of smaller dailies vary by market?

## METHOD

Telephone interviews were conducted with 131 advertisers in six Rocky Mountain region communities that each contained a small daily newspaper. Initially, 139 potential respondents were identified through a visit to each community and with the assistance of representatives from the newspapers. However, eight of the advertisers were unable to take part in the survey resulting in a final sample of 131 advertisers (a response rate of 94 per cent).

Since the intent of the study was to investigate decision making by advertisers in smaller daily markets, the primary market areas in which the communities were located ranged in size from 9,500 to 69,000 with an average size of approximately 30,000. Each of the communities contained a single daily newspaper whose circulations ranged from 3,800 to 17,000 with an average circulation of 7,633.

Only one community contained a local television station, but all six contained cable franchises that offered local advertising options. Four of the communities contained five local radio stations each, one contained two radio stations, and another contained six radio stations. None of the communities had a local weekly newspaper, but four had overlap from a weekly published in another community, and one of the communities contained a student daily newspaper that was published during the university academic year. Shoppers were distributed in all six communities, through the mail in two and by newsstand in four.

A respondent was defined as the person who made the advertising decisions for a business. In each community, advertisers were sought from businesses representing a full range of types and sizes (from mom &pop to chain department stores). Advertising decisions were made locally at 106 of the 131 businesses in this sample. Decisions at the remaining 25 were made at the regional or national headquarters for chain stores.

In the interviews, respondents were asked:"What are the most important factors that help you decide with which media to place your advertising? In other words, how do you decide who to advertise with?" These initial questions were then followed with probing questions both to ensure an accurate interpretation of the respondent's answer, and to help determine with validity the sophistication of the respondent. Respondents were encouraged to provide more than one factor that entered into their decision making; many provided either two or three factors.

Following Greer, advertisers were categorized as sophisticated when their answers indicated that they had accurately assessed what their advertising should achieve, were aware of all media available to them and which were best suited for their purposes, and knew the comparative costs of the advertising outlets (which requires a knowledge of the audience size of each medium as well as the advertising rates). Of the 131 respondents, 103 (79 per cent) were classified as unsophisticated. Only seven of the 106 local decision makers (7 per cent) proved to be sophisticated, compared to the national decision makers, 21 of 25 (84 per cent) of whom were sophisticated.

## RESULTS

The 103 respondents classified as unsophisticated provided 195 responses. From those responses, 28 different factors were identified that helped to account for their media choices. Of those 28 factors, the one cited more frequently than any other was the return generated by the advertising as measured by customer comments (cited by 18 respondents). Another factor cited almost as frequently was a general perception that one medium is best for the advertiser's purposes (cited by 17 respondents).

Each of the 28 factors was grouped with others that were closely related to it resulting in the 11 general categories. The single category that contained the most responses was factors relating to return, cited by 38 respondents. A close second with 36 citations was factors relating to a belief that different media are best suited for specific purposes. One category that received a surprisingly low number of citations was factors relating to cost. Only 23 respondents mentioned cost as a factor in their media choices.

Most of the factors cited by respondents were decidedly subjective, based more on perceptions than objective and rational measures. The most relevant factors cited were those that related to return. That is, respondents would select media based on a comparison of the response generated by previous advertising with those media.

Return that was measured by traffic counts or a tabulation of sales receipts was the most objective and relevant factor of all those cited by respondents. Fourteen respondents measured return by one of those methods. Other respondents used less objective measures in which return was measured by customer comments or simply by their own perception of the response generated by the advertising.

The cost of the advertising was a factor that would seem to be objective and relevant, but not as it was used by the respondents. Six of those who cited cost were simply concerned with the willingness of the media to offer a special deal.

For another 15, cost was merely a perception. In those instances, respondents would indicate one medium was less expensive than others, but they could not support this belief with actual figures. The most objective measure of cost observed was cost per column inch in the newspaper vs. cost per spot on the radio - cited by two respondents. None of the respondents cited cost per thousand - the most effective measure of cost because it allows for a comparison of media - as a factor in their decision making.

Similarly, audience size would seem to be an objective and relevant criteria for selecting media, but not as used by respondents. They did not display a knowledge of the actual size of each medium's audience. Rather, their comparisons of media were based on mere perceptions of audience size. A comparison of those criteria by market showed no real trends based on market size. Some similarities were observed in that the same four factors - Return, Media serve different purposes, Preference for certain media, and Cost-tended to be ranked among the highest in most markets. However, a comparison of the rank orderings of those four factors showed little similarity among markets.

A comparison of those four factors by the percentage of respondents who cited them also showed little similarity among markets. Apparently, then, advertisers in different markets did display a tendency to use the same small group of criteria most frequently in selecting media, but the importance of those criteria varied by market and appeared to be based on conditions other than market size.

The vast majority of advertisers in the markets of smaller daily newspapers are not very sophisticated when it comes to advertising, and as both economic and sales theory suggest, their lack of sophistication affects their purchasing decisions. The results of this study lend support to the idea that these advertisers do not base their selection of advertising media on the types of objective and rational factors that would result in the greatest benefits for their businesses.

Instead, their decisions are much more subjective in nature, often based on personal or emotional rather than business factors. For example, one respondent's media choice was based on the willingness of salespeople to do the coop advertising paperwork, a factor unrelated to the medium's suitability.

Even those factors cited by respondents that might appear more relevant, measures such as return, cost, target audience, or audience size, were typically based on subjective perceptions rather than actual figures. If the assumption is that business managers attempt to maximize profits, the results of this study suggest that the advertising behaviour of local merchants in small daily markets does not always work toward that end. Rather, their behaviour tends to support Frederick-Collins' contention that because of the"daunting task" of gathering advertising information, many local businesses settle for profit levels that are merely satisfactory.

The implication for sales representatives is that they need to be aware of the different degrees of sophistication that typify their advertisers. The large majority of decision makers located outside the community are knowledgeable about advertising conditions. They are already aware of the purpose for which each medium is best suited and of the target audience each is likely to attract. Their primary concern is with the media's reach (circulation or ratings) and its cost per thousand.

The salesperson should recognize that they seek only objective data. Any attempts to embellish the product would probably not be very effective. For example, the salesperson who attempts to convince out-of-town decision makers to place ads with a local newspaper because they should support other businesses in the community is not likely to enjoy much success.

The vast majority of local decision makers are not as sophisticated when it comes to advertising. They select media based on a diverse number of factors, with return being the factor cited most frequently in this study. This supports what Margaret Carter writes, that the retailer is not really buying a newspaper ad, but wants to buy a response from the newspaper's readers.

While a response (or the lack of a response) seems to be a realistic measure by which to gauge advertising effectiveness, return as defined by unsophisticated advertisers is often ambiguous and not based on valid measures. Some advertisers do use somewhat formal measures such as counting coupon returns or adding up sales receipts. However, a large number merely base their assessment of return on customer comments -- on those who say, I saw your ad. Even those advertisers who use more formal measures of return to gauge advertising effectiveness do not always base it on complete information.

For example, they may measure return by totaling sales receipts, but they may not take into account the influence of outside factors such as an announcement of layoffs by a major employer.

It should be noted that return as used by the unsophisticated advertisers in this study is a reactive measure. They run an ad and attempt to gauge the response it generates. To sophisticated advertisers, return typically is more proactive. Prior to placing an ad, they know the size and composition of the media's audiences. Plus, they know the purposes for which each medium should be used. In other words, they know what to expect from different media before an ad ever runs. When an advertising campaign does not generate the return they envisioned, they do not automatically assume any failure should be attributed to the media.

Another factor that seems to weigh heavily in the decision making of local advertisers is the idea that different media are most suitable for different purposes. Some advertisers recognize that certain media are best for reaching specific target audiences. Others believe that some media are best for advertising specific items.

Thirteen respondents noted that,"Broadcast is best for name recognition, print for sales," a simplified interpretation of the idea that different media do have their strengths. The idea that many local advertisers recognize that media do serve different purposes suggests they are partially sophisticated. However, without a recognition of all the factors that should go into media choice, even these advertisers usually base their selection on incomplete information and, therefore, may not be making the best choices.

Ironically cost effectiveness is not as important a factor in selecting media as might be assumed. Media personnel probably believe cost is the most important issue because advertisers ask about it Oust as any consumer wants to know the cost before buying), many complain about it, if for no other reason than to gain an edge in negotiating better rates, and like many other businesses, media perpetually worry that their costs are too high. Yet, the results of this study suggest that advertisers in smaller communities do not base their media selections on cost as much as might be expected since only 23 of the 103 unsophisticated advertisers (22.3 per cent) and 51 of all 131 advertisers surveyed (38.9 per cent) cited cost as a factor in their choices.

Even those unsophisticated advertisers who select media based on cost usually do not make those choices based on a relative cost per thousand between media. Many newspapers salespeople are familiar with advertisers who complain about the cost of a quarter page at $150 and then buy $100 worth of radio spots. In their estimation, these radio spots that reach 1,000 listeners are a better buy than a newspaper ad that reaches 8,000 readers simply because they are less expensive. Given that most local advertisers in smaller markets are unsophisticated and often select media for reasons that may defy logic, sales representatives need to be aware of the sophistication of their clients. For unsophisticated advertisers, the salesperson needs to analyse the basis for their purchasing behaviour and base the sales pitch on these concerns.

As Stout wrote in recommending sales strategies for national advertisers, salespeople need to be aware of the behavioral influences that affect media selection. With local advertisers, this is even more crucial since their purchasing behaviour is less predictable than that of national advertisers. Once a salesperson is able to determine the basis for an advertiser's purchasing behaviour, it provides a strategy for selling.

A commonly held axiom is that the advertising salesperson should, Never walk in the door without something to sell. Knowing the concerns of their clients will help to provide sales representatives with something to sell, something they can discuss with their clients whenever the situation calls for it.

When in doubt, return is an especially effective idea for newspaper ad representatives to discuss with unsophisticated advertisers since it relates to the two most frequently cited factors used to select media. While return was cited most frequently, the second most frequently cited factor was the belief that different media are most suitable for different advertising purposes. Since a major strength of newspaper advertising is its ability to generate traffic, or, as many respondents put it, Use newspaper for sales, newspaper is the medium most suitable for generating return. Thus, return is a sales tool that can easily be related to two of the most frequently cited concerns of respondents.

This study did not examine how newspaper representatives sell advertising, so the type of information they provide their clients was not determined. However, the idea that unsophisticated advertisers do not always make media choices that contribute to profit maximization offers evidence that ad reps could provide a valuable service to their local advertisers by working to make them more knowledgeable about advertising. If a more sophisticated base of advertisers leads to a healthier Main Street, the newspaper ultimately stands to be one beneficiary.

Working to make advertisers more knowledgeable can contribute to' long-term success. For the short term, newspaper salespeople need to be aware of the behavioral influences that affect media selection. Sophisticated advertisers want primarily objective data. Unsophisticated advertisers are much less predictable. This study reveals many of the criteria they use in selecting media, but the criteria are far from universal.

Determining the criteria a specific advertiser uses should be done on an individual basis. From there the, son would be well advised to amend the sales strategy to meet the demands of the individual advertiser. The large number of subjective criteria used by unsophisticated advertisers in selecting media indicates that a one-sales-pitch-fits-all approach may miss the mark with too many clients.

# 12

# Emergence of "New" Media Moves

Once upon a time there were only a comparatively few major media that conscientious public relations practitioners could use to reach their target audiences with any certainty: magazines, newspapers, radio and television. The professionals who staffed these media were often referred to as"gate keepers" because they pretty much controlled whether a PR practitioner's offering was"newsworthy" enough to interest their audience/s and therefore had earned the right to appear in public. In return for giving up this control, PR practitioners gladly settled for being able to espouse the strength and purity of"third party credibility."

There were certain other benefits when your story appeared in a newspaper or magazine or on a radio or TV newscast. For the most part, the"gate keepers" were trained professionals and their judgment as to what was"newsworthy" could usually be respected.

The public didn't have to search for"news;" they could depend on their daily newspaper plopping on their front porch at a specific time; on a monthly magazine appearing in their mailbox or on the newsstand on a specific day; on being able to tune in radio news programs on the hour and half hour; and on being able to watch their favourite local or national TV anchor/s at a specific time every night.

Despite the more recent advent of 24/7 news cycles, this"timeliness" tended to create built-in audiences that could be measured with some degree of accuracy. Although there were some variances, you could pretty much depend on the same number of people reading their newspaper, listening to radio or watching TV at the same time every day.

Public relations agencies have earned a good living based on being able to reach these controlled audiences in a way and with a volume level that pleased their clients and earned them profitable hourly rates.

## THE EMERGENCE OF "NEW/EMERGING" MEDIA

The arrival of a plethora of new or"emerging" media in the past few years has posed an entire array of new agency challenges. The growth and popularity of consumer/user-generated news and information has lessened to some degree the power of"third party credibility." As print and electronic media management cut staffs and reduced the size of the"news hole" to burnish profits, the strength and credibility of the"gate keepers" have weakened.

What exactly does a new or emerging media look like? Think"blog." At least 14 - undoubtedly more - types of"media" probably qualify as"new" or"emerging" (not in any particular order): corporate blogs; grass roots blogs; RSS feeds; podcasts; client wikis; collaboration wikis; Technorati tags; social media (including Facebook, Myspace and YouTube;) webcasts; video blogs and virais (All of which may incorporate"emoticons/smileys" to help clarify digital communications.). This list isn't meant to be all-inclusive, but you get the idea. I've probably missed some media that should be included, or perhaps included some that don't really qualify.

## THE DIFFERENCE BETWEEN TRADITIONAL AND NEW MEDIA

There are some pretty striking differences between traditional and"new" media: Many of the"citizen journalists" manning various"new" media can hardly claim the same experience, objectivity and credibility as a traditional print or electronic journalist. So their output often tends to lack objectivity and"third party credibility." Instead of waiting patiently for the scheduled evening/morning newscast or print run, the public has developed a crushing need to access news and information practically before it exists, and so there is a growing dash - particularly in the younger age brackets so precious to clients - to find out what's new or breathtaking as quickly as possible via the thousands/millions of blogs, podcasts, social network sites and other"new" media that mushroom exponentially on a daily basis.

In addition, it has become disturbingly clear that the growing popularity of new media - particularly at the client level - and its ability to address specific target audiences has the potential to impact negatively on PR agencies' ability to continue to earn a good living - and must be reckoned with. Especially if an agency is still running largely in tandem with traditional media to meet client business and communications needs and has not developed awareness of or the skills necessary to cope with new media challenges. Witness the following: A well-respected, mid-size, Southeastern U.S. agency recently came in second in a new business shootout because the client was impressed with the strength of the winning firm's new"emerging media" division. Agency principals should view this example of a client's preference as the tip of an iceberg that is growing rather than shrinking in typical iceberg fashion and which could loom up in the middle of the night and sink their ship.

To help agencies meet these new"new media" challenges, I asked the presidents of four mid-size U.S. agencies - who regularly factor new/emerging media into their client plans and programs - to outline some of the things every agency principal should know about new media but may be too timid to ask. Herewith:

## THE EVOLUTION OF THE PRESS RELEASE

"In today's networked world, the definition of a news release has expanded. The press release is no longer exclusively a media relations tool; now, with the Internet's search capabilities, consider it a directto-consumer online page of Web content."The news release changed forever in September 2002, with the launch of Google News. From then on, all major public relations wire services - BusinessWire, PR Newswire, Market Wire, et al - became searchable online. Yahoo! News and AOL News soon launched their own news search portals. Today, each has more site traffic than the New York Times' website. "This sea change for news releases (and the PR industry) means that consumers now access releases simultaneously with journalists. This has important implications for news release content, style and format.

"Integrating multimedia assets, anchor text, hyperlinks and social media tags can enhance a release's intrinsic value and make it a portal to other information on the topic. A news release, as a page of web content, is now competing with a forum filled with news and multimedia elements including video and images. Even if you don't have photography or film, embedding a company logo is better than nothing.

"Press releases are no longer one-dimensional. Rather, they initiate a dialogue between an organization and its audience and engage an entire online community in an integrated conversation. Creative use of online content, from graphics to PDFs, logos, pre-approved executive quotes, and creative formatting can keep the conversation going longer and with more intensity. Adding hyperlinks in press releases to help viewers find interesting, related content on specific pages within your client's Web site is another way to provide the'bread crumbs' that guide a journalist (or a consumer) to the content or specific action desired on a Website.

"Search engine optimization (SEO), an activity previously reserved primarily for websites, may be the most important (and easiest to incorporate) technique for the'new' news release. Without SEO, a release will be buried - and anything lower than top ten on a Google News search, is buried.

"News search engines search by algorithms that are based on that old-school/J-school standard the inverted pyramid. Thus, from a search perspective, headlines are the most important areas of content, followed closely by the lead and second paragraphs. Descriptive headlines are a must, and if you can work important keywords into the head, all the better. A great place to determine appropriate keywords is Google Trends, where you can enter specific keywords to discover how often they are being searched online. Find them, and include these in your headline and first two paragraphs.

"Finally, public relations pros today have to consider consumer generated social media and the myriad'Web 2.0' tools and technologies that are expanding the opportunities for online public relations. At the top of that list are blogs. The most direct path to bloggers is via RSS feeds -'real simple syndication.' "How should public relations pros approach blogs? First of all, by respecting the medium's noncommercial conventions. In many ways, pitching a blog is just like Grafting a tailored pitch to a top tier print media outlet. Consider the blog's audience and how your client or product can benefit that community. Work it into a trend angle. Don't expect to see your news release posted on the blog, but do expect a spike in Web traffic if your pitch succeeds in sparking a blog mention or dialogue.

"The pace of change in new media is ever accelerating, and the ability to identify and leverage your agency's knowledge resources is paramount. The major wire services all have experts ready to share the latest tips on SEO, RSS, Technorati tags and (fill in the next new thing here). Seek their help, guidance and recommendations. After all, shiny new bells & whistles for what used to be plain-Jane news releases represent revenue opportunities for us as the distributors of Optimized' news releases. And get ready for the next new thing. Change is what we can count on - embrace it!"

**GETTING UP TO SPEED WITH THE CHANGING PR LANDSCAPE**

"Whether you're a technophile or a technophobe, you'd probably agree that technology continues to transform the public relations industry: how we communicate; how the media does its job; what the very definition of the media is. "However, many of our peers are in veritable denial and in need of a new media makeover. Are you one of them? Signs and symptoms include:

- You find yourself unable to engage in intelligible - much less intelligent - conversation when the discussion turns to blogs, podcasts, RSS, social media, Web 2.0 (or whatever all the buzz is about this week).
- You don't know how to use IM (instant messaging), have no idea what'LOL' means and are certainly not skilled in the art of communicating by emoticons.
- You use your cell phone only for talking.
- The time for excuses is over.'Not my thing' doesn't cut it. It's time to pull your head out of the digital sandbox and embrace your inner tech self. The success of your firm and your career depends on it.
- Here are three simple steps to getting up to speed with the changing PR landscape:

*Step* 1: Learn the lay of the land.

The younger people in your organization are your lifeline to what's happening on the front lines. Spend time with them, ask them to walk you through the hottest websites, to send you links to some of the more influential blogs, to set you up with IM, to teach you to use text messaging. While you're at it, learn the lingo - it's actually easier than a foreign language (No verbs to conjugate!). Most of your younger colleagues will get a kick out of showing you the way. And they'll respect you more for keeping up.

*Step* 2: Take the plunge.

Visit a blog a day. When a new website suddenly becomes the hottest thing (Think YouTube, MySpace or second Life.), go visit it right away. Navigate it or even try registering and using the site. Listen to podcasts. Subscribe to RSS feeds. Follow developments in technology, media and communications. Don't be surprised when you suddenly become the life of the new media party. The jaws of your technophobic friends and colleagues will drop in awe at your transformation.

*Step* 3: Use it or lose it. Today's market is increasingly competitive. Whether or not you're incorporating new tools and tapping technologies in your public relations programs, you can bet your competitors are. Think of ways to begin using the new tools at your disposal. Monitor the so-called blogosphere for conversations about your company and your clients. Post video from your latest event to YouTube. Incorporate a text messaging component into your next community relations programme.

You may never become an expert in new media and technology but at least you can keep pace - because if you don't, your competitors and your clients might just leave you in the digital dust."

From podcasts to blogs, text messages to vlogs, the communications world continues to advance beyond traditional media. Our clients know these channels exist; our job is to sort out the critical, the useful and the one-day wonders, and then match the appropriate tools to each element of the communications strategy.

*Here's what I've learned so far*:

- These are tools, like any other. They need to be integrated into your overall communications plan, not added on like shiny ornaments on a Christmas tree.
- Search engine optimization should be embraced for your firm's Web position as well as your clients'. There are companies that specialize in helping to ensure that your site moves up Organically' when people search for key words. Key word techniques also can be applied to individual press releases, for example, to further their Internet exposure.
- Build measurement into the budget whenever possible. You can learn whether people are really engaging with a Website or flocking to it in an initial flurry of activity, only to leave just as quickly.
- Your youngest employees are already early adapters. They're using these tools in their everyday lives. Let them lead the way in exploring the many ways you can use emerging media to achieve client objectives.
- Social networking sites seem like a natural fit for social issue campaigns, but it's not a given. It's important to manage client expectations. We present these communication tools as value-driven

assets to strengthen an existing audience base and generate new support in a cost effective manner, not as a magic bullet.

- We used emerging media for the"Donate Life Illinois" campaign, an 18-month effort to register Illinois residents in the state's new organ/ tissue donor registry. The client is Gift of Hope Organ & Tissue Donor Network. In planning the campaign, we knew that we wanted to implement a strong web presence, given that the campaign is situated around online registrations and deals with a public issue. As part of the interactive component of our campaign strategy, we created a campaign blog and Donate Life Illinois MySpace page to: a) Spark initial interest about the issue among 18-45 year olds; and b) Expand our social network by creating a centralized location for supporters to receive regular campaign updates and learn about how they can contribute to the campaign.
- We also used Facebook to facilitate conversation among student leaders from colleges and universities throughout Illinois who were participating in the college component of the campaign. We quickly realized that e-mail was not their tool of choice for communicating with the outside world.

**EMERGING MEDIA HAS EMERGED**

"'Emerging media' is no longer on the cutting edge. It's here. Blogs, podcasts, vblogs, virais and the like have fully emerged and are actively engaged every day by PR and marketing pros all over the country. Every agency has (or should have) its own strategic approach to these media. At McClenahan Bruer, we deploy tactics across these areas every day, but rather than package them as a separate practice area, we integrate them into our daily approach to PR, advertising, and marketing communications. The key to successful implementation is simple; do your homework.

"Just as you would if a new magazine or other media outlet was launched, start by investigating the players, the target audience and the rules of engagement before you pitch a client's story. In fact, we decided to use ourselves as a guinea pig. We launched a blog for the agency and'played' with it for nearly a year before offering blog strategy and management programs to our clients. That allowed us to find and figure out the'gotchas' on a more forgiving client (ourselves) than those that actually pay for services.

"We did the same thing with e-newsletters and podcasts, testing them for ourselves before offering those services to paying clients. In addition to avoiding beginner's mistakes on the client's dime, it allowed us to speak with integrity and authority when we told clients we knew how to effectively deploy such programs for them.

"One final thought: Seek out the input and advice of your interns and other young team members. For them, there is nothing new about these media.

They are likely far more sophisticated about online platforms than senior team members, and will welcome the opportunity to share what they know. Their knowledge of the tactics and your strategic expertise could be a very powerful combination."

**THE OTHER SIDE OF THE COIN**

Coming at the topic from a different direction, Kelly Rossman-McKinney, CEO, The Rossman Group, Lansing, MI, notes:"Obviously, the availability of'new media' puts more tools in our arsenal, but they're only good if they work. Just because they're the new shiny thing doesn't mean they work. We need to ask some basic questions such as: Who's the client? Who are their target audiences? Could one of our new media tools reach those audiences effectively?"

Commenting that some of the"shine" may already be wearing off"new media," PR Week editor Julia Hood asked recently in an editorial,"Is it possible that we all engage in overkill in promoting the impact and influence of user-generated (new) media at the expense of other marketing platforms? Far too much of the buzz relates to the opportunities of consumer content in isolation, rather than part of a complex and multifaceted programme. This is both over-simplifying the'new media' strategy and disproportionately diminishing others."

# 13

# Undesired Advertising Effects

Ever since James McNeal recognized children as a distinct consumer market, advertisers have been interested in developing strategies to reach the child consumer. The growing interest in children as consumers has been paralleled by increased concern about the consequences of marketing aimed at children, in particular television advertising. These concerns have been fueled by empirical evidence that children's exposure to television advertising may indeed lead to materialistic attitudes, increased purchase requests, and parent-child conflict.

This study investigates which types of parental mediation are most effective in counteracting potentially undesirable advertising effects. In a parent-child survey, we investigated how various types of parental mediation affect the influence of television advertising on materialism, purchase requests, and parent-child conflict. Parental mediation is often considered the most effective tool in the management of television's influence on children.

Children usually watch television in a family context that is largely provided by their parents. This family context not only influences how children use the medium and the messages they get from it but also how literate children become as television viewers.

There is an impressive body of research on parental mediation of television content. Parents can reduce undesirable media effects, including media-induced aggression, fear responses, and alcohol use, and they can increase desirable effects, such as learning from educational television programs. Although the mediation literature has burgeoned in the past two decades, research on parental mediation of advertising effects is still relatively scarce. A number of studies have investigated the effectiveness of media literacy programs about advertising. However, these studies have usually been conducted in school settings and have therefore disregarded the role of parents.

## TWO TYPES OF PARENTAL MEDIATION

Two types of parental mediation of children's advertising exposure have been identified in the literature. The first type involves parental mediation strategies specifically related to advertising; the second type is related to more general family consumer communication patterns.

## ADVERTISING MEDIATION

The advertising mediation literature has so far identified two strategies that parents can use to modify the effects of advertising: active and restrictive advertising mediation. Active mediation includes making deliberate comments and judgments about television commercials and actively explaining the nature and selling intent of advertising. Restrictive mediation involves sheltering children from advertising by reducing their exposure to it. This type of mediation includes family rules restricting children's viewing of commercial television channels. It has been argued that because young children lack the cognitive abilities to resist commercial messages, reducing their exposure to television may sometimes be the only effective way to counteract negative effects.

The few studies that have investigated parental advertising mediation have focused on the effects of mediation on children's understanding of advertising, their skepticism towards advertising, and their preferences or requests for advertised products. Thus far, no study has investigated mediation effects on the undesired effects of advertising, such as materialism or parent-child conflict. The two studies that compared the effectiveness of active versus restrictive mediation on children's under standing and skepticism arrived at opposite conclusions. Bijmolt et al. concluded that active mediation was the most effective mediation style, whereas Wiman found that restrictive mediation was the most effective way to mediate advertising effects.

The findings on how active and restrictive mediation influence advertising effects are indecisive, and in the case of the undesired advertising effects, they are nonexistent. There is a need to investigate and compare how the two styles of mediation affect the relations between advertising exposure and materialism, purchase requests, and parent--child conflict. Earlier research evidence is too scarce and inconclusive to enable us to formulate specific hypotheses, which is why we investigated the following research question:

*RQ*: How do active and restrictive mediation affect children's advertising-induced materialistic attitudes, purchase requests, and parent child conflict, and which type of mediation is most effective in reducing them?

## FAMILY CONSUMER COMMUNICATION

In addition to specific advertising-related mediation, more general consumer-related family communication styles can influence children's responses to advertising. In the literature, two types of family communication patterns are distinguished:

- Concept-orientation, which stresses negotiation, individual ideas, and opinions;
- Socio-orientation, which emphasizes obedience and harmony.

Studies on family consumer communication patterns have shown that adolescents from families with a concept-oriented communication style have more knowledge about consumer-related matters, are better able to see through selling techniques in advertising, and display less materialistic values. In contrast, adolescents from families with a socio-oriented communication style are more susceptible to the influence of external sources such as television advertising.

There is as yet no research on the effects of family communication styles on children's advertising-induced purchase requests and conflicts with their parents. The study on the effects of family communication on materialism only included adolescents (12- to 18-year-olds). However, because children learn consumer skills well before they reach adolescence, it is important to investigate the influence of consumer communication styles on children under the age of 12. The following hypothesis was posited:

*H*: Concept-oriented consumer communication is more effective in reducing the relations between advertising exposure and materialism, purchase requests, and parent child conflict than socio-oriented consumer communication.

## METHOD

### SAMPLE AND PROCEDURE

The results of this study are part of a larger parent-child survey into the unintended effects of television advertising on children. The children in our sample were recruited from five elementary schools in urban and rural districts in the Netherlands. In all, 427 children completed a paper-and-pencil questionnaire previously tested in a pilot study among 10 children. The questionnaires were administered in the children's regular classrooms by a trained examiner. After completing the questionnaire, which took about 25 minutes, the children were given a parent questionnaire to take home. They were told they would get a present when they returned the completed questionnaire. A total of 360 questionnaires (84%) were returned, yielding a total sample of 360 parent child dyads from various economic backgrounds.

The final child sample consisted of 175 boys (48.6%) and 185 girls (51.4%) between the ages of 8 and 12 (M = 10.0, SD = 1.25). The parent sample consisted of 291 mothers, 61 fathers, and 8 parents who did not indicate their gender. The parent questionnaire was accompanied by a letter asking the parent who spent the most time with the child to fill it out.

If more than one child in a family brought home the questionnaire, the parent was asked to complete one for each child with that child in mind. After all the questionnaires were collected, the parents were informed about the nature and purpose of the study via the school newspaper. All the children, including those who had not returned the questionnaire, were given a present.

## MEASURES

A parent-child sample was chosen because we were interested in behaviors and responses of both parents and children. In the case of the mediation variables, we were interested in the parents' estimates of their frequency of using the different mediation styles. In the case of advertising exposure and effects, we were primarily interested in children's estimates. Therefore, we chose to measure the mediation variables (i.e., advertising mediation and family consumer communication) among parents and the advertising exposure and effects variables (i.e., advertising viewing frequency, materialism, purchase request behaviour, and parent child conflict) among children. However, to check whether children were able to produce reliable responses on the advertising effects variables, we measured these variables (i.e., materialism, purchase requests, and parent-child conflict) among both children and parents. Only the advertising exposure variable was exclusively measured among children because our operationalization of this variable has been validated in earlier research.

All child and parent advertising effects measures were significantly correlated, and none of the analyses yielded substantial discrepancies between the correlations investigated in the child and parent samples. We therefore based the remaining analyses in this study on the advertising exposure and effects variables measured among children.

## ADVERTISING MEDIATION AND CONSUMER COMMUNICATION

To determine advertising mediation, we used a television mediation scale developed by Valkenburg, Krcmar, Peeters, and Marseille. We adapted the items representing an active mediation style (e.g., how often parents try to help their children understand what they see on television) and a restrictive mediation style (e.g., how often parents forbid their children to watch certain programs) to reflect communication strategies more directly relevant to television advertising. The 10 items dealt with the frequency (often, sometimes, rarely, or never) of the various mediation strategies used by parents. To measure consumer communication patterns, we used the original Family Communications Patterns scale developed by Chaffee et al. The items on this scale were adapted to measure consumer-related communication patterns.

Our final list of items measuring types and styles of parental mediation consisted of 24 items, 10 for advertising mediation and 14 for consumer communication. The items were simultaneously entered into a principal components analysis, yielding four factors explaining 48.2% of the variance.

*These factors were*:

- Active advertising mediation,
- Restrictive advertising mediation,
- Concept-oriented consumer communication,
- Socio-oriented consumer communication.

The correlations among the four scales ranged from r =.00, ns, between restrictive advertising mediation and concept-oriented communication, to r =.29, p <.001, between active advertising mediation and concept-oriented communication.

Scales were constructed for each of the four factors by averaging the scores on the items loading on each factor. For the moderator analyses, each scale was recoded into dichotomous variables by way of mean splits.

## ADVERTISING VIEWING FREQUENCY

The frequency of viewing television advertising was measured by presenting the children with the titles of 10 commercials broadcasted on several television channels in the data collection period. We asked the children to indicate whether they had seen each commercial; response options were 1 (never), 2 (sometimes), or 3 (often).

This method has been demonstrated to be a valid measure of children's television exposure among elementary school children. We conducted a principal components analysis with varimax rotation on the 10 commercials. This analysis yielded one factor, which explained 33.1% of the variance. A total score of children's advertising exposure was calculated by averaging the unweighted scores on the 10 commercials.

## MATERIALISM

To ascertain the children's level of materialism, we adopted a scale used by most studies on the relation between advertising and materialism.

*Examples of the questions were* :

- "Do you think it is important to have a lot of money?"
- "Do you think it is important to own a lot of things?"
- "Would you like to be able to buy things that cost a lot of money?"

Children responded to the questions on a 4-point scale, ranging from 1 (no, not at all) to 4 (yes, very much). A principal components analysis with children's responses on these five items yielded one factor, explaining 35.7% of the variance. A materialism scale was constructed by averaging the scores on the five items.

Purchase Requests. To measure children's purchase request behaviour, children were presented with a list of nine product types selected to appeal to boys and girls alike and to younger and older children (toys, CDs, school stationery, candy, clothes, computer games, snacks, athletic equipment, and money).

The children were asked to indicate whether they asked their parents for each product type; response options were 1 (never), 2 (sometimes), or 3 (often). Principal components analysis on children's responses showed a one-factor solution explaining 23.5% of the variance. The total purchase request variable was constructed by averaging the scores on the nine items.

## PARENT--CHILD CONFLICT

To measure parent--child conflict about purchase requests, children were asked to indicate on a 4-point scale, ranging from 1 (never) to 4 (often), how often there was a conflict after denial of a purchase request for each of four product types (toys, candy, school stationery, and clothes). Principal components analyses yielded one factor explaining 45.0% of the variance. Total conflict scores were constructed by averaging the scores on the four items.

## RESULTS

The aim of this study was to investigate and compare the moderating influence of advertising mediation (active vs. restrictive) and consumer communication (socio-oriented vs. concept-oriented) on three effects of television advertising (materialism, purchase requests, and parent--child conflict). To do so, we compared the outcomes of the children of parents who scored either high or low on each of the parental mediation styles.

Research on the unintended effects of advertising has demonstrated that children's advertising exposure is directly related to their materialism and purchase requests. Children's advertising exposure is also related to parent--child conflict, but this relation is mediated by children's purchase requests (advertising exposure influences purchase requests, which in turn enhance the chance of parent--child conflict).

To measure these direct and mediated relations, we first investigated the zero-order correlations between (a) advertising exposure and materialism, (b) advertising exposure and purchase requests, and (c) purchase requests and parent--child conflict. We then investigated the third-order correlations for the same relations, controlling for the children's age, sex, and socioeconomic status.

By means of our research question, we aimed to investigate how active and restrictive advertising mediation affect advertising-induced materialism, purchase requests, and parent-child conflict, and which type of mediation is most effective in reducing these advertising-induced effects. Two of the three investigated relations (i.e., between advertising exposure and materialism, and between advertising exposure and purchase requests) were significantly stronger for children whose parents rarely use active mediation than for children whose parents often use this strategy. This pattern also emerged when controlling for children's age, sex, and socioeconomic status, although differences for the relation between advertising exposure and materialism only approached significance.

The use of restrictive mediation only moderated the relation between advertising exposure and materialism and not those between advertising exposure and purchase requests as well as between purchase requests and parent--child conflict. Contrary to expectations, the relation between advertising and materialism was stronger among children whose parents often use a restrictive mediation style. However, this difference did not hold when controlling for age, sex, and socioeconomic status.

In our hypothesis, we stated that concept-oriented consumer communication would be more effective than socio-oriented consumer communication. Each of the three investigated relations was weaker for children whose parents often use concept-oriented consumer communication than for children whose parents rarely use this type of communication.

However, the moderating effect on the relations between advertising exposure and materialism and between purchase requests and parent-child conflict only approached significance, probably due to the small sample sizes of the subgroups. The same pattern emerged when controlling for children's age, sex, and socioeconomic status. Socio-oriented communication did not moderate any of the relations. The observed trends are in agreement with our hypothesis that concept-oriented consumer communication is a more effective moderator of advertising effects than socio-oriented consumer communication. The aim of this study was to investigate how various parental mediation styles affect the relations between children's advertising exposure and materialism, purchase requests, and conflicts with their parents. We distinguished two styles of mediation: advertising mediation and family consumer communication.

## EFFECTIVENESS OF ACTIVE VERSUS RESTRICTIVE ADVERTISING MEDIATION

Our first aim was to investigate how active and restrictive mediation affect children's advertising-induced materialistic attitudes, purchase requests, and conflicts with their parents as well as which type of mediation is most effective in reducing these relations. Our results indicate that active mediation was significantly more effective in reducing advertising effects than restrictive mediation.

These results are in line with the findings of Bijmolt et al., who compared the effects of restrictive versus active mediation on children's comprehension of advertising. They noted that active mediation increased children's comprehension of advertising and that restrictive mediation had the opposite effect.

In the first instance, our finding that restrictive mediation did not lead to a decrease in purchase requests may seem counterintuitive. After all, various studies have shown that children who watch more television advertising make more purchase requests. One would expect that a parental restriction of children's exposure to advertising would lead to a reduction in their purchase requests.

A possible explanation for the ineffectiveness of restrictive mediation policies is that in reality these policies do not lead to sufficient reductions in children's television viewing. After all, children watch commercial television for several hours a day, and it is often unfeasible to avoid their exposure to advertising. Because both children's television viewing and parents' restrictive mediation were variables in our data set, we could test this explanation by turning back to the data and verifying the relationship between television advertising exposure and restrictive mediation. The correlation between the two variables was indeed nonsignificant, suggesting that parental restriction methods do not necessarily prevent children from being exposed to television advertising.

## EFFECTIVENESS OF CONCEPT-ORIENTED VERSUS SOCIO-ORIENTED CONSUMER COMMUNICATION

Our findings suggest that concept-oriented consumer communication is more effective in reducing the relations between advertising exposure and children's materialism, purchase requests, and conflicts with their parents than socio-oriented consumer communication. Although more research is needed to come to decisive conclusions about the observed trends, these findings are in agreement with our hypothesis about family consumer communication. As noted previously, concept-oriented communication involves active discussions with children about consumer matters, whereas socio-oriented communication involves promoting obedience and harmony.

Concept-oriented communication might be more effective in counteracting advertising effects because it actively teaches children to become critical consumers, which may in turn reinforce their defenses against advertising. Socio-oriented communication may be less able to counteract the effects of advertising because it does not teach children about advertising and consumer matters, and thus does not help them to learn and apply defenses against advertising.

In sum, active mediation and concept-oriented communication are both more effective mediation styles than restrictive advertising mediation and socio-oriented consumer communication. This result is plausible because active mediation and concept-oriented communication are conceptually related, as are restrictive and socio-oriented communication.

Active mediation and concept-oriented communication are focused on family discussions and increasing children's understanding and autonomy, whereas restrictive mediation and socio-oriented communication are mainly focused on protecting children from advertising. Our study suggests that strategies like these are less useful than active communicative strategies.

## PRACTICAL AND THEORETICAL IMPLICATIONS

The results of this study have implications for those involved in the daily care of children as well as for academics investigating advertising effects.

Our findings can help parents and educators learn how to deal with potentially undesired consequences of advertising.

Even though most Western countries have protective policies concerning child-directed advertising, the lion's share of the responsibility of dealing with the negative effects is still shouldered by the parents, who are usually the first to experience inconvenience as a result of advertising.

Our results indicate that parents are able to counteract the effects of advertising by talking with their children about advertising and consumer matters. Parental attempts to restrict children's exposure to commercial television content have a negligible effect, whereas actively interacting with children is an effective way to modify children's responses to advertising.

There is a need for further research to explore the specific ways in which talking with children can reduce potentially undesirable advertising effects.

Future studies could draw from the more developed research line on parental mediation of children's responses to televised violence.

Mediation research on media violence suggests that the outcomes of parental mediation depend on:

- Child and family characteristics, such as children's age and parents' perceptions of television influence;
- The content and form of the mediation.

Nathanson has compared different types of active mediation (i.e., factual vs. evaluative mediation), which could be adapted to investigate advertising-related mediation strategies. Future advertising mediation research should encompass survey studies, to determine the role of different child and family variables, as well as experimental studies to compare the outcomes of different mediation strategies. Such research will not only benefit parents and educators but also designers of curriculum-based educational programs aimed at increasing children's advertising literacy and consumer skills.

# 14

# Analysis of Political Advertising Across Media

Much has been written about political advertising. This is hardly surprising given the huge amounts of money devoted to political spots. Jamieson observes correctly that"political advertising in now the major means by which candidates for the presidency communicate their messages to voters". Research on two different campaigns has confirmed that four times as many voters obtain more issue information from television spots than from the news. Clearly, political spots (advertisements) merit scholarly attention.

Devlin has chronicled presidential television advertising each campaign starting with 1976. Benoit, Diamond and Bates, Jamieson and Levine discuss the history of presidential TV spots. James and Hensel, Johnson-Cartee and Copeland, and Procter and Schenck-Hamlin have focused on negative or attack ads in particular.

Several studies adopted a rhetorical approach to political advertising. While direct mail has become an increasingly important medium, little research has investigated its nature. Political candidates are increasingly using webpages, but again, research on this new message form is still in its infancy.

The literature that is most relevant to this project analyses television spots on the two primary dimensions of such messages: functions and topics. Most research on presidential television spots divides ads into positive and negative (attacking) spots. However, the Functional Theory of Political Campaign Discourse acknowledges that there are three possible functions: acclaiming (self-praise; positive), attacking (criticism of opponent; negative) and defending (responses to attacks; refutation).

Three works offer an overview of the functions of political advertising. Kaid and Johnston found that 71% of the 830 presidential television commercials they studied from 1960 to 1988 were positive and 29% negative. However, the number of negative ads varied over time: Negative spots spiked at 40% in 1964, dropped to 22-28% in the 1970s, and increased to 35-37% in the 1980s. Kaid and Johnston found no difference in use of negative spots by challengers than incumbents.

West studied 379 spots from 1952 to 1996, reporting that 46% of the ads were positive (and the rest negative). Benoit's analysis of 829 presidential spots from every presidential campaign to use this message form found that 60% of the utterances were acclaims, 39% attacks, and 1% defenses. He also reported that challengers were prone to use attacks more frequently than incumbents (45% to 33%) while incumbents used more acclaims than did challengers (66% to 54%). Thus, research reveals that presidential television advertising uses acclaims (positive ads) more than attacks (negative ads), and, rarely, defenses.

## POLICY VERSUS CHARACTER ADVERTISING

The second major dimension employed to analyse political ads is topic: policy (issue) and character (image or personality). Kaid and Johnston reported that 67% of the positive ads and 79% of the negative ads provide issue information, and that 65% of the positive spots and 64% of the negative spots include image information. West reported that 61% of the ads in his sample mentioned issues.

Benoit found that 60% of comments in presidential television spots addressed policy and 40% character (recent spots have emphasized policy more than earlier ones). Jamieson, Waldman, and Sherr report that their analysis of presidential spots from 1952-1996 found that"the majority of verbal content in political advertisements is not discussion of policy". They divide ads by type, reporting that 39% of attack (negative) ads, 39% of contrast (comparative) ads, and 32% of advocacy (positive) ads discuss policy.

However, this research has a relatively low inter-coder reliability ("the reliability was greater than the 0.6 level using the stringent Krippendorf reliability alpha"), which could explain the divergent results. Most research in this area suggests that policy (issues) is a more common topic of TV spots than character (personality).

Johnson-Cartee and Copeland developed a list of topics from negative political ads and asked respondents to rate them as fair or unfair. The topics clustered into two groups,"Political Issues" (political record, stands on issues, criminal record, and voting record) and"Personal Characteristics" (personal life, marriage, family, religion, medical history, and sex life).

At least 83% of the respondents rated every political issue as a fair topic for an attack; no more than 36% considered any of the personal characteristics acceptable grounds for an attack. This study shows that people do not necessarily reject all political attacks as unfair, and that attacks on policy are considered more appropriate than attacks on character.

Of course, these two topic areas (policy/issue, character/image/ personality) are not as discrete as it might appear Benoit and Wells argue that a politician's position on issues influences that person's image, and that a candidate's image influences perceptions of his or her issue stands. Devlin noted that Carter's campaign"used issues or themes as a vehicle for Carter to achieve an image as a legitimate candidate". Policy and character must be viewed as interrelated concepts.

Thus, we have seen a great deal of research on presidential television advertising. The race for the highest elective office in the land ought to command interest. However, this focus on presidential spots is unfortunate, because there are literally thousands (if not tens of thousands) more non-presidential than presidential candidates.

## NON-PRESIDENTIAL TELEVISION ADVERTISING

There have been fewer studies of non-presidential ads. A few studies focused only on certain types of spots. Joslyn analysed presidential, gubernatorial, and senatorial television spots from 1960-1976. He found overall that issue-related content was more common than candidate information. Payne and Baukus analysed 1984 Republican Senate spots with Diamond and Bates' typology. Attack, argument, and ID (identification) ads were far more common than resolution or biographical spots. Positive ads are more common than negative ads and incumbents used more attack spots than challengers.

Several studies describe political newspaper advertising. Bowers' analysis of 1970 ads found that issues accounted for 46% of the assertions and candidate characteristics accounted for 37% of the statements in these ads. Humke, Schmitt, and Grupp studied ads from 1932 to 1960. The central theme was candidate or party in 62% of the ads and issue in 38% of the advertisements.

Latimer examined newspaper ads from Alabama from 1982, while Latimer analysed newspaper advertisements from 1986 in seven state campaigns. Both found image was more common than policy. Latimer's study of ads from 1978-1984 seems to have found the same result. Thus, most research on newspaper ads tends to indicate more reliance on character than policy.

Internet campaigning has produced several studies of this new medium. Warnick examined parody on the web, but not serious candidate web pages. Klotz reported that in 1996, 50 of 68 Senate candidates had web pages, which tended to include a photograph, biography, issues, and contact information. Klotz found that 94% of congressional web sites in 1996 were positive, 4% comparative, and 2% oppositional. Some had no attacks: 47% of challenger pages, 69% of incumbent pages and 77% of open-seat pages were entirely positive.

Margolis, Resnick and Tu analysed presidential web sites in the 1996 primary campaign. The standard features of candidate web sites included signing a guest book, volunteering to help the campaign, fact-sheets and speeches, and links to political party organizations, groups, and people. Selnow noted that candidate sites in the general election included biographies with photos, quotes, links to speeches and news stores, policy positions, and

E-mail addresses for the candidate. Thus, most campaign web advertising includes biographies, photographs of the candidate, issue information; speeches and press releases; and opportunities to volunteer, contribute, and sign up for e-mail newsletters. Unfortunately, we don't have a clear understanding of the functions or topics of presidential candidate webpages at this point.

This chapter will begin by describing the theory which undergirds this study, the Functional Theory of Political Campaign Discourse. Then will explain the purpose of this study, justify use of this approach, and describe the research questions and hypotheses.

## FUNCTIONAL THEORY OF POLITICAL CAMPAIGN DISCOURSE

The Functional Theory of Political Campaign Discourse posits that citizens vote for the candidate who appears preferable (on whatever criteria are most important to each voter). Candidates have but three discursive options to increase their apparent desirability. First, they may acclaim, or engage in self-praise.

The better a candidate appears to voters, the more likely that candidate will be preferred over opponents. Second, candidates may attack, or reduce an opponent's desirability. Because voting is essentially a comparative judgment, a successful attack makes the opponent appear worse to voters, giving the attacker a net gain in desirability (of course, it is possible that an attack will backfire and damage the source of the attack).

Third, if attacked, an opponent may engage in defence, refuting accusations so as to restore lost desirability. So, a candidate has these basic options to persuade voters that he or she is preferable to opponents. These are the three functions of political campaign discourse, instrumental effects or means to an end (i.e., persuading citizens to vote for one candidate over another).

Citizens can assess candidates based on what they do (what they have done or will do if elected) and on who they are. Thus, these three functions (acclaims, attacks, defenses) occur on two broad topics: policy and character. Each topic area has three subdivisions. Policy utterances are divided into three categories: past deeds (actions related to governance), future plans (specific policy proposals, means to an end), and general goals (desirable policy ends). The categories used in this analytical method will be illustrated with excerpts from 1996 presidential TV spots, which guided the analysis reported here.

Clinton acclaimed his past deeds:"President Clinton cut the deficit 600%. Signed welfare reform--requiring work, time limits. Taxes cut for 15 million families." These utterances concern policy--deficit, welfare, taxes--and he praises his first term accomplishments. Dole however, attacked Clinton's actions on welfare reform:"But he [Clinton] vetoed welfare reform not once, but twice. He vetoed work requirements for the able-bodied. He vetoed putting time limits on welfare." This utterance addresses a policy topic, welfare, and Clinton's actions (past deeds) are the subject of the attack.

Dole turned to the future, acclaiming one of his specific policy proposals in this future plan utterance:"Bob Dole's economic plan will cut taxes 15 per cent for every single taxpayer. The typical family of four will save over $1,600 a year." Clinton, in contrast, offered a different perspective on this proposal, attacking Dole's future plan:"Dole's risky tax scheme would balloon the deficit, threaten Medicare cuts--again." At times candidates discuss more general policy concerns.

One ad for Clinton acclaimed this general goal:"President Clinton says balance the budget." Clinton also attacked two of Dole's alleged general goals:"Bob Dole. Raising taxes. Trying to cut Medicare." Thus, the three forms of policy are used in acclaims and attacks.

It is worth noting that the Functional Theory assumes that candidates' discourse is shaped by the opportunities available to them. Specifically, incumbents have a record in the office sought, so they are presumed likely to acclaim and, in particular, to acclaim on past deeds.

Challengers may have a record in other offices, but not in the office sought. Therefore, they are expected to attack, especially on past deeds (aspects of the incumbents' record). Challengers also frequently acclaim general goals and future plans, telling voters what improvements they will make if elected.

Character utterances are subdivided into three categories: personal qualities (e.g., honesty, determination, compassion), leadership ability (competence, experience in governing), and ideals (principles, values). Once again the categories that guided the analysis performed in this study are illustrated with spot excerpts from the 1996 presidential race.

One personal quality candidates can discuss is courage, as this excerpt from a Clinton advertisement illustrates:"President Clinton had the courage to take on the special interests." Dole uses various policy statements about the time it would require to achieve a balanced budget to attack Clinton for engaging in double-talk, an undesirable personal quality: [various video clips of Clinton]:"I would present a 5-year plan to balance the budget. We could do it in 7 years. I think we could reach it in 9 years.

Balance the budget in 10 years. I think we could reach it in 8 years. So, we're between 7 and 9 years. [Announcer]:... Talk is cheap. Double talk is expensive." Dole's ad uses various video clips from Clinton to impeach Clinton's consistency and honesty (notice how Clinton's various statements about a question of policy are used to indict his honesty, illustrating the potential overlap between policy and character noted above).

Dole acclaimed his leadership ability when he declared:"I am not afraid to lead America. I know the way." A Clinton spot, however, questioned the kind of leadership ability Dole had demonstrated:"He told us he would lead. He told us he could do his job and run for President. That he was a doer, not a talker. Then he told us he was quitting, giving up." Dole's decision to resign his Senate office is used to impeach his leadership ability.

In this passage, Dole acclaimed an ideal:"I see an America with a government that works for us, not the other way around." A Dole ad attacked Clinton's ideals in this passage:"From Day 1, Bill Clinton shocks America with his liberal agenda." Thus, the three forms of character are also used in both acclaims and attacks.

Notice how this theory relates to other approaches to understanding voting. Some voters want to know what a candidate has done, successes and failures, as an indication of what he or she is likely to do if elected. Discussion of past deeds, one form of policy discourse, helps voters engage in this kind of retrospective voting (What have you accomplished, good or bad, in the past?). On the other hand, some voters are more concerned about the future than the past, or about what the candidate will try to accomplish if elected.

Discussion of future plans and general goals (campaign promises) allow prospective voting (What are you likely to do if you are elected?). These three policy sub-topics together are helpful for voters who decide more on policy (issues) than on character (image). On the other hand, personal qualities, leadership ability, and ideals--character topics--appeal to citizens who tend to base their vote on the candidates' character.

Partisanship comes into play as well, especially in ideals and general goals (e.g., Republicans are often seen as the better party for controlling inflation, while Democrats are usually seen as the better party for fighting unemployment; Popkin, 1994). Thus, the Functional Theory of Political Campaign Discourse is compatible with other approaches to understanding voter behaviour.

## PURPOSE

Systematic studies of non-presidential spots--or on other forms of political advertising besides television or newspaper--are relatively rare. Furthermore, most research considers but a single medium at a time--and usually just television spots. Nor does every study examine both dimensions, functions (positive, attacking) and topics (policy, character). This study is designed to extend our knowledge of political advertising in two directions: by conducting a functional analysis (functions and topics) of advertisements from candidates for a variety of non-presidential offices and by considering advertisements produced for a variety of media.

Jacobson reported that broadcast campaign messages have more impact on voting behaviour in non-presidential than presidential races (presumably because citizens have less information about nonpresidential than presidential candidates), justifying analysis of advertisements by non-presidential candidates. Furthermore, research has found that in the 1996 presidential campaign television spots were more negative than speeches or debates, and that defenses were more common in debates than in other media. Thus, there is a reason to investigate multiple media for potential differences in candidate advertising.

This study applies the Functional Theory of Political Campaign Discourse to political advertising in four media (television spots, newspaper ads, direct mail, and World Wide Web pages) in the 1998 Missouri election. The functions (acclaims, attacks, defenses) and topics (policy: past deeds, future plans, general goals; character: personal qualities, leadership ability, and ideals) of these ads will be analysed, looking for similarities and differences across media. This theory is employed in this analysis for four reasons. First it is appropriate for the purpose and the discourses studied here. Second, it has advantages over competing approaches to analyzing political advertising. It addresses both functions (acclaims, attacks, defenses) and topics (policy, character) of campaign discourse. Some research (as can be seen in the literature review above) examines but one of these two areas.

Clearly, both are important to a complete understanding of political campaign discourse. A third advantage is that this approach analyses discourse thematically. It is more common for research on political advertising to analyse entire spots. However, most spots are not entirely positive (acclaiming) or completely negative (attacking); few spots discuss either policy (issues) or character (image, personality) exclusively.

For example, consider the following two spots. In the traditional method of analysis, both would be classified as negative or attacking spots. A recent study offered this Clinton spot from the 1996 campaign to illustrate a negative spot: America's values. The President bans deadly assault weapons; Dole/ Gingrich vote no. The President passes family leave; Dole/Gingrich vote no. The President stands firm: a balanced budget, protects Medicare, disabled children; No again. Now Dole resigns, leaves gridlock he and Gingrich created. The President's plan: balance the budget, protect Medicare, rearm welfare. Do our duty to our parents, our children. America's values.

Notice that the italicized portions of this ad are positive, acclaiming Clinton and his accomplishments. These passages are ignored when the entire ad is classified as either positive or negative. Compare the previous ad, containing both positive and negative elements, with the following Clinton spot: Let's go back in time. The'60s. Bob Dole's in Congress. Votes against creating Medicare. Against creating student loans. Against the Department of Education. Against a higher minimum wage. Against Family and Medical Leave. Against Vaccines for Children. Against Medicare--again. Dole/Gingrich tried to cut $270 billion. Bob Dole. Wrong in the past. Wrong for our future.

This spot, in sharp contrast, consists entirely of attacks. However, the traditional method of classifying entire spots would consider these two ads to be the same: Both are negative or attacking spots. The Functional approach analyses by themes (ideas), and would report (with greater accuracy) that the first spot contains both acclaiming and attacking, whereas the second consists exclusively of attacks. A final reason for adopting the Functional Approach is that it has been used to analyse other campaign messages, like television spots, Acceptance Addresses, Keynote Speeches, and debates. This gives us the opportunity to contextualize the results of new studies with findings on other message forms or other kinds of races.

Four research questions are answered in this study:

1. *RQ.sub*.1: What is the proportion of functions (acclaims, attacks, defenses) in these ads?
2. *RQ.sub*.2: What is the proportion of policy and character utterances in these ads?
3. *RQ.sub*.3: What is the proportion of the forms of policy (past deeds, future plans, general goals) in these ads?
4. *RQ.sub*.4: What is the proportion of the forms of character (personal qualities, leadership ability, ideals) in these ads?

This study also tests three hypotheses. Previous research on presidential television spots found that Democrats attack more than Republicans, who in turn acclaim more than Democrats.

*H.sub*.1: Advertising from Republicans uses a greater proportion of acclaims than ads from Democrats, while Democrats uses a larger percentage of attacks than Republicans. Second, prior study of presidential television ads found that incumbents used more acclaims than challengers, who in turn use more attacks than incumbents.

*H.sub*.2: Advertising from incumbents uses a greater proportion of acclaims than challengers, who in turn use a larger percentage of attacks than incumbents. Previous research has found that incumbents particularly differ from challengers on use of past deeds:

*H.sub*.3: Incumbent advertising acclaims more than it attacks on past deeds, while challenger advertising attacks more than it acclaims on past deeds. This investigation will provide a better understanding of non-presidential, and nontelevision, advertising.

## METHODS

The categorical content analytic procedure employed in this study had four steps. First, ads were unitized into themes. Themes are the smallest units of discourse that are capable of expressing a complete idea. Berelson defined a theme as"an assertion about a subject". Similarly, Holsti characterized a theme as"a single assertion about some subject". Basically, a theme in this study is an argument about the candidates. Because discourse is inherently enthymematic, themes can (and do) vary in length from a phrase to several sentences. Second, the function of each theme was then identified according to these rules:

- Acclaims portray the sponsoring candidate in a favorable light. Attacks portray the opposing candidate in an unfavorable light.

- Defence respond to (refute) an attack on the candidate. Third, each theme was classified as concerning policy or character according to these rules:
- Policy themes address government action or problems amenable to such action.
- Character themes address characteristics, traits, abilities, or attributes of the candidates.
- Fourth, policy themes were broken down into past deeds, future plans, and general goals, while character themes were analysed into personal qualities, leadership ability, and ideals.

For example, Dan Fischbach ran this newspaper ad in his 1998 campaign for County Clerk:

- Dan Fischbach for Boone County Clerk.
- Dan Fischbach has 19 years training and management experience as a flight instructor in the Navy--he is a qualified professional.
- Dan Fischbach will build public confidence in election fairness by publishing election results online.
- Dan Fischbach will never serve on a campaign committee while Clerk, because you can't be the umpire and play the game.

Each theme is numbered in this transcript. Although it is a coherent idea, the first sentence is not coded because it announces the candidate and office but gives no reason to vote for the candidate. The next theme acclaims his leadership ability (administrative experience). The third sentence is a campaign promise. Because publishing election results online is quite specific, this is considered to be a future plan (rather than a general goal).

The last sentence is divided into two themes. The first part of this sentence begins by expressing a principle (the County Clerk should be above partisan politics), which acclaims an ideal expressed by the candidate. The last statement functions as an attack on his opponent for participating in a campaign while she occupies the office of County Clerk. Thus, this ad contains four themes, three acclaims (leadership ability, future plans, ideals) and one attack (past deed).

In the race for one of Missouri's Senate seats, Jay Nixon attacked Kit Bond for having released prisoners. Bond's the one who brought back the death penalty law and expanded our prisons 74% so we wouldn't have to let criminals out. But Jay Nixon's hunger to get elected is so bad he'll say anything but the truth. Give it a rest, Mr. Nixon, nobody's buying it.

The first sentence is not coded because it only establishes the source's credentials (by itself, it does not give a reason to vote for Bond or against Nixon). The next sentence attacks Nixon for running negative ads.

Because these negative ads are not governmental policy, this is an attack on Nixon's personal qualities as exemplified in his campaign tactics. The third sentence defends against Nixon's attack, denying that Bond was soft on criminals. Sentence four functions much like sentence one and is not coded. There are two themes in the next sentence: The fifth theme acclaims Bond's past deed of restoring the death penalty, while the sixth theme also acclaims past deeds, expanding prisons. Both actions are likely to be perceived as desirable by voters.

The next sentence attacks Nixon's personal qualities (he is dishonest). The last sentence reiterates the denial (defence) of Nixon's accusations ("nobody's buying" Nixon's attack). Thus, this spot contains six themes: two attacks on Nixon (both on personal qualities), two defenses denying Nixon's attack (simple denial), and two acclaims of Bond (both on past deeds).

Two coders analysed the advertisements and intercoder reliability was calculated on 20% of the sample (including all four ad types). Cohen's kappa was calculated to control for possible agreement due to chance. Kappa for identifying function (acclaim, attack, defend) was.96.

Kappa for classifying utterances as policy or character was.68. For classifying policy themes (past deeds, future plans, general goals) kappa was.77 and for classifying character themes (personal qualities, leadership ability, ideals) it was.71. Fleiss explains that"values [of kappa] greater than.75 or so may be taken to represent excellent agreement beyond chance... and values between.40 and.75 may be taken to represent fair to good agreement beyond chance". Thus, reliability ranges from good to excellent for this analysis.

## SAMPLE

This study used a purposive sample of sixteen candidates who campaigned in Missouri in 1998: US Senator, US Representative, State Senator, State Representative (two districts), State Auditor, County Clerk, and County Commissioner. These offices were selected to represent a balance of levels of government and races: four federal, eight state, and four local candidates (because the number of candidates running at each level varies, no attempt was made to proportionately represent the number of candidates running at each level). The sample includes 118 advertisements from four different media: 49 television spots, 19 direct mail pieces, 17 newspaper ads, and 29 web pages ("web page" was defined as a document with a unique URL, so some candidates had only a single page on their web site, while others had several).

Painstaking efforts were made to obtain every instance of these message forms from these candidates. For example, every issue of the major state newspapers was closely examined during the two months preceding the election to locate newspaper ads.

Similarly, several search strategies were employed to locate the candidates' WWW pages (e.g., multiple web search engines were used; the state political party web pages were examined for links to candidate pages). Candidates and political party headquarters were contacted to obtain direct mail advertising. The sample obtained seems reasonably complete; however, no objective evidence is available to determine whether the sample is utterly exhaustive. As with other studies of presidential advertising, there is no evidence concerning how frequently each message appeared (e.g., some television spots are broadcast more frequently than others).

## FUNCTIONS

The first research question, concerning the proportion of acclaims, attacks, and defenses in these advertisements, will be answered for each medium: television spots, direct mail, newspaper ads, and Webpages. Then these three functions will be compared across the four media represented in this study. Because the first two hypotheses concern functions of these ads, they will be tested before turning to the other research questions.

### TELEVISION SPOTS

Candidates used more acclaims (67%) than attacks (31%) in these commercials. For example, this spot illustrates an acclaim:"Chuck Graham is fighting to make our schools safer. That's why a stoplight is being installed by Rock Bridge Elementary School." This spot praises one of his accomplishments (a past deed). In contrast, consider this attack from Steelman:

$853 more for each student in St. Louis and Kansas City, only $45 more per student here? That's the school funding plan Mike Lybyer voted for. It gets worse. In the last six years, Lybyer has voted to raise our taxes and fees MORE THAN 10 TIMES. This 20-year political incumbent has voted himself 11 pay raises and twice has voted to raise his own tax paid pensions (emphasis original).

Here, Lybyer's record in office is condemned. Several specific past deeds (voting for an unfair school funding plan, tax increases, pay increases, pension increases) are recounted.

**Table. Functions of Advertisements by Medium**

| Medium | Acclaims | Attacks | Defenses |
|---|---|---|---|
| TV Spots | 207 (67%) | 99 (31%) | 6 (2%) |
| Direct Mail | 322 (92%) | 28 (8%) | 0 |
| Newspaper | 154 (83%) | 31 (17%) | 1 (0.5%) |
| Web Page | 237 (98%) | 5 (2%) | 0 |
| Republicans | 529 (83%) | 107 (16%) | 7 (1%) |
| Democrats | 391 (87%) | 56 (13%) | 0 |
| Incumbents | 510 (91%) | 45 (8%) | 4 (1%) |
| Challengers | 410 (78%) | 118 (22%) | 3 (0.5%) |
| Total | 920 (84%) | 163 (15%) | 7 (1%) |

Defenses were relatively rare in these television advertisements (2%). For example, Steelman used a defence in response to this attack from her opponent, Lybyer:"Steelman opposed smaller classes and returning money to local schools.

Steelman fought the Safe Schools Act and opposed expanding drug free zones." Steelman's defence spot began with video from Lybyer's ad, and then declared"I was surprised to hear what Mike Lybyer says Sarah Steelman was voting for. I'm Sarah Steelman, and I've never served in the state legislature. Mike Lybyer just invented a voting record for me. He knows that as a mother of three boys, I'm for smaller class size, for safe schools, and zero tolerance for drugs and violence." This defensive spot from Steelman explicitly refuted Lybyer's attack, using simple denial. Direct mail. These candidates used far more acclaims (92%) than attacks (8%) in their direct mail advertising.

For instance, a flier for Noren reported that"Wendy Noren drafted one of the most sweeping election reform laws in our state's history and fought successfully for its passage. She later led a reform effort to reduce last minute lawsuits on ballot issues, saving legal expenses to taxpayers."

This passage lists two specific past deeds (election reform, reducing lawsuits), acclaiming her record in office. Vogt charged that her opponent"favors dismantling public schools with private vouchers," attacking her opponent's future plan. Several candidates used no attacks in these messages, relying exclusively on acclaims. No defenses occurred in these ads.

Newspaper ads. Acclaims also predominated in newspaper ads: 83% of their statements were positive. Stamper's ad told voters that"We will need Don Stamper's experience on all these matters during the next four years," acclaiming leadership ability.

Attacks accounted for 17% of the comments in these messages. For example, Spickert told readers that her"opponent, Chuck Graham, is soft on crime" and that he"voted against strengthening the penalties for carrying a weapon or ammunition onto a school bus." These comments clearly function to attack, and do so on the basis of past deeds. Only one defence (0.5%) occurred in these newspaper ads.

Chuck began his career in the state auditor's office more than fifteen years ago, starting as a staff auditor and worked [sic] his way up through the ranks to become an audit supervisor. During this time, he supervised the state audits of the City of St. Louis, audits that uncovered waste, fraud, and numerous mismanagement issues in city government. Pierce's audit work resulted in criminal convictions and the ouster of a city official from office.

He began by touting his experience in office (leadership ability) and his accomplishments in office. Two per cent of the themes in web sites were attacks. For example, Vogt attacked her opponent on past deeds, lamenting the fact that"Hulshof's votes against popular measures like the Family and Medical Leave Act." No defenses were used in these web pages.

Comparisons of media. Overall, these campaign messages were positive: 84% acclaims, 15% attacks, and 1% defenses. However, these candidates' use these media in different ways. Web pages were by far the most positive of these four media, with 98% acclaims. Direct mail (92%) and newspapers (83%) were also mostly positive. Television spots were the most negative with 31% attacks. Defenses only occurred in two media-television spots and newspaper ads--and were not especially common in either (spots: 2%; newspapers: 0.5%).

The first hypothesis was not supported. There was no significant difference in acclaims versus attacks (defenses were excluded because of their relatively small number) for Republicans versus Democrats. Thus, function does not appear to be influenced by the candidates' political party in these advertisements.

The second hypothesis was supported. There was a significant difference in acclaims versus attacks (defenses were excluded because of their relatively small number) for incumbents versus challengers. As predicted incumbents used acclaims (91%) significantly more than did challengers (78%), while challengers tended to attack (22%) much more than incumbents (8%). Not surprisingly, the third hypothesis was also supported. Incumbents were significantly more likely to acclaim (115) than to attack (12) on past deeds, while challengers were more likely to attack (80) than to acclaim (28) on past deeds. *Topic*: This section answers the second research question, on the proportions of policy and character discourse, by comparing these topics across the four media represented in this study. Next, the three forms of policy (past deeds, future plans, general goals) will be broken out to answer RQ3. Finally, the last research question, concerning the three forms of character (personal qualities, leadership ability, ideals) will be discussed.

Television spots. Candidates devoted two-thirds (66%) of their comments to policy topics, and one-third (34%) to character. These candidates devoted 64% of their policy utterances to past deeds, 35% to general goals, and only 0.5% to future plans. For instance, this ad attacked on the basis of past deeds:"Chuck Pierce doesn't tell us that year after year he audited the Highway Department and missed a $14 billion shortfall." Another spot articulated general goals:"I'm Patrick Henry. I'm running for state representative because we need to put families first, revitalize our children's education, and cut government waste." These excerpts illustrate the common policy utterances.

**Table. Policy Versus Character by Advertising Medium Medium Policy Character**

| | | |
|---|---|---|
| TV Spots | 203 (66%) | 103 (34%) |
| Direct Mail | 233 (67%) | 117 (33%) |
| Newspaper | 106 (57%) | 79 (43%) |
| Web Pages | 75 (51%) | 167 (69%) |
| Total | 617 (57%) | 466 (43%) |

Most character utterances concerned personal qualities (58%). Others addressed leadership ability (26%) and ideals (16%). For example, this advertisement praised Bond's leadership ability:"The Kansas City Star says Bond is the superior candidate because of his leadership." This spot began with several personal qualities (it ends with an appeal to leadership ability based on governmental experience):"I'm Linda Vogt.

This is my husband of 39 years and our family at Christmas. I farmed, worked and had babies, and been elected to our County Commission." After discussion the importance of helping seniors with their medical bills, Steelman declared this ideal:"After all, there is nothing more precious than life, no matter what your age."

Thus, these examples illustrate television spots' use of character. Direct mail. Utterances in these direct mail pieces spent twice as much time on policy (67%) as character (33%). Policy utterances stressed past deeds (56%) and general goals (39%). Tim Harlan's flier praised his accomplishments:"His hard work put in place the toughest standards in the country for dealers of methamphetamine." Kenny Hulshof emphasized the future when he articulated these goals:"reforming our complicated and antiquated tax code, limiting the terms of members of Congress and keeping the promise of Social Security to our seniors." These excerpts illustrate the use of policy in direct mail advertising.

Character utterances focused on leadership ability (48%), but also discussed personal qualities and ideals (26% each). For example, Carrington acclaimed his leadership ability:"Proven leadership in local area Army Reserve and National Guard units." This passage acclaims personal qualities:"I think what people like about Claire [McCaskill] is that she's forthright." Patrick Henry embraced ideals in this message:"Patrick Henry will... preserve Missouri's values of family and integrity." So direct mail messages also used the forms of character in their persuasive appeals.

**NEWSPAPER ADS**

Advertisements in newspapers also favored policy (57%) over character (43%). When discussing policy, these candidates addressed past deeds (52%), general goals (39%), and future plans (9%). This ad for Graham reported that"We've been able to cut taxes for senior citizens and working families, while also increasing funding for our public schools and the University of Missouri," clearly acclaiming his past deeds.

Spickert used a newspaper ad to promise this goal:"As our state representative, Donna will work to eliminate unnecessary government spending and bureaucracy that waste government dollars." Fischbach pledged to"reduce voter fraud susceptibility by providing absentee vote results," an example of a policy acclaim based on future plans. These examples show the use of policy in newspaper ads.

Character appeared in newspaper ads as leadership ability (41%), personal qualities (38%), and ideals (22%). One ad argued that"Patrick [Henry] has the talent and ability to make an outstanding State Representative," praising his leadership ability. An ad for Bond proclaimed that"he is the right combination of compassion and conservatism," using both personal qualities (compassion) and ideals (conservatism). So, newspaper ads entice voters with character appeals.

**WWW PAGES**

Web pages were the only message form to privilege character (69%) over policy (31%). These candidates stressed leadership ability (45%) and personal qualities (44%) over ideals (10%). For example, Hulshof acclaimed his leadership abilities on this page:"Congressman Hulshof was appointed to the Committee on Ways and Means where her [sic] serves on the oversight and Social Security Subcommittees. Hulshof recently completed his term as President of the Republican Freshman Class and participated in the first-ever Great Social Security Debate with President Clinton." McCaskill's web page included eighteen photographs, one of which showed"Claire McCaskill with Bob Costas at an important charity event in Kansas City."

This acclaimed one of her personal qualities (charity). Steelman also declared that"private solutions are better than bureaucratic programs," acclaiming an ideal on her web page. Thus, these messages used character to encourage voters to prefer the candidates.

Policy utterances were split about equally between past deeds (52%) and general goals (48%). Nixon's web page told voters that he"created the Environmental Protection Division to enforce Missouri's environmental laws. In 1994, cases won by the division resulted in more than $2 million in civil penalties and more than $1.8 million in other damages." This acclaim used past deeds to praise Nixon.

In contrast, Bond indicated that"I will fight for tax relief for farmers, small businesses and middle class families, including capital gains relief." These are clear examples of acclaims based on goals. So, web pages also discussed policy.

**COMPARISONS OF MEDIA**

As noted above, three of the four media (television spots, newspaper advertisements, and direct mail ads) emphasized policy over character: Only web pages devoted more comments to character.

Given the exponential growth of the web--Buie predicts that by 2000,"more than half of Americans will be connected to the Internet" --and the use of Internet by voters--a Washington Post poll found that"one-third of voters said the Internet was a source of information about the election"--this will become an increasingly important campaign advertising medium in the future.

However, given its relative newness, this advertising medium is not well-understood. Research question 3 concerns the allocation of the three forms of policy utterances. The distribution of policy utterances was generally consistent across media. Past deeds were the most common form of policy remark, ranging from 52% to 64%.

Future plans were uniformly the least common form of policy utterance, ranging from none to 9%. General goals varied from 35% to 48%. Attacks and acclaims are not evenly distributed across these message topics. In general, 83% of policy comments are acclaims, and 17% are attacks.

However, acclaims were more common than this norm (83%) for general goals (98%) and less frequent than the norm for policy on past deeds (72%).

Acclaims were near the norm for future plans: 85%. Attacks on past deeds were more common than the norm (17% of all policy remarks were attacks, but 28% of past deeds were attacks), while attacks on general goals were less frequent than the norm (17% of all policy remarks were attacks, but only 2% were on general goals). Attacks on future plans occurred nearly at the norm for all policy attacks (17% of all policy comments are attacks; 15% of future plans are attacks).

The final research question addressed the allocation of forms of the three forms of character utterances. There is somewhat more disparity in the percentage of remarks deployed in support of each form of character, but there still is a fair amount of consistency.

Ideals are the least common form of character in all four media (10% to 23%). Personal qualities are the most common form in television spots, while leadership is most common in direct mail. These two forms of character are roughly equivalent in the other two message forms.

Overall, acclaims accounted for 88% of character appeals, while attacks were 12%. Utterances on personal qualities (76%) acclaimed less than the norm for character acclaims (88%). Acclaims on both leadership ability (95%) and on ideals (99%) were both higher than the norm of 88% character acclaims. Personal qualifies were used for attacks more frequently than the norm (of 12% character attacks) at 25%. Both leadership ability (5%) and ideals (1%) were used as grounds for attacks far less frequently than the norm (of 12%).

There is important consistency across these message forms. Acclaims are the most common function in all four media, followed by attacks. Defenses are the least common function. Past research on non-presidential TV spots has found positive ads are more common than negative ads. Previous research on presidential (general) television spots found generally consistent results: Presidential ads acclaim (60%) more than they attack (39%) or defend (1%).

Notice also that while defenses are relatively uncommon, they do occur, even thought past research (other than research using the Functional Approach) ignores them. These figures are fairly close to those obtained in this study of non-presidential television spots: acclaims: 67%, attacks: 31%, and defenses: 2%. This distribution of functions--more acclaims than attacks, and more attacks than defenses--also has been found in presidential nomination Acceptance Addresses, nominating convention Keynote Speeches, the 1960 presidential debates, the 1988 presidential debates, the 1992 presidential debates, and the 1996 presidential debates.

An emphasis on acclaims is not surprising because voters have consistently reported that they do not like mudslinging. Candidates consistently acclaim more than they attack. However, voters need to know the costs or drawbacks of each candidate, and these must be learned from attacks. Attacks are an important component of political discourse, but they are usually less common than acclaims. Defenses, in contrast are relatively uncommon in political communication.

One reason is probably that candidates prefer to appear proactive rather than reactive, and defenses are inherently reactive. Furthermore, defending is likely to take a candidate"off-message," forcing him or her to spend limited time discussing issues that likely favour one's opponent.

Notice that these factors--no drawbacks to acclaims, some risk to attacks, several drawbacks to defenses--are true regardless of campaign level, so it makes sense to find consistency across message forms as well as in both presidential and nonpresidential advertising.

With the exception of web pages, the advertising forms analysed in this study stressed policy over character. These findings are consistent with earlier research on TV spots. Earlier studies of newspaper advertising, is mixed on this point. Bowers found that issues (policy) were more common than personal characteristics. However, studies by Humke, Schmitt, and Grupp and Latimer reported that candidate characteristics occurred more often than issues. Discrepant results could reflect a shift in emphasis from character to policy in newspaper ads over time, or it could reflect a difference in method (previous research tends to note when image or issues are"mentioned" in ads rather than analyzing each statement in an ad). Further research is necessary to settle this question.

Research on other message forms also has found a preference for policy over character in Acceptance Addresses, Keynote Speeches, the 1960 presidential debates, the 1988 presidential debates, and the 1996 presidential debates. Thus, this finding is consistent with much, but not all, previous research. Why would these advertisements focus more on policy than character? A Princeton Survey Research Associates poll of 1714 registered voters revealed that in 1998, more citizens reported that issues make the biggest difference to their vote (59%) rather than character/experience. Thus, politicians may again be adapting their discourse to the audience. The fact that more voters consider policy more important than character (than those who rank character above policy) leads campaign messages across medium and across level of campaign to emphasize policy over character.

In these non-presidential ads, past deeds (58%) are more common than general goals (39%), which in turn occur more frequently than future plans (3%). These general proportions were found in presidential television spots as well, and they intuitively make sense. Past deeds, whether good (acclaims) or bad (attacks) appear more concrete and objective than future plans or general goals.

Campaign promises (future plans or general goals) may or may not be fulfilled, so past performance may appear to be better evidence of a candidate's likely performance if elected. Furthermore, general goals are easier to develop than the other (more specific) form of campaign promise, future plans. Future plans are, by definition, more specific than general goals, and may be used ("broken campaign promises") against the politician in future campaigns.

This possibility may encourage candidates to moderate their use of future plans. General goals may also pose less risk of alienating portions of the electorate: A general goal of reducing the deficit is less likely to upset voters than a specific proposal (future plan) to increase taxes or cut a specific form of spending, like Medicare or Social Security.

Once again, these factors apply to presidential and non-presidential campaigns, leading to the consistency in political advertising found in these studies. Turning to policy utterances, attacks occurred more on past deeds than the norm. Past deeds are concrete, so they are an attractive basis for an attack (17% of policy utterances were attacks, but 28% of past deeds are attacks). That is, they may appear more objective or"true" than attacks on other bases. On the other hand, general goals served more often as the basis for acclaims than attacks (83% of policy comments were acclaims, but 98% of general goals were acclaims).

It is much simpler to acclaim, and more difficult for an opponent to attack, a general goal like"balance the budget" than a specific future plan to accomplish this goal like"raise taxes,""close military bases," or"cut Social Security and Medicare." Thus, the forms of policy do not lend themselves equally well to each function. However, the attractiveness of past deeds for attacks applies to campaigns at various levels and messages in different media.

Turning to character utterances, ideals are far easier to acclaim than attack (74 acclaims, 1 attack). This probably occurs for the same reason acclaims are more common on general goals than attacks: It is far easier to acclaim a goal like educational opportunity than to attack it. Similarly, it is probably easier to attack an opponent's personal qualities (24%) than his or her leadership ability (5%). This is the case for presidential and non-presidential candidates alike. These non-presidential advertisements focused most on personal qualities (42%) and leadership ability (42%), and least often on ideals (16%). Presidential spots stressed personal qualities the most (49%), followed by leadership ability (34%), and then ideals (17%). Again, while the percentages are not identical, personal qualities and leadership are the two most common forms of character utterances in both studies, with ideals the least common form of character comment at 16-17%. Although most citizens report that policy or issues determines their vote, they must be able to trust their elected officials to remain true to their principles (to try to enact their campaign promises). Thus, character utterances can play a useful role as well. Thus, there are clear consistencies in use of topics across media. However, there are also notable differences among these media.

While all four message forms stressed acclaiming, web pages were the most positive (98%). Web pages are the newest medium for campaigns and candidates (and their advisors) know the least about them. The web pages examined here tended to resemble a vita or resume, which would account for few (attacking) references to the opponents.

It seems likely that as candidates, and their campaign advisors, become more comfortable with this medium, it may tend to resemble other message forms. All four message forms used attacks, but television spots were clearly most negative at 31% (almost twice as many attacks as the next medium, newspapers). In the 1996 presidential campaign television spots were the most negative medium, using more attacks (46%) than radio addresses, free television remarks, or debates. Thus, these candidates may have been following the lead of national politicians in attacking most via TV spots.

Furthermore, two of these media (direct mail, www) had no defenses. While Benoit, Blaney, and Pier's study of the 1996 presidential campaign found defenses in every form of message they studied, they did find that some message forms used far fewer defenses than others (debates had the most defence at 7%; free television time used only 0.2% defenses).

Furthermore, in Missouri ads the media with the fewest attacks included no defenses, which is consistent with previous research: The incidence of defenses has a direct relationship to the frequency of attacks. Benoit and Wells found that in the 1992 presidential debates, the candidate who defended the most had been attacked the most. The same was true in 1996.

Furthermore, candidates presumably prefer to respond quickly to attacks. Direct mail and webpages in particular provide no guarantee of a prompt defence (e.g., voters must seek out the webpage, unlike television spots, which arrive on voters' television screens without action by the voter). Thus, there are differences in the candidates' use of these media for political advertising.

The first hypothesis predicted that party would influence advertising function. No significant difference between the two major political parties was found in these ads. Previous research on the relationship between party and function is mixed. Republicans were more positive than Democrats in presidential television spots and in Keynote Speeches.

However, Democrats were more positive than Republicans in Acceptance Addresses. Therefore, research suggests that the effect of political party on function is not powerful or consistent. Nor is there any reason in the Functional

Theory to expect a partisan difference in advertising function. In contrast, as expected, advertising from incumbents used more acclaims than ads from challengers, while challengers relied more heavily on attacks than incumbents. This finding is strong and consistent in previous research into presidential campaign messages. Studies of presidential television spots, Acceptance Addresses, Keynote Speeches, and debates all found that incumbents were more positive in their messages than challengers.

Benoit's study of presidential television spots considered just those candidates who ran first as challengers and then ran again (as incumbents) after being elected. In every case these candidates attacked more when they were challengers than when they were incumbents.

Only one study found that incumbents attack more than challengers, and it was limited by party and office. Thus, the tendency of incumbents to acclaim more than challengers, and of challengers to attack more than incumbents, occurs in non-presidential campaigns as well as well as presidential ones.

This result makes perfect sense, because incumbents, by definition, have a record in the office sought (established during their first term). This record is arguably the most relevant evidence for assessing their merit as politicians, and so past deeds is a very attractive source both for acclaims by the incumbent and for attacks by challengers. This is why the third hypothesis was also supported: an incumbent acclaims more than they attack on past deeds, whereas challengers are more prone to attack than acclaim past deeds. Thus, the difference between campaign discourse from incumbents and challengers is a function of the situation, not campaign level.

As noted earlier, web pages were the one medium that addressed character more than policy. This probably occurred because the web is the newest tool available to candidates for reaching voters, candidates aren't quite sure yet what to put on their web pages. As a result, much of what was available on the web read like a resume, stressing personal qualities and experience (leadership ability). Indeed, about 90% of the character-related comments on the web were leadership ability and experience. It seems likely that candidates in the future will devote more space to policy than in current web-pages.

While these non-presidential advertisements did not use functions (acclaims, attacks, defenses) or topics (policy, character) in exactly the same proportions as presidential spots, the similarities are quite striking. It is quite possible that local candidates (and their campaign advisors) consciously emulated national campaign advertising. It seems quite reasonable for local campaigns to look to national campaigns and to incorporate the features that seem to be effective. Second, it is also possible that the inherent nature of the campaign situation--i.e., desire to impress voters with positive traits and to reduce the desirability of opponents; desire to avoid backlash from voters against advertising that is excessively negative; interest in both policy and character topics--have a natural tendency to encourage candidates to use these functions and these forms. Nor are these possible explanations mutually exclusive (i.e., there could be a natural tendency that is reinforced by conscious emulation of national spots). Given the sheer number of candidates for non-presidential offices, and the lower levels of citizen knowledge about such candidates, understanding non-presidential advertising is an important task facing political communication scholars.

Given the fact that multiple media are available to, and employed by, these candidates, we also need to understand the differences between those media. This study analysed political advertising at the state level in four different media: television, direct mail, newspapers, and web pages. It found several similarities in general proportions of function (acclaims [is greater than] attacks [is greater than] defenses), of topic (policy [is less than] character; except for web pages), and of the specific forms of policy and character utterances employed.

There are also differences (spots were most negative; more character on web pages) across these media. It seems likely that web pages in the future will shift topic emphasis more towards policy, and away from character, as this medium becomes better understood. Attacks, understandably, appear to provoke defenses. Acclaims and attacks are not distributed evenly across the various forms of policy and character (more acclaims than attacks on general goals and ideals; more attacks on past deeds). Some media (direct mail, www pages) seem less effective for defenses. These results were contextualized with the findings of previous research on presidential campaign discourse.

Any study has limitations and this one is no exception. First, the advertisements analysed in this study were a convenience sample, selected purposively to include various levels of elective office (federal, state, local). This sample is also limited to political advertising in a single state (Missouri), a single campaign, and to a particular group of candidates and races.

Nevertheless, it is a beginning. Second, this method focuses on functions and topics, but not on other textual features. Analysts could, for example, examine these texts for such factors as the use of evidence or metaphor. Hart focuses on language in his campaign research.

Similarly, Bormann's fantasy theme analysis could provide useful insights into political advertising. Recent research has applied Burke's concept of identification to presidential TV spots (Benoit, in press). Any of these approaches could supplement this analysis of non-presidential campaign advertising. Still, this study adds to our understanding of non-presidential and non-television campaign advertising.

# 15

# Web Advertising: Print vs. Online Media

The recent and rapid growth of web advertising into a multi-billion dollar industry has sparked renewed interest in the age-old question: Does this new medium work better than traditional media in spreading the advertiser's message? While this question is of obvious practical importance to media planners and other advertising professionals, it raises more fundamental theoretical questions about cognitive processes for media scholars: Do people remember advertisements on the internet any differently-or perhaps better-than they do ads in newspapers and television? How much memory do they have for online ads compared to print ads? Are these memory differences, if any, unique to advertising content or are they generalizable to all content?

The present investigation makes an effort to address these questions through a controlled experiment designed to measure memory differences for identical content transmitted via different media. Specifically, the experiment measures recall and recognition of advertising as well as news story content on a newspaper front page and compares it with recall and recognition of the same content presented on a website.

The purpose is to track differences, if any, in incidental memory for print and online ads while controlling for memory differences for other, non-ad content. The independent variable is medium, with two values: print and online. The dependent variable is incidental memory for ad content.

The control variable is memory for news story content. The research question maybe summarized as follows: For media consumers, controlling for story memory, what is the relationship between the type of medium and the level of memory for advertisements?

This chapter will first explicate the concepts of medium and memory in the context of advertising effects. It will then present the methods and results of an experiment designed to answer the above-mentioned research question. Finally, it will discuss the findings with a view to enhancing academic understanding of the psychological effects of online media.

Almost all classical models of communication have conceptualized"medium" as a transmission vehicle, channel, or device through which messages are transmitted from senders to receivers. Implicit in this conceptualization is the idea that the medium of communication is a variable capable of altering the nature of communication between senders and receivers. McLuhan was among the first to problematize"medium" when he proclaimed that the psychosocial effects of media on audiences far outweigh the effects of message content. He theorized that technologies in general and media technologies in particular were transmitting their own messages, which were much more powerful and all-encompassing than the effects of"content" on the masses.

With a broad social-psychological sweep that would forever change generations of humans, new media introduce changes in scale, pace, and pattern into human affairs."The effects of technology do not occur at the level of opinions or concepts, but alter sense ratios or patterns of perception steadily and without any resistance."

The advertising profession, more than any other media enterprise, has long recognized the psychological effects of media technologies by explicitly comparing different media while making campaign decisions regarding media mix. This is especially the case since the arrival of the latest"new media," meaning computers and the Internet. In addition to measuring various media for their relative reach of audiences, the advertising industry keenly pursues audience reactions to different media by trying to assess the"standing of the media vehicle" in the minds of the audience.

The idea of viewing"medium" as a function of the receiver has spawned a number of psychological definitions of media technologies. Instead of considering media purely in terms of industry-based delivery systems (cable, film) or whole technologies (radio, TV) as scholars in the effects tradition do, these definitions adopt a receiver-centered perspective by aligning media stimuli along a number of psychological dimensions to one such dimension is modality, which refers to the mode of presentation-- text, audio, picture, video-that corresponds to human senses used for processing the presented material. Other dimensions include the degree of notationality, repleteness, mental representation, intended symbolicity, informational and computational equivalence, realism or vividness,and interactivity.

Such definitions of medium-based as they are on user-centered criteria-facilitate a variable-based approach to communication research 199 by helping to isolate the precise variables of media technologies-and the values on those variables-that cause the observed changes in receivers' processing as well as responses to media stimuli. For example, research on modality of presentation has shown us how visual stimuli and auditory stimuli are differently processed2 and how an interaction of the two stimuli could lead to behaviour changes.

The variable-based approach has also led some researchers to pinpoint the precise features of media technologies that contribute to changes in cognitive spaces devoted to-and cognitive effort expended for-paying attention to stimuli, information processing, and memory.

Just like these definitions of medium, theories about media effects have historically used receiver-centered criteria to distinguish between various media vehicles. While uses and gratifications theories document user expectations of-and patterns of exposure to--different forms of media, cognitive response theories such as the elaboration likelihood model posit that certain stimuli in certain media are processed"centrally" (i.e., with considerable expenditure of cognitive energy) while stimuli in other media are typically processed"peripherally," with little or no cognitive involvement or effort.

This distinction between central and peripheral processing echoes the distinction made by McLuhan between"hot" and"cold" media wherein the former elicit active engagement by audience members while the latter are responded to passively.

Krugman and Wright have both empirically documented the wide differences in the amount of brain activity while using different media technologies such as television and print.

In sum, converging evidence from theory and research suggests considerable psychological differences in the processing of stimuli transmitted by different media. However, as Stewart and Ward point out, much of the research has focused on differences between traditional mass media such as radio, television, and print, with little or no attention being paid to new media such as computer information services. It is an empirical question whether past research on advertising effects of different media are applicable to new media.

The present investigation is designed in part to answer this question. Since the study reported here attempts to compare the traditional print medium with the new online medium, important questions about differences in the psychological importance of"medium" and"modality" come to the fore.

As the modality of both print and online media is predominantly textual, a good case could be made for the absence of any psychological differences between the two. On the other hand, the difference in the delivery vehicle (paper versus computer) could be argued to have significant psychological effects, as suggested by the growing literature on the socialness of human-computer interaction.

## MEMORY

The concept of"memory" has enjoyed a long, rich tradition as a criterion variable in communication research-not just because advertisers are interested in finding out how effective their campaigns were in"getting through," but because scholars have continually used memory as an operational indicator of a variety of higher-order concepts in information processing such as attention, involvement, arousal, habituation, and learning.

Human memory is a complex phenomenon, with different locations in the brain used for different mental operations.

Among the components of memory are cues affecting the sensory organs. The memory structure is divided into short-term and long-term sub-structures. The former is the locus of consciousness and has limited capacity."

The latter is comprised of semantic long-term memory concerned with structural information and episodic long-term memory for contextually dependent information. Memory is commonly measured in two ways: recall and recognition. Recall is affected by almost all substructures of memory while recognition tasks typically entail a less rigorous involvement of memory structures. Recall and recognition of news stories have been measured by numerous investigators studying differences in the amount of learning from different media, especially print versus television. Surveys of television viewers minutes after they voluntarily watched the evening news have shown that they remember very little.

This has been used as a measure of attention by some researchers who contend that people generally do not give television news their full attention because they are simultaneously engaged in a variety of competing activities like eating and cooking.

Agenda-setting researchers have used recall and recognition of major issues in the news and correlated them with the level of newspaper and television coverage of those issues.' However, such survey-based measures of memory have proved less reliable than recall and recognition measures administered in experimental settings.

DeFleur and colleagues conducted an experiment that made an intermedia comparison between TV, radio, newspaper, and computer. Their subjects recalled about the same amount of news information from newspaper and computer, but differed significantly from television and radio. The researchers accounted for the lack of differences between the newspaper and computer conditions by proposing that both these media represent the same modality. They claimed that both are"print media requiring a quite similar cognitive processing unlike that of the audio-visual or audio-only versions related to TV and radio." A cross-cultural experiment showed that while Spanish audiences learned least from computer presentations (compared to newspapers and other traditional media), American subjects found the computer as effective as the newspaper for learning details of a news story.

Other studies involving online news have concluded that online information is not all processed in a cyber-haze but attended to as deliberately as printed news stories. Extending these findings with news information to the present study, it may be tempting to speculate that recall and recognition of advertising content will not differ between print and online conditions.

However, numerous studies have documented the enormous differences in the nature of processing of news and advertisements. Typically, news occupies the centre-stage of any publication. Ads are often relegated to the corners of the newshole, face greater informational competition, and hence have a lesser chance of gaining reader attention and retention. Therefore, in general, readers' memory for ad content may be conceptualized as"incidental memory" (short-term or episodic long-term memory) Memory for ad-related material may be all the more incidental in online media because of the"I-readsomewhere-that" phenomenon wherein readers are believed to be incapable of remembering the origin of the different pieces of cyber-information because of the multiplicity of sources in online media. Given the paucity of past research on such incidental memory for advertising content, no specific directional hypotheses can be proposed for the current study. Nor can we predict that there will in fact be a difference in ad memory between print and online conditions. The works of McLuhan and other technological determinists detailed in the previous section would lead us to expect differences between print and online media.

However, the findings with news recall and the fact that both print and online share the same mode despite being different media could be strong arguments for finding no differences. Therefore, this study performs a test of two competing schools of thought on the processing of print and online stimuli.

## METHOD

All subjects in a between-subjects experiment were exposed to the front page of a fictitious newspaper featuring two news stories and one advertisement. Half the subjects read the page in print form while the other half read the same content in online form. After subjects read the page, their memory for ad content as well as story content was measured by a battery of recall and recognition questions administered via a paper-and-pencil questionnaire. The independent variable, Medium, was operationalized in terms of the two manipulated conditions while the dependent variable, Ad Memory, was operationalized as a ratio measure computed from the number of correct responses to ad-related memory questions on the questionnaire. The control variable, Story Memory, was operationalized in terms of the number of correct responses provided by subjects to story-related memory questions in the questionnaire.

### SUBJECTS

Forty-eight undergraduate students enrolled in communications classes participated in the experiment. Half the subjects were randomly assigned to the print condition while the other half were assigned to the online condition. Both genders were equally represented in both conditions. All subjects signed an informed consent form prior to their participation in the experiment.

### STIMULUS MATERIAL

In order to increase the generalizability of the experiment's results, the news stories and the ad were taken verbatim from actual newspapers and edited only for length. However, in the case of the advertisement, which offered free installation of car stereos, the name of the store was changed to prevent any influence of subjects' familiarity with the local business.

The ad was exclusively textual, but featured a lot of bold lettering, size and font variations, and a distinct border much like the display ad seen in newspapers and websites. It also included a vertical banner proclaiming"Big SALE." The news stories were carefully chosen to include typical, routine content which would be unlikely to evoke strong positive or negative emotions.

*The first story was titled Malpractice Law:* A Defective Product." It dealt with medical malpractice lawsuits in the state of New York. Since the story originally appeared in the news over three years ago, it reduced the likelihood of respondents' memory being affected by its recency or timeliness.

The other news story was an international story entitled"King Hussein's visit makes statement." This was a report about the visit of Jordan's King Hussein to Jericho since the Palestinians took control of the West Bank as part of the Middle East Peace Accords. The domestic story was considerably longer (thirty-two lines) than the international story (seventeen lines).

At the very top of the page was the masthead featuring the name of the newspaper, the Daily Star, in bold letters and stylized font. This was followed by a line indicating date, volume number, and issue number. Below this line, occupying two-thirds of the width of the page on the top left-hand side was the domestic story with a headline and byline. Below that was the international story with a headline and byline. On the right-hand side of the page, occupying the remaining one-third of the width, was the ad for a car stereo store featuring names of car stereo brands and company names, as well as larger font sizes compared to the font of the news stories.

## EXPERIMENTAL TREATMENT CONDITIONS

Both the print and online versions of the stimulus were made to look similar in order to optimize treatment equivalence. The two news stories and the advertisement read by subjects in the two conditions were identical in content as well as layout. Moreover, the size of the print version of the newspaper was that of a 11" x 14" tabloid. This was done in order to maintain consistency with the online version, which was displayed to subjects on 11" x 14" computer monitors.

The only discrepancy between the conditions was in font size: While the font size of the news stories for the print condition was twelve point, it was only ten point for the online condition. This was necessary not only to accommodate all the content on a single computer screen without having the subjects scroll down, but also to enhance the resemblance between the overall appearance of online and print versions.

In addition to the print-online manipulation, there was another manipulation unrelated to the present study: One-half of the subjects in both print and online conditions was exposed to a black-and-white version of the ad while the other half was exposed to a colorized version of the same ad.

## DEPENDENT MEASURES

The dependent variable of ad memory was operationalized in the form of five different questions in the paper-andpencil questionnaire. All five questions tested subjects' memory for various aspects of the ad's content. Two of the five questions were recall measures (e.g.,"What do you know about the advertiser's sale/installation procedure based on the advertisement?) with an open-ended response option.

The other three questions were recognition measures (e.g.,"The advertisement made which one of the following claims?) with multiple-choice, closedended response options (e.g., a. lowered prices; b. free after-sale service; c. free gift with purchase; d. free car batteries with purchase; e. free car upholstery with purchase).

Control Measures. In order to test whether memory differences between print and online content were unique to ads or generalized even to news stories, measures were included in the questionnaire to assess subjects' memory for story content. In all, 14 questions were used to test for story memory-four recognition questions and three recall questions relating to each of the two stories.

In addition, two questions about subjects' media habits (one each about their use of newspapers and online media) were included as potential control measures. For each of the two media, subjects' frequency of prior use was measured on a five-point scale anchored between 0 ("never") and 4 ("daily".

## PROCEDURE

The experiment was administered to groups of subjects in a classroom with computers. However, all subjects in a given group administration belonged to the same condition (i.e., print or online). Subjects were informed that they were participating in a study that compared different formats of a newspaper.

After the informed consent forms were signed, copies of the print version of the newspaper were distributed to the subjects in the print condition. In the online condition, experimenters directed subjects to view the Daily Star website on the computer monitors in the classroom? Subjects in both conditions were encouraged to read the newspaper as they would read any other newspaper.

No time constraints were placed on subjects. Once all subjects had finished reading the Daily Star front page, they were handed a paper-and-pencil questionnaire and asked to answer the questions without referring to the news stories. After all the subjects handed in their questionnaires, they were debriefed, thanked for their participation, and dismissed.

## DATA ANALYSIS

Both recall and recognition questions pertaining to ad content as well as story content were given numerical values for correct and incorrect answers. Correct responses were coded as 1 and incorrect answers as 0. Since all questions pertained to factual aspects of ad and story content, the recall and recognition items could be coded without any ambiguity. Questions that were left blank or answered as"don't remember" were coded as incorrect.

Additive indices were constructed to arrive at composite measures of ad memory and story memory before entering them as dependent variables in analyses of variance to detect memory differences between print and online subjects.

In order to increase the precision of the experiment by statistically controlling for extraneous variability and removing biases due to possible non-randomness in assignment of subjects to conditions, a series of analyses of covariance (ANCOVA) was run with each of the three control measures (story memory, newspaper frequency, online frequency) as the covariate.

## RESULTS

All 14 items measuring subjects' memory for content of the two stories were subjected to a factor analysis in order to determine if the recall items would load under a factor distinct from the recognition items. No such pattern emerged. Additionally, the factor analysis revealed that subjects' memory for the domestic news story was not systematically different from their memory for the international story. Therefore, it was decided to construct an additive index of all 14 items pertaining to the two stories and use that index as an overall measure of story memory. Similarly, an additive index of all 5 items pertaining to ad content was created as an overall measure of ad memory.

When the story memory index (Cronbach's ax =.72) was entered as a dependent variable in a two-tailed t-test between the two medium conditions (print vs. online), no significant difference in means was discovered between print subjects ($M = 6.33$) and online subjects ($M = 6.04$), $t(46) = .32$, $p = .74$. Subjects in both conditions averaged about 6 correct responses out of 14 questions.

However, when the ad memory index (Cronbach's ai =.68) was subjected to the same test, there was a significant difference in the means of print ($M = 3.91$) and online ($M = 2.87$) subjects, $t(46) = 2.54$, $p < .05$. Given a total of 5 memory questions about the ad content, subjects in the print condition provided nearly 4 correct responses on average while subjects in the online condition provided less than 3 correct responses.

An analysis of covariance with the ad memory index as the dependent variable and the story memory index as the covariate echoed this significant finding. Similarly, the analysis of covariance with newspaper frequency as the covariate showed a significant effect of medium on memory, F (1, 45) = 6.49, p <.05, as did the analysis with online frequency as the covariate, F (1, 45) = 6.48, p <.05. None of the three covariates varied significantly as a function of medium.

The next set of analyses pertained to the two different types of ad memory: recall and recognition. The two open-ended dependent measures were additively combined to form the ad recall index and entered as a dependent variable in an analysis of covariance with medium as the independent variable and story recall index (a composite of the 6 recall items in the 14-question battery aimed at capturing story memory) as the covariate, the difference between print (M = 1.25) and online subjects (M = 0.87) in their amount of recall of ad material was in the same direction as with the overall ad memory index.

However, this difference was not statistically significant. When the 3-item ad recognition index (Cronbach's ax =.55) was used as a dependent variable in a similar analysis (with story recognition serving as the covariate), the difference in scores between print subjects (M = 2.66) and online subjects (M = 2) was statistically significant.

When gender and colour were entered as independent variables, both separately and together with the medium manipulation, they failed to show significant results on any of the dependent variables. Therefore, these two variables will not be discussed henceforth in this chapter.

In summary, results from the analyses suggest that individuals exposed to news stories and ads in the print medium tend to remember (specifically, recognize) significantly more of the ad content than comparable individuals exposed to identical stories and ads in the online medium. There is no significant difference however on memory for story content between the two groups of individuals.

Even when story memory and prior frequency of newspaper and online media are statistically controlled, memory for the print version of the ad is significantly higher than memory for the online version of the same ad.

The absence of a significant difference in story memory between subjects in the two conditions not only confirms earlier findings with memory for news information, but also eschews the need for a separate control variable of story memory for the present investigation. Given that print and online subjects were about equal on the story memory index, our control variable is automatically controlled for in this study.

Furthermore, the absence of differences in story memory serves to highlight the fact that ad memory differences between the two groups of subjects is not due to any attentional differences between the two conditions. It is clear that subjects in both conditions were about equal in paying attention to the stimulus because they scored about the same in a test of their memory for story content. Therefore, we cannot conclude that print and online media command different levels of attention from readers.

The lack of differences in story memory also rules out another explanation for differences in ad memory between the two media. This explanation is based on the difference in font size between the print and online conditions. As mentioned in the methods section, the news stories in the online version had smaller font size than in the print version. If this size difference was driving the memory difference for ad content, it would first have to affect memory for story content. Since it did not, font size difference can be ruled out as an explanation for the study's result.

The reasons for finding higher ad memory scores among subjects exposed to the print medium are more likely to be related to the specific features of print as a medium when compared to online, than to any artifact of the experimental design.

To begin with, the study's result might be a reflection of a novelty effect. Since online advertising is relatively new (compared to print advertising), users of the online medium may be less prone to notice peripheral attributes like advertising. Therefore, while receivers show no media-based differences in their processing of news content, they seem to exhibit somewhat lower level of processing of ad cues in the online context.

Whether this is due to differential processing of different media or due to differential storage and/or retrieval is unclear. Since the recall measure did not show statistical significance (while the recognition measure did), it may be argued that the difference exists in retrieval, not encoding of information.

However, given the closeness of the recall measure to statistical significance (not to mention the high likelihood of this measure being significant if it had more questionnaire items than just two) and the general empirical tradition of always finding low recall and high recognition for advertising content, it is premature to conclude that online media and print media differ only in recognition memory, not recall memory.

All that can be stated at this stage is that people remember more ad content from print medium than from online medium.

An important theoretical implication of this study is that in order to find cognitive differences between two media, it is not necessary for the media to differ in their modality. Both print and online media, at least in this experiment, shared the same mode: text. Therefore, the psychological distinction between these two media is not rooted in modality, but in some other factor(s) central to the media.

Perhaps the differences are due to the delivery mechanism. It may be speculated that the paper on which the newspaper is printed allows for the readers' eyes to consume the news page in its entirety, including all peripheral aspects like advertising, while the computer screen, with its thick boxed boundaries, limit readers' attention to the centre of the screen.

Another explanation for the study's finding could be related to receivers' expectations as well as estimations of the appropriateness of advertising in the online medium. It may be argued from a uses-and-gratifications perspective that readers are purposive in their use of online medium, such that they associate this new medium as a channel for news and information and consider it inappropriate for advertising.

The image of the Internet as a free information network perhaps engenders a psychological predisposition to consider all of its content as free-floating sharing of information rather than as carefully packaged products of advertising and marketing. This attitude may be reflected in readers' careful consideration of the central content of the online news page (namely, news stories) while, at the same time, ignoring peripheral content like advertising.

This is of consequence to the recently formed Internet Advertising Bureau which has undertaken the task of making the web medium a"measurable" entity in order to standardize space-selling and ad spending? While advertisers have measured traditional media in terms of their reach of audience members (circulation size or viewer ratings), such an approach would be insufficiently informative in the online medium.

Given the relatively poor memorability of online ads noticed in this study, reader access data of web pages is not a good indicator of the reach of advertising on those websites. Perhaps, the bureau could recommend placement of hyperlinks, which may help in tracking the number of users clicking on a given advertisement. This would be a stronger indicator of the reach of the ad in the new online medium. An important practical implication of this study is that, in order for web advertising to work, advertisers have to do more to attract readers than they would in the print medium. For example, animated ads as opposed to still ads might be needed to attract online users. To the extent advertisers use the new features of the online medium that are nonexistent in print (audio and video downloads, animated images, hyperlinks, site-maps, etc.), they are probably more likely to enhance user attention to advertising.

Future research should investigate the psychological merits of the new features of online media in the advertising context. Experimental studies in the selective exposure paradigm might be conducted to determine not only how many users consciously process ad material by clicking on them but also which technological features attract what kind of audiences. Information-processing experiments may then be conducted to determine the mechanisms by which these new features help or hinder reception as well as reaction of audience members to online advertising.

# 16

# Cable Advertising and the Future

As the highly touted" high culture" cable network, CBS Cable, prepared to launch in 1981, it offered 30-second advertising spots for $6000 each. Even given a projected audience rating of 2.5 - comparable to PBS ratings at the time for similar programming - the CBS Cable price worked out to a cost-per-thousand (CPM) rate of about $48, more than seven times the average broadcast network rate for that year. Even after dropping this price drastically, CBS Cable sold very little advertising, and less than a year later, it ceased operations.

CBS Cable's woes were extreme, and many other cable networks have, of course, survived and prospered. The cable advertising industry, however, has never realized the high expectations that inspired launches like CBS Cable's in the early 1980s. According to the"narrowcasting" model of cable television, cable networks had remarkable advertising opportunities; by segmenting toward higher income or special interest audiences, they could charge much higher CPM rates than the"mass appeal" broadcast networks.

The inspiration for these expectations was magazines. Specialized publications such as Photography and Architectural Digest, for example, charge CPM rates several times greater than do general interest magazines such as Readers Digest or TV Guide. On average, however, CPM rates of basic cable networks have remained much lower - not higher - than network or national spot broadcast rates, in spite of the fact that many basic cable networks evidently do reach more sharply segmented audiences.

In this chapter, we hypothesize that a primary reason for the gap in broadcast and cable advertising rates is that cable networks are able to reach a relatively small proportion of their total target audience nationally. Even the most widely distributed basic networks, such as Discovery and ESPN, could reach no more than the"multi-channel" TV household universe (including cable, DBS, MMDS, and other competitors to cable) of about 78% of all TV households by June, 1998.

Most of the 100 plus basic networks now in business reach far fewer homes. We operationalize our general hypothesis by testing the extent to which the CPM rates of various basic cable networks can be explained by their TV household penetration, or by similar audience reach variables.

Understanding the reasons for basic cable's paradoxical failure to command healthy advertising rates has important implications for the eventual ability of cable networks to successfully narrowcast to sharply segmented audiences - or more generally, to compete successfully with broadcast networks and local stations. On average, advertising has accounted for about 65% of each dollar of revenue received by basic cable networks since 1990, the remainder coming from per-subscriber fees paid by cable operators.

As the penetration of multi-channel media--including cable, but especially faster growing alternatives such as DBS--increases, cable TV networks will achieve higher penetration. Similarly, the diffusion of digital compression technologies should improve penetration by relieving the channel capacity constraints of cable systems. Cable networks thus may become more viable advertising vehicles in the future. The chapter continues in the next section with a brief discussion of literature relevant to the economics of advertiser-supported cable networks. We then describe our method and data, followed by results. We conclude and discuss implications of our analysis for the future of narrowcasting on basic cable and for FCC policy with respect to size limits on MSOs.

## THE ECONOMICS OF BROADCAST AND CABLE ADVERTISING

Research on television advertising has suggested many factors affecting the rates which broadcast television networks and stations charge advertisers. Webster and Lichty provide a summary of numerous factors found to affect broadcast advertising revenues, including audience size, demographic composition, geographic location, and daypart. Fisher, McGowan, and Evans empirically estimated audience revenues using a sample of broadcast programs, and found that daypart and median household income in the local market area affected revenues (and implicitly, CPMs).

They also found an elasticity greater than one for the effect of average station audience share within the market area on total advertising revenues within that market - thus implying that greater ratings within a given market area have a positive effect on CPM rates.

A later study by Fournier and Martin explicitly estimated advertising prices and found that the demographic characteristics of particular programs affected those prices. Other empirical studies treating broadcast advertising revenues or prices include Levin, Poltrack, and Wirth and Bloch.

Textbook authors such as Eastman and Klein and Batra and Glazer discuss cable advertising, the widely assumed motivations of advertisers to reach large, demographically desirable audiences, and cable's shortcomings in fulfilling its promises. In commenting on special interest services and cable advertising, Poltrack noted that the combination of the low absolute audience levels of these cable services and their limited penetration made it difficult for them to get the premium charges they want from advertisers. We were unable, however, to find other empirical analysis relevant to an understanding of cable advertising rates.

Certainly, a similar menu of basic factors is likely to affect both cable and broadcast advertising rates. A key difference between broadcasting and cable networking, however, is the importance of household reach. The technology of television broadcasting puts at least VHF stations on basically the same footing in terms of reach, thus making reach a relatively minor issue; within a given geographic area, that is, the overwhelming majority of all homes are able to receive the same local stations.

On a national level, the four major broadcast networks have affiliation agreements that permit them to reach over 95% of total U.S. households with most programs (though shortfalls are more common with Fox Network programs). In the cable industry, however, household reach is a critical concern. Though all U.S. TV households have access to a multichannel service of some kind, we noted above the approximately 78% upward bound in 1998 on household reach of non-terrestrial broadcast television programming. In turn, nearly all cable networks reach fewer than 100% of these multichannel homes, because cable and other multi-channel operators choose to carry only a subset of the available networks.

Descriptive data and other sources suggest the importance of household reach to cable networks in order to attract advertising. One trade press report maintains that no basic network can interest national advertisers at all with under 20-25% total US TV household penetration.

A number of claims have been made that cable networks cannot effectively compete for major advertising dollars without virtually complete coverage of the cable universe. Descriptive data lend credence to such claims. In 1995, 84% of total basic cable network advertising revenues were earned by networks which reached 90% or more of cable homes.

Based on the existing literature about broadcast advertising and these observations, we proceed to set out our empirical models.

## METHOD

### Basic Structural Model

The underlying structural economic model from which our statistical models are derived consists of basic demand and supply functions for cable television advertising. The demand for advertising time on a given cable network, expressed in per-household-delivered terms, is hypothesized to depend on its price (or CPM), the TV household reach of the network, the network's rating within that household universe, the audience's demographic characteristics, and the prices of available substitute vehicles, notably broadcast television.

In turn, the supply of cable advertising that will be offered by a given network depends on the CPM that can be charged and on its cost per delivered household or rating point. That cost basically consists of the expense to operate the network and the production cost investment necessary to attract the network's audience.

Setting demand equal to supply in equilibrium, the result is a general reduced form, single equation model for a given cable network's CPM which depends on the following: that network's household reach, its household rating, the demographic characteristics of its audience, the network's costs per rating point, and the characteristics and prices of available substitute advertising vehicles. Quarterly CPMs for the 18 cable networks are reported in Paul Kagan Associates' Cable TV Advertising, based on surveys of basic network advertising executives. The annual CPMs used in this study are averages of the four quarters of each year.

Included are all networks for which CPM reports were available for any of the seven years for which we had data. These networks tended to be the more popular and widely penetrated of the basic cable networks, although some of the larger networks, such as ESPN and MTV, did not report data in usable form or did not cooperate with the survey. The Kagan sample also increased in size over the period. The result is an unbalanced cross-section/ time series data set of 106 observations, in which somewhat more observations were available for later than for earlier years.

Consistent with prior studies of broadcast advertising, we might expect RATING to have a positive influence on CPM. We do not have firm a priori expectations for this sign, however. To a point, a higher rating should indicate that a higher percentage of an advertiser's target audience is being reached.

Relatively low cable network ratings, however, may also reflect programming that is more finely targeted, or"narrowcast," toward special interest audiences. Such special interest audiences should command higher advertising prices, independently of quantifiable demographic characteristics also in the model. The data for PENETRATION and RATING are collected from various issues of Cable TV Programming, derived from Nielsen data. To represent demographic characteristics of the various cable network audiences, we include the following measures for gender, age, and income:

WOMEN = the average percentage of women in the network's audience divided by the average percentage of women in the general TV audience;

AGE1849 = the average percentage of viewers aged 18-49 in the network's audience divided by the average percentage of 18-49 viewers in the general TV audience. Specifically, we want to measure not only the extent to which a given network reaches certain more desirable demographic groups, but the extent to which each cable network successfully narrowcasts to any particular demographic category. For example, although men are relatively less desirable to advertisers than are women in general, a network which delivers men relatively efficiently should increase its CPM rate, other things equal. We do not include a squared term for income since we expect the effect of higher income to be positive and monotonic.

The basic cable network demographic data, all for prime time and for the second quarter of each year, were obtained directly from quarterly Nielsen Media Research publications.

Note that we do not include a variable in EQ1 for costs per rating point, as our general reduced form model calls for. This omission reflects our implicit assumption that production investment and other costs follow the same general time trend as those of broadcast television. Those costs should be reflected, then, in the right hand side variable, CPMB. Finally, we hypothesize one basic variation on EQ1. In this variation, we omit the independent variables, PENETRATION and RATINGC, but include a new variable, RATING multiplied by PENETRATION. Except that it is here defined in terms of percentages, this product term is interesting because of its equivalence to total household delivery, a commonly used industry measure of a program's total audience reach. This specification allows us to infer whether household reach conveys the same, more, or less useful information than the penetration and rating terms separately.

Following Fisher, McGowan, and Evans and Fournier and Martin, we specify both of these model variations in log linear and linear form. The log linear specifications permit us to interpret key coefficients in terms of elasticities. Estimation Our cross-section/time series data base of cable network data makes necessary the use of a fixed effects, feasible generalized least squares (FGLS) estimation model. The selection of 18 cable networks is not random and the available observations are skewed toward certain (later) years. A random effects estimation method is thus generally inappropriate.

Also, the use of a random effects model requires that the individual network effects not be correlated with the explanatory variables in the model. The Hausman tests soundly rejects that hypothesis. We thus use a fixed effects estimator. We also tested and rejected the hypothesis that the network effects, u: are equal to each other in the fixed effects model. There are heteroscedasticity problems in the models.

We therefore used FGLS to correct for heteroscedasticity. We do not encounter serious multicollinearity problems in our data. That is, other things equal, a 1% increase in PENETRATION (for example, an increase of 50% to 50.5%) permits the average cable network to increase its CPM by approximately 1.18%. The linear effect of PENETRATION on CPM, is.17. That is, a 1% rise in the network's penetration rate leads to a 17 cent increase in CPM. At least Model II shows that the network's average minute household rating has a significantly negative effect on CPM. This result suggests that the advantage of attracting special interest audiences tends to outweigh the advantages of audience size per se with respect to advertising prices - at least for the more popular cable networks in our sample. The effects of competing media prices, as represented by CPMB, are insignificant, as are nearly all of the demographic variables. A principal reason for the mostly insignificant demographic variables is the nature of the fixed effects estimator. Whereas a pooled estimator uses the variation both between and within cross-section units, the fixed effect estimator uses only the variation within units over time. As might be expected, the values of the demographic variables changed little over time for the individual cable networks in our sample.

Results indicate, as expected, significant and positive effects of total households delivered (penetration x household rating) on cable CPMs. The unexplained variance in these models, however, rises significantly. Other variable specifications, including different specifications for the demographic variables, also yielded qualitatively similar results. In all of these models, measures of the elasticity of CPM with respect to household penetration were also within a narrow range.

Our analysis consistently supports the hypothesis that the TV household reach of advertiser-supported basic cable networks is a critical factor in determining the CPM advertising rate which those networks can command. Our results thus reinforce a conventional wisdom in the cable industry that obtaining a high rate of cable system carriage is the most critical business objective of cable television programming suppliers.

These results have broad implications. First, they suggest that compared to traditional broadcast television media, limitations on the TV household reach of cable networks have - so far - overwhelmed the narrowcasting advantages that cable networks appear to have in targeting more sharply segmented demographic or special interest groups. From the advertiser's perspective, this result is reasonable. Advertisers want to plan nationwide campaigns that blanket their target audience.

The over one-fifty of US TV households which still cannot be reached by even the most widely distributed cable television networks tend to be lower income and probably in rural areas. But those households as a group are very difficult to efficiently reach using any other media. The reach problem is especially acute for less widely distributed cable networks, because the gaps in coverage of those networks are likely to be arbitrarily scattered throughout the nation depending on where cable systems happen to carry them.

To illustrate the apparent narrowcasting advantages of cable networks to advertisers - separated out from the coverage handicap - consider the following calculations. In 1996, the final year of the sample period, our 18 cable network sample reached 60.9% of all the TV households on average, and charged an average prime time CPM rate of $8.62, about 22% less than the averaged 1996 broadcast network CPM rate of $11.00.

Based on the estimated elasticity of cable CPM with respect to household penetration of 1.18 in the log linear model, the average cable CPM would have been \$15.15 - 38% above the broadcast rate - if those cable networks had reached 100% of TV homes, network household ratings and all other factors being equal. The linear model predicts a very similar cable network CPM, \$15.26, at 100% cable network penetration.

Of course, cable networks are unlikely to reach very near to 100% of TV households anytime soon. Also, the projected gap between cable and broadcast rates is exaggerated to the extent that broadcast programs themselves typically fall short of 100% penetration. Such large scale projections should not be taken too literally in any case.

Our results nevertheless imply an optimistic economic future for cable networks if the household penetration of multi-channel video distribution systems continues to rise. Continued penetration of DBS and other multi-channel technologies, as well as digital compression technology, is likely to substantially increase cable network CPMs, and thus the viability of basic cable networks as competitors to broadcasting.

Our negative estimated relationship between cable CPMs and cable network household ratings is contrary to findings for broadcast television reported by earlier studies. Our result suggests that in the case of cable networks, a sharper, more narrowcast focus of cable programming increases the desirability of cable audiences to advertisers.

The significance of these coefficients, however, is fairly marginal. Certainly, however, our results suggest that increased household ratings in and of themselves do not permit higher advertising prices in cable. Cable's household coverage problem, that is, cannot be blamed on household ratings levels.

Finally, our results are relevant to an important policy issue in the cable industry. Numerous claims have been made that larger cable MSOs, such as TCI and Time-Warner, have excessive influence over entry and competition of cable networks. Our analysis lends credibility to these claims.

A basic cable network whose household reach was reduced from a 70 million to a 60 million household multi-channel universe due to an MSO's carriage decision, for example, would not only have 10 million fewer homes to offer advertisers, but would be able to charge substantially less per household (about 17% less according to our log linear estimate) for the 60 million homes that are reached. The leverage of an MSO controlling access to a significant proportion of all U.S. multi-channel subscribers is thus greater than its percentage market share alone suggests. By threatening to withhold access to its cable subscribers, an MSO with a relatively small national market share by usual antitrust standards might extract input price concessions from the network, or otherwise engage in anticompetitive behaviour that reduces programme quality or diversity.

# 17

# Analysis of Prime-Time Advertising

Social cognitive theory (SCT) suggests that under certain conditions, such as the repeated, simple, and rewarded messages that typify television ads, viewers can and do learn from what they see in the media. Although not every learned behaviour is emulated, SCT submits (and empirical research supports) that the manner in which images are presented on television influences how viewers interpret and respond to the modeled acts. One contextual feature in particular that may be considerably influential for audience members exposed to television commercials is the extent to which the models are believed to be similar to self.

The character's race/ethnicity has been found to be an especially salient indicator of this perceived similarity as evidenced in research indicating that Black viewers prefer ads and programming featuring Blacks, and that Latinos favour Spanish-language programs. Additionally, studies reveal that children are more likely to report identifying with and wanting to be like media characters of their own racial/ethnic background. Given that Blacks and Latinos also have been found to be among the heaviest television consumers, examining how often and in what context characters from different racial/ethnic groups are depicted in commercials becomes consequential.

## COMMERCIAL IMAGES

Typically, researchers interested in evaluating images in advertising have focused on three primary areas:

- Frequencies,
- Selective presentation,
- Presentation quality.

### FREQUENCIES

Examining numeric representation is meaningful as presence in the media is seen as an indication of social relevance in larger society. Despite their actual proportions in the population, racial/ethnic minorities have been chronically underrepresented in television commercials. This finding has been supported by longitudinal and cross-sectional studies of television advertising. Two exceptions include Licata and Biswas' and Taylor and Stern's results revealing elevated occurrences of Black portrayals in television ads (finding Blacks in 35% and 31.8% of ads, respectively). Further, Taylor and Stern found Asian Americans to be depicted in 8.4% of commercials, Latinos in 8.5% of ads, and Whites in nearly every advertisement (98%).

## SELECTIVE PRESENTATION

Examining the quality of these portrayals in terms of product association and setting is necessary as these provide implicit cues regarding the cultural worth of the individuals associated with them. Typically, Blacks appeared in integrated ads for food, cars, alcohol, or institutional/service advertisements, with the value of the product inversely related to interaction with Black models.

Comparatively, Whites appeared most often in advertisements for cosmetics and were most frequently found at home. Asians were most often in ads for retailers while Latinos were primarily located in banking/finance ads or ads for food and entertainment.

Presentation quality. Although arguably the most illuminating measure of the value of the characterization, relatively little is known about the qualities associated with these presentations. On average, studies suggest that racial/ ethnic minorities appear most regularly in minor or background roles and group settings; are less likely to be pictured as parents or spouses; and are less likely to give orders.

## RESEARCH QUESTIONS

When the potential impact of exposure to television commercials is considered from the perspective of social cognitive theory, the quality of these ads assumes increasing social significance. As such, based on the assumptions of SCT and existing content analyses, the following research questions were formulated:

- *RQ*1: What is the comparative frequency of portrayals of race in television commercials?
- *RQ*2: Do characters' age and sex vary by race?
- *RQ*3: What occupational and familial roles are associated with which groups?
- *RQ*4: What physical attributes are associated with which groups?
- *RQ*5: What personality characteristics are associated with which groups?

## METHOD

A one-week sample of prime time television programming (8:00 p.m.-11:00 p.m. EST, Mondays-Saturdays and 7:00 p.m.-11:00 p.m. EST, Sundays) across the six broadcast networks (ABC, CBS, NBC, Fox, UPN, and WB) was recorded over a 3-week period in February 2001. Programme time periods were assigned numbers from a random numbers table and these were then blindly drawn to construct a complete week. All national advertisements were coded, yielding 2,880 ads. Consistent with existing research, the use of a simple random sample was deemed appropriate to allow for generalization. While no uniform standard exists regarding sample size, using standard error estimates to calculate confidence intervals around the current measures provided 95% confidence in the generalizability of findings.

## RELIABILITIES

Four undergraduate students, extensively trained on commercials outside the actual sample, served as coders. Scott's pi was used to assess intercoder reliability for nominal level variables. Ordinal/interval data were appraised with Krippendorff's alpha. Reliabilities based on the actual sample are individually reported alongside each variable definition to follow.

### UNITS OF ANALYSES

The present study involved two units of analysis. First, consistent with current research on prime-time advertising, all national commercials were coded including repeated ads. Local commercials, political advertisements, trailers for television shows, movies, and sports events were excluded. Second, the first three speaking human characters in each ad were coded.

A speaking part was defined as a singular, discernible voice emanating from an identifiable character. Pilot testing revealed that the majority of prime-time commercials contained fewer than three identifiable speaking characters. Thus, a maximum of three characters per commercial was coded thereby providing a systematic assessment while avoiding the uncertainties that arise when identifying "primary" or"background" characters.

In addition, because social cognitive theory posits that audience members are more likely to prefer and identify with characters similar to self and are more inclined to attend to notable and distinctive characters, only human speaking characters were included.

## VARIABLES

At the commercial level, product type (Pi =1.0) was coded to identify the best description of the product using a 30-product coding scheme. At the character level, several variables assessing context, roles, behaviors, and attributes were coded. To address the context, setting (Pi =1.0) was coded as the primary location where the character was found (including work, home, other indoors, and outdoors). Characters' relationship to the product (Pi =.92) was also addressed and categories included using, endorsing, both, or neither.

Characters' primary behaviour (Pi =.83) (i.e., work, domestic, recreation, and other) was assessed to determine principal function within the ad. Another measure, job authority, (Pi =.75) was used to estimate characters' primary professional relationship with other characters at work, including order giver, order receiver, both, and neither. Similarly, a social authority(Pi =.86) measure designating giving advice, receiving advice, both and neither was utilized to determine character's social status.

Family status (Pi = 1.0) was recorded in terms of whether or not the character was depicted as a family member. Alluring behaviour (Pi = 1.0), measured as a dichotomy, indicated whether or not the character took part in behaviors such as flirting. To assess the extent to which a character engaged in sexual gazing (Pi = 1.0), the following four options were provided: receiving a sexual gaze, giving a sexual gaze, both, or neither.

Characters also were examined to establish the presence or absence of an accent (Pi =.91), and their affective state (Pi = 1.0) was coded to determine if the characters laughed, cried, and/or shouted in anger.

Several other character attributes were assessed on a 5-point scale. Degree of dress ([alpha] =.88) measured the attire of the character ranging from conservative (1) to suggestive (5). Hierarchy position ([alpha] =.88) addressed the status of the characters from superior (1) to subordinate (5). The extent to which characters were respected ([alpha] =.94) was evaluated from highly (1) to not at all respected (5).

Each character's activity ([alpha] =.72) was rated ranging from active (1) to passive (5). Physical attractiveness ([alpha] =.88) gauged characters' physical beauty by mainstream U.S. standards from attractive (1) to unattractive (5). An affability item ([alpha] =.95) described the disposition of the character from friendly (1) to hostile (5). In addition, body type ([alpha] = 1.0) was measured on Stunkard, Sorensen, and Schulsinger's 9-point pictorial scale ranging from extremely thin (1) to extremely overweight (9). Finally, age (Pi = 1.0) was measured from child (1) to senior (5).

## RESULTS

To examine differences based on the race of the character, chi-squares were performed. The sizeable imbalance in appearances across racial/ethnic groups presented too great a violation of analysis of variance assumptions to employ such analyses with ordinal/interval variables. It was further necessary to collapse the following variables into three levels to avoid violations of the chi-square minimum frequency requirement: degree of dress, hierarchy position, respectability, activity level, physical attractiveness, affability, body type, and age. Across the 2,880 commercials coded in this sample of prime time television, the race of 2,290 of the 2,315 speaking characters was identified. The majority of these characters was White (n = 1907, 83.3%) followed by Black (n = 285, 12.4%), Asian (n = 53, 2.3%), Latino (n = 24, 1.0%), Native American (n = 9, 0.4%), and"other" (n = 12, 0.5%). Males of all races appeared more often than females with the exception of Latinos, among whom the number of males and females was equivalent.

## COMMERCIAL LEVEL CHARACTERISTICS

Black characters were most commonly depicted in commercials for financial services (n = 56, 19.7%) and food (n = 50, 17.6%). Asians appeared most commonly in ads for technology (n = 16, 30.2%). The commercials most frequently featuring Latinos were for soap/deodorant (n = 10, 43.4%). White characters were seen most in commercials for technology (n = 285, 15%) and food (n = 277, 14.6%). Native Americans, rarely shown, were most often depicted in ads for macro-retailers (e.g., Wal-Mart) (n = 2, 22.2%) and automotives (n = 2, 22.2%). Due to the small number of appearances of Native Americans, they were excluded from further analyses.

The setting in which characters were located in commercials was found to vary significantly by race, [X.sup.2] (9, n = 2239) = 36.22, p <.01. While both Black (n = 83, 29.4%) and Latino (n = 10, 43.5%) characters were most often located outdoors, Asians (n = 22, 45.8%) were most often found at work and Whites (n = 574, 30.4%) were most often at home.

### CHARACTER LEVEL ATTRIBUTES

Chi-squares revealed significant differences in characters' relationship to the product based on race. Blacks (n = 103, 36.4%) and Whites (n = 667, 35.4%) were predominately seen using the product. Alternatively, Asians (n = 34, 65.4%) and Latinos (n = 12, 50.0%) most often had no relationship with the product being advertised. The primary behaviour of characters did not differ significantly by race. However, while Black (n = 94, 33.0%), Latino (n = 12, 50.0%), and White characters were most often found engaging in activities other than work, domestic activities, or recreation, Asians were most often seen working (n = 22, 44.0%).

If shown in occupational roles, the job authority of characters differed based on race. Findings indicated that while Blacks (n = 51, 44.7%) and Asians (n = 10, 45.5%) typically did not give or receive orders, Whites were nearly as likely to give orders (n = 226, 32.4%) as they were to neither give nor receive orders (n = 279, 40.0%). An insufficient number of Latinos appearing in occupational roles barred them from inclusion.

Measures of characters' social authority demonstrated no distinctions based on race. Among Black (n = 241, 84.6%), Asian (n = 39, 78.0%), Latino (n = 15, 62.5%), and White (n = 1524, 80.1%) characters, the most common representation was neither giving nor receiving advice. Characters' family status also did not vary by race. The majority of Black (n = 214, 76.2%), Asian (n = 35, 71.4%), Latino (n = 21, 95.5%), and White (n = 1365, 72.0%) characters were not identified as family members.

Statistically significant differences by race did emerge in chi-square tests of sexual gazing. The vast majority of Black (n = 264, 93.0%), Asian (n = 48, 96.0%), and White (n = 1762, 93.0%) characters did not give or receive sexual looks. Latinos, however, were more evenly divided between those who did not give or receive sexual gazes (n = 13, 54.2%) and those who did (approximately 45.9%). A similar pattern surfaced for use of alluring behaviour.

Although Blacks (n = 262, 92.3%), Asians (n = 50, 100.0%), and Whites (n = 1777, 93.8%) rarely engaged in alluring behaviors, Latinos were more closely divided between behaving alluringly (n = 10, 41.7%) and not demonstrating such behaviour (n = 14, 58.3%). Whether or not a character had an accent was significantly associated with race.

Overall, Blacks (n = 271, 95.8%), Asians (n = 43, 87.8%), and Whites (n = 1842, 97.7%) spoke with no discernable accent. In contrast, Latinos (n = 14, 73.7%) were likely to speak with an accent. Although statistically significant, differences in laughter were not found to be associated with the race of the character. Race was not significantly associated with crying or shouting.

The race of the characters was significantly related to their age. Black characters (n = 138, 48.6%) and White characters (n = 1020, 53.5%) were most commonly depicted as older adults, while Asians (n = 22, 41.5%) and Latinos (n = 10, 41.7%) were typically portrayed as young adults. Significant differences for degree of dress also were revealed. Whereas Blacks (n = 167, 58.6%), Asians (n = 35, 70%), and Whites (n = 1219, 64.1%) were shown to be conservatively clad, Latinos tended to be more suggestively clad (n = 12, 50.0%).

Differences in hierarchy position and respectability, did not vary meaningfully based on race. The characters were typically deemed to be average/neutral on both variables. However, the characters' activity level, was significantly related to character race. Although Blacks (n = 114, 40.0%) and Whites (n = 747, 39.3%) were moderately active, Asians (n = 29, 58%) were most often found to be more passive. Latinos, were evenly divided between highly (n = 10, 41.7%) and moderately (n = 10, 41.7%) active. The attractiveness of characters also varied significantly by race. Both Black characters (n = 127, 44.6%) and White characters (n = 904, 47.7%) were average in attractiveness. Asians, however, were nearly evenly divided between very attractive (n = 20, 40.0%) and very unattractive (n = 18, 36.0%). Most often, Latinos (n = 15, 62.5%) were identified as very attractive.

Chi-squares for affability were conducted separately for men and women. Latinos were excluded due to an insufficient sample size. For men, no meaningful differences existed based on the race of the character, as each group was most often depicted as average in affability. Although not significantly different, both Asian women (n = 12, 66.7%) and White women (n = 370, 48.7%) were identified as highly affable while Black women (n = 74, 56.5%) tended to be depicted as average in affability.

Last, significant differences in body type emerged by race for both males, and females. Among males, Black (n = 78, 53.8%) and White (n = 770, 70.4%) characters were typically average in weight, while Asians (n = 17, 58.6%) and Latinos (n = 6, 60.0%) were most commonly extremely thin. An examination of the women revealed that Black (n = 72, 55.8%), Asian (n = 12, 70.6%), and White (n = 464, 61.9%) women were most frequently depicted as extremely thin. Latino women (n = 11, 100.0%) were identified exclusively as extremely thin.

## DISCUSSION

Overall, this analysis of contemporary television advertising indicates both progress and stagnation for racial/ethnic minority representations. While Blacks are generally portrayed in a more diverse, equitable manner, and at a rate commensurate to the population, Asian Americans, Latinos, and Native Americans remain underrepresented and, at times, negatively depicted.

Because television commercials not only promote consumption, but also shape images and"sustain group boundaries that come to be taken for granted", it is important to consider how such representations might influence racial/ethnic minority viewers.

However, linking exposure with consumer outcomes certainly will require micro-and/or macro-level effects studies that incorporate audience and production level variables together with content characteristics.

According to SCT, the process of learning from the media begins with the act of attending to the media event. Similarity and identification with the model facilitate this process. Given this, Blacks and Whites have the greatest number of potential models in current television advertising among all racial/ethnic groups. When compared with U.S. Census (2000) figures, Blacks are represented in commercials proportionately (12.3%) while Whites are over-represented (75.1%).

Black characters are typically found in ads for financial services or food, and are attractive, respected adults commonly located outdoors. This is largely comparable to the depictions of Whites, who tended to be fairly average in their roles and attributes. Based on SCT, then, it would be expected that Black and White viewers might be less likely than others to develop harmful self-perceptions as a result of exposure, especially when considering that characters' mere presence in ads suggests social relevance and group legitimization.

Latino and Asian consumers may acquire substantially different sets of messages. Although Latinos comprise 12.5% of the U.S. population, they make up only 1% of speaking characters in commercials. These models are highly attractive, younger adults with noticeable accents, who are more suggestively clad than their commercial counterparts and more frequently found engaging in alluring behaviors and sexual gazing. In applying SCT, Latinos exposed to these ads may learn to identify physical appearances and sexuality rather than intellect, for example, as the most important components of self. Alternatively, Asians attending to images of self will typically find young, passive adults at work in technology ads. Potentially, this may serve to reinforce perceptions of Asian Americans as dedicated to work only, ultimately tying self-worth to submissiveness and superior achievement. Unfortunately, Native Americans are so infrequently represented in television ads that it is impossible to speculate about the type of social learning that may result from exposure.

## LIMITATIONS AND IMPLICATIONS FOR FUTURE RESEARCH

Given that these results reveal dissimilar patterns in the portrayal of different racial/ethnic groups, empirically testing their consequent implications for viewers will be essential in future research. Until such time, assumptions regarding the impact of media exposure on consumers remain largely theoretical. As Shoemaker and Reese point out, it is by integrating information about media production constraints, audience characteristics, and media content features into effects studies that we are able to more fully explain and predict the outcomes of exposure.

Although this study provides insight into representations of minorities in contemporary television commercials, the picture is far from complete. Future content analyses in this area should consider carefully the constraints presented by coding only the first three speaking characters in each ad. This practice limits confidence that all primary characters have been included and privileges primacy effects over recency effects.

Further, this analysis, like much quantitative research on television content, utilized sampling and analytical techniques that, despite their ability to provide objective and generalizable information, preclude the inclusion of groups with minimal representation (i.e., Native Americans). As a result, continued research aimed at assessing the impact of the absence of representation on perceptions of self should consider, at minimum, the use of longitudinal data to detail and match changes over time.

# 18

# Various Forms of Political Advertising

"You sell your candidates... the way a business sells its products" one-time Republican National Chair Leonard Hall noted. One of the most effective methods to"sell' candidates is televised advertising, which is designed to provide viewers with information about current issues as well as the traits and qualifications of candidates and opponents. There is a link between political advertising and attitudes toward the political process and voting, as ads may increase general awareness despite negative reactions to them. Given that candidates typically spend over 60 per cent of their campaign budget on television advertising, and over 200 million dollars (part of which comes from taxpayers) is spent on TV ads during a campaign, examination of the linguistic construction of various political ads is important.

Televised political advertising can take many forms. Positive ads promote the personal characteristics of the sponsoring candidate in attempt to convince people that the candidate has strong leadership abilities and other favorable qualities. Such ads focus on the good things that the candidate has done or will do, and may not tacitly or explicitly mention the opponent. Negative ads are intended to make the opposing candidate look bad by attacking personal characteristics, political issues, or affiliated party. Negative ads may not even note the name of the sponsor. Finally, some political ads may contain elements of both positive and negative ads in order to promote the sponsor while denigrating the target. These comparative or mixed-format ads are designed to hurt the opponent and to engender positive feelings about the sponsor.

Positive, negative, and mixed (comparative) ads have distinctly different formats: most attention has been given to the content and effects of negative ads. A positive ad includes the candidate, highlighting character or issues, without mentioning the opponent. If candidates discuss issues in these ads, the ad tends to be evaluated more highly. Negative ads take several varied formats, although they often employ a narrator to impugn the ethics or abilities of the opposing candidate.

Johnson-Cartee & Copeland describe 11 distinct presentation methods in negative ads (ranging from"person-in-the-street" interviews to mock news bulletins), all of which have one common element: the sponsoring candidate never appears. Different types of negative ads utilize varied argumentation formats, including direct attack, implied comparison (where the opponent is never mentioned, and the sponsor is only mentioned as a"tag" at the end), and direct comparison (which explicitly contrasts the sponsor and the opponent). Although containing negative components, the direct comparison ad can also be classified as a comparative or mixed ad, as it describes positive aspects about the sponsor while attacking the opponent.

Immediate affective reactions as well as the long-term effects (on voting, attitudes toward politics and advertising, etc.) of negative ads provide insight as to why candidates employ them. Negative ads were once considered a tool used only by politicians who were untrustworthy and immature. These ads now account for over half of ad budgets. Candidates may choose to use negative ads in their campaigns for good reason; for example, some incumbents have been defeated in part because they refused to answer negative ads.

Although many think negative ads are unethical and disapprove of them, some voters are more likely to remember negative ads. Negative ads can be effective for candidates who are behind in a political race, increasing simple name recognition. Negative ads may provide information about political contests, and are perceived as particularly informative by those voters who value advertising as an important source of political information.

Moreover, negative ads may be memorable, possibly because such ads arouse emotion and initiate thought about the political process in general. People process negative information faster and more deeply than positive information, making that information salient as they ponder claims.

There may be unintended effects associated with sponsoring a negative ad, although such effects vary by voter population. The victim syndrome occurs when the target is seen positively because of the negative ad, whereas a double impairment occurs when both the sponsor and target are seen negatively. The backlash (or boomerang) effect occurs when the sponsor (but not the target) is seen more negatively. A backlash effect may be avoided if the negative ad is sponsored by someone other than the candidate, although the effects are exacerbated if the ad attacks the character (rather than issue stance) of a target, or if charges are perceived as undocumented.

The influence of comparative ads has received less attention in the literature, although these, like negative ads, seem to produce a mixed pattern of findings. In many respects, comparative ads may be like negative ads, because they contain attack elements. Hill found that the sponsors of mixed ads were viewed as poorly as they were when they produced negative ads, although Pinkleton reported that sponsors of mixed ads were not perceived badly. Effects on the target have also varied, as in some cases the ad does not lower perceptions of the target while in others it does. Such discrepant findings may be due to generalized negative affect toward political advertising, or may be a function of the amount of negativity in the ads, as those ads with many damaging items are less well-received than those with a better balance of positive and negative elements.

Various forms of advertising produce differential reactions on the part of voters. While affective and cognitive reactions to ads have been documented, little is known about how language is used to construct different types of ads. On an individual level and in everyday conversation, people select and use different types of language, and we form impressions of people's character and abilities based on such language selections.

It is likely that the language used in ads may reflect an advertiser's perception of what will influence voters. The goal of our study was to describe language use in the three different types of political ads placed by both winners and losers from different political parties in an effort to examine how ads are created on a linguistic basis, with a particular focus on the content of mixed ads (as less in known about their content and effects). Therefore, we sought to determine: *RQ.sub*.1: What standard linguistic dimensions are employed in positive, negative, and mixed ads? What elements of language are in common and different among the three ad types?

Language representing the psychological themes of thinking, feeling, and interacting with others is prevalent in political advertising, which often directs viewers to consider certain issues and candidates. The literature leads clearly to predictions that language describing negative emotions will be present in negative political ads and positive emotions will be contained in positive ads. However, a delineation of the specific types of positive and negative emotions conveyed is missing. Attention to social concerns and cognitive mechanisms may vary according to ad focus;

*RQ.sub*.2: What is the specific nature of negative and positive emotional expressions in political advertisements as a function of ad focus? How prevalent is language representing thinking and interacting in the three different types of political ads?

Personal concerns about jobs, money, and the future are at focus in political ads. Therefore, our last question is:

*RQ.sub*.3: How much focus is given to personal concerns (occupation, money, schools, the future) in differing types of political ads?

## METHOD

### SAMPLE

Political ads appearing on four major television networks (ABC, CBS, FOX, and NBC) during prime-time viewing hours (8-11 p.m.) were taped from the middle of September through the eve of the November, 1996 election. All programming was taped from these slots on a rotating basis (e.g., one network on one evening, another on the next). Volunteers taped ads in the South (Charlotte NC for both NC and SC, and in Memphis TN), the Northeast/Mid-

Atlantic (Boston MA and Pittsburgh PA for Pennsylvania), and the upper Midwest. The sample was one of convenience, as regions were included depending on the availability of volunteers. Several important regions (notably the West, including California) were not included. All ads were approximately 30 seconds long. After eliminating duplicates, political debates, and infomercial-style programming, 167 ads were transcribed word-for-word, typed, and checked for spelling accuracy.

## LINGUISTIC CONTENT OF ADS

In order to examine word usage in the text of the ads, the Linguistic Inquiry and Word Count: The Second Version (SLIWC) programme was applied to the transcripts. The SLIWC programme analyses written samples of normal, spoken language or other text and calculates the percentage of certain types of language that appear in text. Individual words are then compared against comprehensive dictionaries; if found, the words are distributed into four general categories.

The dictionaries and corresponding categories are standardized from the programme and have emerged from over 40 studies examining written and spoken language used by a wide variety of people in several different contexts. The category classifications of language are reliable and show validity in predicting a spectrum of behaviour.

The linguistic categories delineated and described by the SLIWC are standard linguistic dimensions (including pronouns, negations, assentions, articles, prepositions, and words unique to the particular communication); psychological processes (such as positive and negative emotions, causation, inhibition, feeling); relativity (including time, space, motion); and personal concerns (i.e., occupation, leisure activity, finances, physical states). Although over 70 different language dimensions within these four categories are generated, only those pertinent to the research questions were chosen for analysis. For example, we would expect that language designed to convey emotions would appear in political ads, and that there would be a focus on personal concerns. Standard linguistic dimensions may inform us as to how different types of ads are constructed moreover; analysis of these dimensions may provide baseline measures for researchers utilizing the SLIWC for political advertisements.

## FOCUS AND GENERAL CONTENT OF ADS

### AD FOCUS

Each ad was classified as either a positive ad, a negative ad, or a mixed ad. A negative ad may concentrate on impugning the character of the opposing candidate (by focusing on greediness, a checkered personal life, or lack of ethics), or may criticize the position on an issue favored by the opponent (by asserting, for example, that the opponent does not (are about the environment). Positive ads focus on the sponsoring candidate's record or on campaign issues, never mention a specific opponent, and usually feature the sponsoring candidate in person.

A mixed ad combines formats to promote the sponsor via the record or character and detract from the opponent according to his or her traits or position/record. To assist in the classification of ad focus, coders noted whether a narrator was employed, and whether the candidate was seen and/or heard in the ad.

## BACKGROUND INFORMATION

The type of office in contention (national, state, local), the candidate's political party (Democrat, Republican, other or unknown), and the candidate's and opponent's sex (if given) were recorded. The candidate's success in securing the office was noted (from the 1998 World Almanac).

Ad coding. Two judges discussed the criteria for classifying an ad as positive, mixed, or negative. Each then separately reviewed the first 30 ads and determined the focus of each, coming to complete (100%) agreement. Thus, the remaining ads were classified by one judge.

# RESULTS

## BACKGROUND OF THE AD SAMPLE

The ads were distributed fairly equally among regions sampled, and were not placed disproportionally by candidates of either of the two major political parties. As well, a fair representation of each type of ad (positive, mixed, negative) was present. However, most of the ads were for candidates for state offices (i.e., Senator, Governor) and few were, as expected, for the National office (President). A larger number of candidates and opponents were men.

Percentages do not always total 100 due to rounding. Before examining language use as a function of ad focus, we first checked to see whether the different types of ads were proportionally represented according to region, political party, and candidate success.

A 3 × 3 (Region × Focus) chi-square revealed no relationship between these two variables, [chi square](4, N = 167) = 8.03, ns, and a 2 × 3 (Party: Democrat/Republican × Focus) chi-square also failed to achieve significance, [chi square](2, N = 167) = 4.40, ns. However, the 2 × 3 (Candidate Success × Focus) analysis was significant, [chi square] (2, N = 167) = 13.28, p [is less than].001. The ads for winners contained a higher percentage of positive than mixed or negative approaches, whereas the ads for candidates who lost were more frequently mixed or negative than positive. Positive ads generally feature the candidate, and a candidate who is familiar to viewers, such as an incumbent, may be received positively. As well as having face recognition, incumbents may be able to construct positive ads, because they have a record to discuss. We could not, however, classify most candidates' incumbency status from the information provided in most of the ads to address this possibility. Finally, background description of the ads included examination of the presence of the candidate's face, voice, and/or a narrator. Narrators were employed in most (130, or 77.8%) of ads, although narrators were more prevalent in negative (95%) and mixed (85%) ads in comparison to positive ads (61%). Not surprisingly, candidates were shown in most (93%) positive ads, although they were shown in a comparable percentage (90%) of mixed ads. However, they rarely appeared on screen in negative ads (12%). The candidate was heard in positive ads (46%) more than in mixed (17%) and negative (2%) ads.

## LINGUISTIC ANALYSES

The SLIWC produces 71 indices tapping four major language dimensions. Not all of these dimensions were examined in this study, either because they were unlikely to appear (e.g., references to grooming) or because they were not of theoretical interest (such as notes regarding television). The following indices (and their corresponding dimensions) were studied: Seven (of 19 possible) areas of personal concern, such as references to occupation, school, jobs, achievement, leisure, home, and money (but not physicality, music, or death); four (of 10) issues of relativity (use of verbs relating to the past, present, future, and time, but not motion or space); 19 (of 25) indices of psychological processes, including general affect and specific types of affect (negative emotion, anxiety), an overall measure of expression of cognitive processes (as well as specific references to mechanisms such as insight, certainty, and causation), a global index referencing sensory/perceptual processes (but not the specific types of senses such as seeing and hearing), and references to social issues including only communication and family. Finally, most (15 of 17) of the standard linguistic dimensions were examined, omitting only article and preposition counts. Each linguistic marker was separately entered in a 3-way (Ad Focus: Positive, Mixed, Negative) ANOVA. Because of unequal n in cells, the unweighted means solution was used, and to reduce the likelihood of Type I error, we lowered to.03 the acceptable p-level for effects to be considered significant. Although test-wise alpha levels can be set at any level, the.03 level was selected, because the likelihood of Type I error owing to the large number of analyses (45) is close to the routinely-accepted rate (i.e., one in 20, or.05), while not overly increasing the probability of a Type II error. Group comparisons were made via Scheffe tests. Given that post-hoc comparisons were made only for significant effects (considerably fewer than the large number of ANOVAs calculated), and the Scheffe procedure is conservative, the alpha level for acceptance for these post-hoc comparisons was set at the conventional (.05) level.

**STANDARD LINGUISTIC DIMENSIONS**

The per cent of words in the ad captured in the SLIWC dictionary varied according to ad focus, as positive ads contained a higher proportion of classifiable words than did mixed and negative ads. Although ads did not differ in total number of words, average words per sentence, unique words, or six-letter (and longer) words, the number of sentences ending with question marks did vary according to focus. Post-hoc tests revealed that negative ads employed questions-probably of a rhetorical sort-more often than did both positive and mixed ads.

Categories are listed in a hierarchy such that indented titles reflect specific types of processes. Except for the first three categories given, numbers indicate percentage of the language in the ad mentioning the processes in question. Same subscripts reflect significant differences between mean percentages within rows, revealed via Scheffe tests.

Use of pronouns in general, particularly in the first person (both singular and plural), differed according to the focus of the ad, all Fs(2, 164) [is greater than] 7.43, all ps [is less than].001. In particular, use of words such as"1","we", and"me" was more prevalent in positive ads compared to mixed and negative ads. However, use of second-person pronouns ("you") was rare in any ads, while references to others (via the third person) varied according to the focus of the ad, F(2, 164) = 3.76, p [is less than].03, as negative ads (which are directed at impugning others) contained a higher percentage of these pronouns compared with positive and mixed ads.

Negations (such as"no") also appeared differentially according to ad focus, F(2, 164) = 4.42, p [is less than].01, and the Scheffe test revealed that mixed ads contained a higher proportion of negations than positive ads. Assents (such as OK, yes), however, were uncommon. Not surprisingly, the ads varied in per cent of time given to use of numbers, F(2, 164) = 8.34, p [is less than].001, as negative ads contained more language concerning figures than did positive ads.

Psychological processes. To address Research Question 2, we compared the language concerning feeling, thinking, and interacting across the different types of ads. The total percentage of ad language concerning all types of affective or emotional processes did not differ according to ad focus, which is not surprising given that different types of emotion would be expected in ads of differing focus.

The analyses for positive and negative emotional expression in ad language were both significant, F(2, 164) = 4.23, both p [is less than].025, and Scheffe tests indicated that words reflecting positive emotion (such as"good") were more common in positive ads than negative, but not in both mixed and negative ads. Although the positive emotion of optimism appeared more often in positive (M = 1.57) than negative (M =.79) ads, this difference was not significant, F(2, 164) = 3.02, ns, and feeling-oriented emotion (i.e.,"joy") did not vary at all according to ad type. Negative emotional expression examined included anger, anxiety, and sadness. The two latter dimensions were very rare and did not differ according to ad focus; however, anger did vary according to focus, F(2, 164) = 3.68, p [is less than].03. Post-hoc tests indicated that mixed and negative ads contained a higher percentage of the language of anger (such as"hate") than did positive ads.

Categories are listed in a hierarchy such that indented titles reflect specific types of processes. Numbers indicate percentage of the language in the ad mentioning the processes in question. Same subscripts reflect significant differences between mean percentages within rows, revealed via Scheffe tests. Language signifying cognitive processes varied according to ad focus, F(2, 164) = 4.69, p [is less than].01, as positive ads included more cognitively-oriented language (such as"know") than either negative or mixed ads.

However, different types of cognitive mechanisms were examined, and differences in these according to ad focus showed no systematic pattern. The language of insight (i.e.,"think"), inhibition (e.g.,"constrain"), certainty ("always"), and tentativeness (such as"maybe") did not differ across ad foci.

However, the analyses for causal language (including"because") and discrepancy (such as"should") were significant, F(2, 164) = 3.55, p [is less than].025. Scheffe tests showed that words indicating causation made up a higher proportion of positive and mixed ads than negative ads, and that positive ads contained a higher percentage of words indicating discrepancy than did mixed ads.

Examination reveals that the amount of language devoted to describing sensory processes differed according to ad focus, as negative ads contained a higher proportion of references to the senses (e.g.,"listen") than did positive or mixed ads.

Mentions of general social processes regarding friendship, people, and interacting also varied according to ad type, and were most common in positive ads. Language describing two particular forms of social interactions (communication and family) differed by ad but demonstrated no specific pattern, both. Post-hoc comparisons showed that references to family were less common in negative ads compared to positive and mixed ads, but that language regarding communication (such as"talk") was given more time in mixed rather than positive ads.

## PERSONAL CONCERNS AND RELATIVITY

The means from the 3-way ANOVAs comparing language use revolving around personal issues and relativity in the three types of ads. Although a fair proportion of the language in political ads not surprisingly concerned occupations in general, and school and work in particular, there were no differences according to ad type. However, words signaling achievement (such as"goal") varied by ad focus, as positive ads more than both mixed and negative ads contained such language.

Issues of leisure in general, and the home in particular, also showed no differential linguistic attention according to ad focus, although (not surprisingly) the analysis of language concerning money was significant. Negative ads focused on money far more often than did positive and mixed ads.

Categories are listed in a hierarchy such that indented titles reflect specific types of processes. Numbers indicate percentage of the language in the ad mentioning the processes in question. Same subscripts reflect significant differences between mean percentages within rows, from Scheffe tests. Issues of relativity included references to time as indicated by the use of past-, present-, and future-tense verbs.

These three verb forms were used differently according to ad focus. Scheffe tests revealed that positive ads devoted more time to discussion of the present and future when compared to negative ads, but that negative ads included a higher proportion of language describing the past than did mixed ads.

Negative ads included more numbers and contained many questions, whereas positive ads had more classifiable (common) language and pronouns. In some cases, mixed ads were like negative ads. For example, both negative and mixed ads contained more negativity and anger, but less of an achievement-oriented appeal, than positive ads. In other cases, mixed ads were like positive ads, as the former contained less language indicative of sensory processes, lesser focus on money, and devoted a higher proportion of language to social processes when compared to negative ads. In contrast to negative ads, positive ads focused more on the present and future, included positive emotion, and contained more language signaling cognitive processes.

The results of the SLIWC analyses revealed marked differences in the language used in various political ads, and provided a description of the linguistic content of these ads. One research question focused on the commonalities and differences in linguistic dimensions among mixed, positive, and negative ads.

Mixed ads were like negative ads and different from positive ads in that these employed less"everyday" language (from the SLIWC dictionary), avoided the first-person singular and plural (using fewer pronouns altogether), and used more negations. Negative ads had many sentences ending with question marks, perhaps reflecting their rhetorical nature. Use of pronouns in positive ads was expected given that candidates often speak for themselves in these ads, while narrators do the bulk of the talking in negative ads.

The close parallel of mixed and negative ads in pronoun usage is not surprising given that candidates rarely spoke for themselves in mixed and negative ads, even though they were shown on the screen quite often in mixed ads. Mixed ads were like positive ads and different from negative ads in that these employed fewer references to others in the third person, which would be expected in accusatory ads. From our data, it is impossible to tell whether pronoun usage corresponded to systematic use of image ads versus issue ads.

The use of first-person pronouns in positive ads could include discussion of both issues as well as image. Given that negative ads focus on impugning a target, but that negative image appeals are highly disliked by viewers, it is possible that third-person pronouns (i.e.,"he") were used in conjunction with issue appeals so as to avoid an explicit and obvious slandering of the traits of the opponent.

On the linguistic level, our sample is consistent with the samples described by Pennebaker and Francis. Words per sentence were comparable with normal spoken discourse, although more unique words were used, indicating a lack of repetition, which is not surprising given the length of an ad and its cost. A larger proportion of words longer than six letters appeared in ads, and more numbers were employed. None of these are unexpected given that the SLIWC dictionary has been generated primarily by examining everyday speech and personal writing, and normal talking and writing may be simpler than political ads.

The SLIWC has seldom been used to examine speech created for the media, and therefore there is no base by which to compare the words-captured counts from this study. Given, however, that a large percentage of words (about 65% overall) were classifiable by the SLIWC, and that this figure is close to the 70% of words normally captured by the programme, it would appear as though the SLIWC is a viable way to examine dialogue from political ads.

Our second research question concerned the amount and nature of language signifying emotional, social, and cognitive processes in the different types of ads. The language of negative emotion was prevalent in negative ads; however, such language was also common in mixed ads. These appeals were neither sadness- nor fear-oriented, but were instead designed to convey anger, perhaps in effort to describe situations that should make voters angry, but not worried. As arousing fear is effective only when a plethora of other variables are controlled, advertisers wisely avoided fear approaches in their negative ads. Positive ads contained more positive emotion overall when compared to negative (but not mixed) ads, although language expressing positive feelings (such as love) was not prevalent in any ads. Instead, positive ads included energy and an upbeat focus on pride, certainty, and winning. Positive ads that stress a visionary appeal may only be effective for incumbents who have a record to fall back on.

Positive ads--more so than negative and mixed ads--included language concerned with cognitive mechanisms, while avoiding language of sensory processes. Positive and mixed ads directed viewers to think, reason, and consider, and occasionally employed logical cause-effect language; in contrast, negative ads appealed to basic sensory processes.

These findings suggest that the content of political ads may be shifting, as long-range study of televised political ads through 1988 revealed that logical appeals were more common in negative ads, whereas emotional and ethical appeals were more prevalent in positive ads. Although positive ads utilized language concerned with higher cognition, the content of these ads revolved around social communication and interaction, particularly that concerning the family.

The results also provide information as to how different types of ads are focused on the personal concerns (i.e., school, work, the future) of the electorate. All ads gave relatively equal weight to many personal concerns, although descriptions of achievement were more common in positive ads. The achievement discussions were not in all likelihood centered around discussion of an incumbent's record, as positive ads tended to focus on the present and future, rather than the past. Negative ads focused on the past, and the language of these ads disproportionately concerned financial issues and money.

In sum, mixed ads did not appear to contain the best aspects of positive ads (e.g., the candidate speaking for him/herself, a focus on the future and present, positive emotion) or negative ads (i.e., money and sensory processes). Moreover, the overall linguistic comparison of the various ad focuses indicated that while positive and negative ads differed along 24 dimensions, mixed ads varied along seven linguistic dimensions from the negative ads and 14 dimensions from the positive ads. Thus, from a linguistic perspective, mixed ads more closely paralleled negative ads.

Although the SLIWC analysis appears to be a helpful tool to understanding the linguistic construction of political ads, future research should include examination of other aspects of ads-the pictures, the music, and the visual images-which may be more powerful in creating responses to ads than language alone.

Our limited sample of negative ads (n = 43) did not afford examination of language use and argumentation as functions of the many different types of negative ads. Finally, attitudes about the text of ads were not assessed. Such attitudes may have long-term consequences, as negative responses to political ads engender disgust and negativity toward the political process, which may in turn decrease reliance on the media as a source of political information.

However, cynicism about the political media is not related to political participation, as the perception that the media may be manipulating voters and considering them naive may actually increase voting behaviour.

A linguistic focus on money, achievement, anger, or relationships may contribute to the affective and cognitive responses of the voting population. Positive ads included a broad vocabulary of ideas and were cognitively sophisticated, but at the same time utilized much pronouns-in essence being more"chatty" about the candidates and the voters, ultimately sounding more like a pep talk. This combination may appeal to a voter population that values interpersonal relationships and that is characterized by a higher educational and economic level. Negative ads had a simplistic and fundamental appeal, and were essentially limited to"dollars and sense," which may address the concerns of less-sophisticated voters.

Both of these types of ads have been shown to be persuasive to certain populations and under specific circumstances. Varying the language of political ads in order to"sell" candidates may be the most effective way to address the disparate concerns of the voting population.

# 19

# Impact of Television Advertising

Advertising to children has always provoked strong feelings and contradictory opinions. Some advocates of child-directed advertising believe that advertising has no or negligible negative effect on children, and that the consequences of advertising are rarely lasting. They argue that children are critical consumers who are capable of defending themselves against the possible harmful effects of advertising. According to other advocates, advertising provides children with valuable product information, so that they learn how to become consumers.

Many opponents of child-directed advertising, however, believe that commercials aimed at young children can have a profound impact on their beliefs, values, and moral norms. Critics fear that children, more than adults, are susceptible to the seductive influences of commercials because they do not have the necessary cognitive skills to protect themselves against the attractive and cleverly put advertising messages. According to these authors, advertising to children can

- Create materialistic attitudes;
- Result in conflicts in the family;
- Encourage bad eating habits.

Finally, opponents argue that advertising can make young children dissatisfied and unhappy because they are less able than adults to resist the temptations in advertisements. Since the mid 1970s, an impressive number of studies on the topic of children and advertising have been conducted. These studies have focused on three types of effects: cognitive, affective, and behavioral effects. Studies examining the cognitive effects of child advertising usually focus on children's ability to distinguish commercials from television programs, and their ability to understand the persuasive nature and selling intent of advertising. Most of these studies have adopted Piaget's theory of cognitive development to guide their research.

Cognitive-effects studies have demonstrated that children who are at Piaget's preoperational stage (2-7 years) react differently to commercials than do children at the concrete operational stage (7-12 years). It has been shown, for example, that children in the concrete operational stage are progressively more able to distinguish commercials from television programs, and show a better understanding of the persuasive intent of commercials.

Studies investigating the affective effects of advertising concentrate on children's liking of and trust in commercials. Affective-effects studies have documented, for instance, that children's responses towards commercials gradually become less favorable as they enter the concrete operational stage. As children get older, they are more likely to display irritation and skepticism while watching commercials.

Finally, studies examining the behavioral effects of advertising focus on the extent to which children are persuaded by advertisements. Since young children usually do not have the means to purchase products, behavioral effects are usually measured by children's preferences for products, or by the requests they make in response to advertised products.

In behavioral-effects studies, children usually watch one or more commercials, after which they are given a choice from a series of products, which include the advertised brand. Researchers then often demonstrate that the advertising of a specific brand makes the child's subsequent choice of that brand more likely. A disadvantage of these studies is that the results that are found within a controlled laboratory setting may not be generalizable to more naturalistic contexts.

A number of behavioral-effects studies have attempted to solve this problem by investigating advertising effects in a field setting. One type of field study has focused on the impact of advertising on children's purchase requests by surveying parents or children. Another, less intrusive, type of research has observed how parents and children in retail environments interact with each other regarding the product requests of children.

A third type of field studies has investigated to which extent children's Christmas gift ideas are determined by television commercials. These studies were conducted in the Christmas season, first because child-targeted advertising reaches a peak in this period, and second because children are generally eager to list their preferred Christmas present choices.

Despite the differences in methodology, both the laboratory and the field studies have yielded a number of consistent findings. First, it has been shown that television viewing is a major source of children's gift ideas, and that children who watch more television are more likely to ask for advertised products.

Second, it has been demonstrated that children's requests for advertised products decrease as they mature. Not only do children become more critical about and, thereby, less susceptible to media offerings in middle childhood, they also become more sensitive to peer influences. Research has found that conformity to the peer group peaks between the ages of 11 and 13 years. There is reason to assume that the norms and values that are created in particular peer groups function as a filter for other socializing forces, including advertising.

Finally, it has been suggested that gender plays a role in children's requests for advertised products. A number of studies have demonstrated that boys are more persistent in their requests for advertised products than girls are. This research finding is consistent with general theories on gender differences in parent-child interactions.

It has been shown that boys are on average less compliant than girls to the requests and demands of their parents. Boys also more often rely on forceful or demanding strategies when trying to persuade their parents to comply with them, whereas girls are more likely to rely on tact and polite suggestions. Gender and developmental level also have been shown to influence the types of gifts requested. Boys tend to ask for activity-oriented items, like computer games, racecars, and action heroes, whereas girls prefer clothing, dolls, and jewelry. In addition, younger children--because of their early cognitive level--often ask for simple, friendly stuffed animals, dolls, and toys, which provide them with feelings of comfort and safety. As children become older, toys begin to lose importance, whereas products with a social function, like clothing and music equipment, take increasingly prominent places as favored objects.

The aim of the present study was to provide an extension of the third type of field studies, which investigated how television commercials influence children's preferred Christmas gifts. This line of research needs extension for several reasons. First, studies of this type were all conducted in the 1970s.

As most western societies have become increasingly child- and consumer-oriented in the past two decades, there is a need to investigate whether the results of these early studies are still valid. Second, in previous studies the sources of children's ideas were measured by asking children directly where they had seen or heard about the presents that they mentioned (e.g., television, catalogs, interpersonal influence). These studies have consistently found that television was the most dominant source of children's gift ideas. However, it is not certain whether the self-report measures that were used in these studies can be considered as valid indicators of young children's information sources of gift ideas.

In the present study we did not rely on children's self-reports to investigate the extent to which television is an information source of their gift ideas. Like the previous studies, we asked children to nominate their preferred Christmas gifts, but rather than asking children directly to list the source of their requests, we compared their requests to the commercials that were broadcast in the period leading up to Christmas.

We specially examined whether and to what extent the brand names children mentioned in their gift requests were identical to the brands that were advertised at the Christmas season. We also explored if and how children's gender and developmental level predict their requests for advertised products.

## RESEARCH QUESTIONS AND HYPOTHESES:

In earlier studies, the percentages of children's requests that were determined by television advertising ranged from 25%, to 49%, and 78%. In the present study, we investigated how these previous statistics compare to elementary school children sampled in 1997. Our first research question therefore was:

*RQ.sub.1*: To what extent are children's Christmas wishes influenced by television commercials shown in the period leading up to Christmas?

As argued above, several earlier studies have demonstrated that:

- Children who watch more commercial television are more likely to ask for advertised products;
- Children's requests for advertised products decrease as children mature;
- Boys are more persistent in their requests for advertised products than girls are.

We therefore investigated the following three hypotheses:

- *H.sub.1*: Children who watch a lot of television commercials ask for advertised products more often than children who are less often exposed to commercials.
- *H.sub.2*: Older children ask for advertised products less often than younger children do.
- *H.sub.3*: Boys make requests for advertised products more often than girls do.

Finally, earlier studies suggested that the types of products children request depend on their gender and developmental level. Since research into the types of wishes of boys and girls in different age groups is too scarce to formulate hypotheses, our second research question asked:

*RQ.sub.2*: What types of products do boys and girls in different age groups request?

## METHOD

### SAMPLE

A total of 250 children between the ages of 7 and 12 participated in the study. The children were recruited from three elementary schools in Utrecht, an urban district in the Netherlands, which consisted primarily of Dutch students with various socioeconomic backgrounds. The sample consisted of 124 boys and 126 girls. The children were grouped into three age ranges: 7-8 (30.6%), 9-10 (40.7%), and 11-12 (28.6%).

This trichotomy was chosen for three reasons. First, it provided us with the opportunity to investigate whether the observed trends in our sample were linear or curvilinear. Second, we wanted to investigate seven- and eight-year olds as a separate age group, because these children are still on the threshold of concrete operations, which qualify them as a separate subgroup. Third, we wanted to investigate 11- and 12-year-olds as a separate subgroup.

As discussed earlier, children in this age group develop an interest in products with a social function and the influence of peers is at its peak in this age group. These developments may affect their interest in advertised products.

**Procedure**

Early in December 1997, children in each classroom were presented with a paper-and-pencil questionnaire. The questionnaire contained questions about children's gender and age, their television viewing behaviour, and their preferred Christmas wishes. Completing the questionnaire took about 20 minutes. To investigate the number and types of commercials children were exposed to in the period leading up to Christmas, we taped the two most popular commercial children's networks, RTL-4 and Kindernet.

We recorded all commercials that were shown on these networks on Saturday mornings from 8.00 to 12.00 a.m. in the period from 8 November 1997 to 20 December 1997. In total, 876 commercials were sampled, 553 on RTL-4 and 323 on Kindernet. Almost 90% of these commercials were about toys, and 80% of them were shown on both channels. RTL-4 and Kindernet have the highest viewing density among 6- to 12-year-olds. Both commercial networks were introduced at the end of the 1980s. We selected their Saturday morning programs because these programs have the highest ratings among elementary school children. The numbers of television commercials shown on RTL-4 ranged from 25 to 113 per four-hour time span, and those on Kindernet ranged from 13 to 78 over the same time period. Overall, RTL-4 showed 71% more commercials than did Kindernet. This difference is due to the fact that RTL-4 has a larger market share (16%) than Kindernet (10%) in the target age group, with the result that advertisers are more interested in this network.

## MEASURES

### CHILDREN'S GIFT IDEAS

We asked the children to write down their two most favourite Christmas wishes. For each present mentioned, we determined whether an advertised brand was mentioned. In some cases this was easy. In other cases we were not sure whether the product was advertised. In these cases, the brand name was traced in the recorded advertisements. Of course, gift ideas like"a doll,""a racecar""money," and"a teddy bear" were not considered as brand names. The intercoder-reliability based on a subsample of 25% of the requests was 99%.

### TELEVISION VIEWING FREQUENCY

The children were presented a list of 12 popular children's programs that were broadcast on RTL-4 and Kindernet. They were asked to indicate whether they always, often, sometimes, or never watched each of the programs. This method of children's television exposure has proved to be the most valid one for elementary school children.

On the 12 items, we conducted a factor analysis with varimax rotation. This factor analysis yielded three factors, which explained 53.8% of the variance. The first factor (4 items, Eigenvalue 2.01) represented the chi ldren's programs that were broadcast on Kindernet, the second factor represented the children's programs broadcast on RTL-4.

The third factor (3 items, Eigenvalue 1.1 8) represented programs that were made for adults and broadcast in the evening hours. Scales were constructed for each of the three factors by totaling the unweighted scores on the items that loaded on each factor. Cronbach's alpha values were.72 for the Kindernet scale.70 for the RTL-4 scale, and.51 for the programs made for adults. Since the latter scale had an inadequate reliability, it was omitted from further analysis.

## RESULTS

Our first research question asked to what extent children's Christmas wishes were influenced by commercials broadcast around Christmas. The analysis of children's Christmas wishes revealed that 51.6% of the children specifically asked for at least one brand that was advertised at the time of the survey.

The brands that were most frequently advertised also turned out to be the most wanted toys. K'nex, Nintendo, Lego, and Action Man were all in the top 10 of most frequently broadcast commercials. Three of these products, Nintendo, K'nex, and Lego, were also in the top five of most requested products in the whole sample. Action Man also occurred in the top 10 of wishes, but only for the youngest boys.

Barbie turned out to be the most advertised toy. The Barbie commercial represented almost 10 per cent of all the commercials that were broadcast during the period of analysis. Barbie occupied the ninth place in the top 10 gift requests for the whole sample. For the youngest girls, this toy was the second most wanted product.

## CHILDREN'S REQUESTS FOR ADVERTISED PRODUCTS BY AGE, GENDER, AND TELEVISION VIEWING FREQUENCY

To investigate our three research hypotheses, which stated that younger children, boys, and children who are more often exposed to commercials ask for more advertised products, we conducted a multiple regression analysis, with the child's age, gender, and television viewing behaviour as independent variables. The dependent variable was the number of gift ideas mentioned by the children that corresponded to one of the commercials broadcast during the period of investigation.

The number of children's toy wishes consistent with the brands in television commercials was predicted by exposure to RTL-4, the network that aired most commercials, and not by exposure to Kindernet.

Consistent with our second hypothesis, younger children asked for products advertised on television more often than older children did. Finally, contrary to our third hypothesis, the child's gender did not predict the number of advertised product requests. To investigate curvilinear patterns and possible interactions between age and gender, which would not be expressed in the regression coefficients, we investigated how many boys and girls in each of the three age groups requested advertised products.

Older children asked for advertised products less often than younger children did. Our cross tabulation revealed that the negative age effect that was found in the regression analysis only held for boys. Seventy-six per cent of the seven- and eight-year-old boys asked for at least one advertised product, whereas only 2 7.5% of the 11- and 12-year-old boys requested at least one advertised product. For girls no significant age effect was found. Older girls asked for as many advertised products as younger girls did.

The cross tabulation yielded an interaction effect between gender and age. Among the seven- and eight-year-olds, boys asked for an advertised product more often than girls did, whereas, among the 11 - and 12-year-olds, girls asked for an advertised product more often than boys did.

## THE TYPES OF PRODUCTS REQUESTED

Our final research question asked whether and how boys and girls differ in the types of Christmas wishes. To answer this question, we investigated the most popular product requests for boys and girls in the three age groups. All children, particularly the youngest, were quite brand conscious in their selection of toys. The most frequently requested Christmas present was Nintendo. Although Nintendo products were popular among all subgroups, boys in all age groups asked for Nintendo products more often than girls did.

Younger children asked for toys and games more often than older children did. For seven- and eight-year-old boys Nintendo, K'nex, and Lego accounted for 72% of all Christmas wishes. The boys in the lower age group mostly requested activity-oriented toys (racetracks and racecars) and construction toys. For the youngest girls, stuffed animals, dolls, and real-life pets were the most frequently mentioned wishes.

Children in the middle age group more often asked for useful items, like school stationery and sports items. For these categories, children generally did not mention a specific brand name, but asked for"a ball" or"a school notebook." Also in this age group boys and girls differed significantly in their toy wishes.

Boys mainly requested sports items, construction toys, computer games, and racecars, whereas girls showed a preference for Spice Girls merchandising, school stationery, stuffed animals, sports items, Fingernail Fun, and Barbie. 11- and 12-year-old children often mentioned products like music equipment and clothing, without mentioning a specific brand name. For the oldest girls, this type of product accounted for 58% of all requests. Popular requests for boys in the highest age group were Nintendo, compact discs, clothing, and a personal computer. For girls of this age, merchandising related to their favourite pop groups, and items related to horses and horse riding were the most favourite gift requests.

The main aim of this study was to investigate to what extent child-directed television advertising influences children's Christmas gift requests. Our findings revealed that in the overall sample more than half of the children (51.6%) asked for at least one brand that had been advertised in the period of investigation. How do our Dutch findings compare to the American results obtained in the 1970s?

In the study by Frideres (1973), 78% of the children reported that they saw their requested toys on television. At first sight this percentage may seem incomparable to the 52% that we found. However, the sample in Frideres' study consisted of children in the ages of five and eight, which is younger than the age group that we investigated. When we compare our youngest age group (seven- and eight-year-olds) with those in Frideres' study, the results are more similar. In our study, 76% of the boys and 57% of the girls in the youngest age groups asked for at least one advertised product.

The relative low percentage (25%) of requests for advertised products found by Caron and Ward can also be explained in terms of differences in age groups between the studies, because their percentages were based on older children than the children in our sample. The 11- and 12-year-olds in our sample also less frequently asked for advertised products than did the younger children.

Finally, Robertson and Rossiter who used the same age groups as we did, found percentages of requests for advertised products (49%) that were virtually equal to ours. In summary, our Dutch percentages are comparable to the American percentages that were found more than 20 years ago. One could argue that our percentages should have been higher because most societies have become more consumer-oriented over the past two decades. An explanation for this unexpected lack of difference could be that media in the Netherlands have only recently been commercialized. Until the end of the 1980s, Dutch children's programming was limited to public television on Wednesday afternoons and Saturdays.

However, since the introduction of commercial television in 1989, children can watch children's programs every day and all day long. While the Dutch public broadcasters have always been reserved with child-targeted advertising, today's children's programs aired by commercial networks are usually loaded with more than 25 child-targeted commercials per hour.

Our first hypothesis predicted that children who watch a lot of television commercials ask for advertised products more frequently than children who view little or no commercials. To investigate this hypothesis we asked children how often they watched a number of programs on the two most popular commercial networks, RTL-4 and Kindernet.

Children who more often watched RTL-4, the network with most commercials, nominated significantly more advertised products as favourite gifts than did children who less frequently watched this channel. No significant differences were found for Kindernet, the network that showed fewer commercials. Our results are in line with prior research. In these studies, it was also shown that children who watch more commercial television have more favorable attitudes toward commercials, and are more inclined to believe the advertising messages, which in turn make them more susceptible to advertising influences.

Our second hypothesis that older children ask for advertised products less often than younger children do also received support. We found that two-thirds of the seven- to eight-year-olds nominated an advertised brand product as their favourite Christmas gift, whereas only one-third of the 11- to 12-year-old children did so.

One explanation for this finding could be that the needs and preferences of younger children were more similar to the types of commercials that were included in our sample of commercials. We recorded all commercials that were shown during two Saturday morning children's programs. We found that 90% of these commercials were toy commercials.

Since younger children are more interested in toys than older children, the commercials that were taped might have been more congruent with the preferences of younger children than with those of older children, resulting in more younger children asking for these advertised brands.

Another explanation for our finding that younger children asked for more advertised brands than did older children could be that the younger children in our study are in a transition period with respect to their cognitive and affective reactions to commercials. As children enter the concrete operational stage (7-8 years), their abilities to understand the selling intent of advertising rapidly increases. They then also become more skeptical towards commercials, and less susceptible to advertising effects. Since the younger children in our sample were only on the threshold of the level of concrete operations, they might have been more vulnerable to the toy advertising campaigns during Christmas than the older children.

Our third hypothesis, that boys would make more requests for advertised products than girls, received support only in the youngest age group. Gender differences were not found among 9- to 10-year olds, whereas for the 11- to 12-year-olds, girls asked for advertised brands more often than boys did. An explanation for the finding that younger boys are more affected by television commercials than younger girls could be that the commercials in the Christmas period were more appealing to younger boys than to younger girls. Our results showed that for the youngest boys, Nintendo, K'nex, and Lego accounted for no less than 72% of all Christmas gift requests in this age group. The youngest girls asked most often for a nameless stuffed animal.

Our finding that 11- and 12-year-old girls tend to ask for more brand name gifts than did boys in this age group could be because they often requested merchandising related to pop groups, which inherently includes a brand name. Boys in this age group were more interested in items like clothes, personal computers, and stereos, items for which no specific brand name was mentioned. Both gender and age played an important role in the types of products children requested. Consistent with Kamptner's findings, younger girls preferred stuffed animals, pets, and dolls, whereas younger boys mainly requested activity-oriented toys and construction toys.

In accordance with earlier findings, children in the middle age group start to attach more value to the usefulness of products.

For instance, they frequently asked for school stationery, electronic organizers, and sports equipment. Although the older children in our sample were only 11 and 12 years old, their product preferences resembled Kamptner's findings among adolescents. Boys and girls in the highest age groups requested products with a strong social function (e.g., clothing), and products that facilitate social ties and the expression of aspects of the self (e.g., music, jewelry).

## STRENGTHS AND LIMITATIONS OF THE STUDY

This field study, conducted in a naturalistic setting, was designed to investigate to which extent television advertising plays a role in the Christmas gift ideas of school-aged children. We asked children to nominate their favourite Christmas wishes.

We then compared their requests to the commercials broadcast on the two most popular Saturday morning children's networks in the Netherlands.

The methodology of combining a two-pronged approach--the content analysis and the subsequent survey--is in certain ways similar to agenda setting methodology. Traditionally, the theory of agenda setting assumes that public judgments of the importance of certain issues are a result of the prominence of those issues in the media. Agenda setting theory claims that the media determine what the audience thinks and talks about.

Although agenda setting theory has traditionally focused on the realm of news and issue salience, this theory might have broader applications to contexts in which a mass medium could influence what an audience perceives as important.

In this study we compared the content of children's commercial media environment with their gift wishes.

We found that the brands that most often appeared on children's wish lists, were exactly the ones that were most frequently advertised. To speak in agenda-setting terms, we found a striking similarity between the agenda of advertisers and that of children.

Although we think that this study has made an important contribution to the literature on behavioral effects of advertising, several limitations do exist. First, our study failed to investigate some alternative sources of children's preferred Christmas wishes. For instance, children could have seen the toy in a store or got the idea from a friend. Second, some toys, such as Barbie, might be popular, irrespective of advertising, because they perfectly connect to the fantasies of young elementary school girls.

Over the years, manufacturers of children's products have developed a diverse spectrum of highly sophisticated research techniques to investigate children's preferences during the product development cycle.

As a result, children have increasingly added their voices to newly developed toys. The extensive research into children's likes and dislikes, together with the wealth of commercial messages meticulously targeted to specific child segments, has made it difficult for researchers to determine whether toy manufacturers set the agenda for children's ideas and wishes, or whether children dominate the dynamics of toy development.

The two basic tasks of marketing communications are message creation and message dissemination. Media planning supports message dissemination. Media planning helps you determine which media to use--be it television programs, newspapers, bus-stop posters, in-store displays, banner ads on the Web, or a flyer on Facebook. It also tells you when and where to use media in order to reach your desired audience.

Simply put, media planning refers to the process of selecting media time and space to disseminate advertising messages in order to accomplish marketing objectives. When advertisers run commercials during the Super Bowl game at more than $2.5 million per thirty-second spot, for example, media planners are involved in the negotiation and placement.

Media planners often see their role from a brand contact perspective. Instead of focusing solely on what medium is used for message dissemination, media planners also pay attention to how to create and manage brand contact.

Brand contact is any planned and unplanned form of exposure to and interaction with a product or service. For example, when you see an ad for Volkswagen on TV, hear a Mazda's "zoom zoom" slogan on the radio, are told by a friend that her iPod is the greatest invention, or sample a a new flavour of Piranha energy drink at the grocery store, you are having a brand contact. Television commercials, radio ads, and product sampling are planned forms of brand contact.

Word of mouth is an unplanned brand contact -- advertisers normally do not plan for word of mouth. From the consumer's perspective, however, unplanned forms of brand contact may be more influential because they are less suspicious compared to advertising. The brand contact perspective shows how the role of media planners has expanded.

First, media planners have moved from focusing only on traditional media to integrating traditional media and new media. New media -- cable and satellite television, satellite radio, business-to-business e-media, consumer Internet, movie screen advertising and videogame advertising -- is playing an increasingly significant role.

Spending on new advertising media is forecast to grow at a compound annual rate of 16.9 per cent from 2005-2009, reaching $68.62 billion by 2009, while traditional media advertising is expected to rise only 4.2 per cent on a compound annual basis during the same period to $192.28 billion. Second, media planners are making more use of product placements now, in lieu of advertising insertions. Advertising insertions, like print ads or television commercials, are made separately from the content and are inserted into it.

The ads are distinct from the articles or TV programs, not a part of them. As a result, the ads seem intrusive. In contrast, product placement (also called brand placement or branded entertainment) blends product information with the content itself.

Whether content is a television programme, movie, video game or other form of entertainment, product placement puts the brand message into the entertainment content. For example, in the movie E.T., the extraterrestrial eats Reese's Pieces candy. The candy was authentically integrated into the movie ?and sales of Reese's Pieces soared 80% after the movie, catapulting the new product to mainstream status. On the other hand, inappropriate or excessive product placements may do more harm than good to the brand. Finally, the role of media planners has expanded as media planners have moved beyond planned messages to take advantage of unplanned messages as well.

Whereas planned messages are what advertisers initiate -- like an ad, press release or sales promotion -- unplanned messages are often initiated by people and organizations other than advertisers themselves.

Word of mouth, both online and offline, is one form of unplanned message. Although advertisers have little direct control over the flow of unplanned messages, they can facilitate such a flow.

For example, advertising agency Crispin Porter + Bogusky (CP+B) created a viral marketing mascot, the Subservient Chicken, for Burger King to illustrate its slogan "Have It Your Way."

Visitors to the www.subservientchicken.com site can ask the chicken to make a move, such as jump, dance or lay an egg. In the first two weeks after the site's launch, the Subservient Chicken story appeared on 63 broadcast segments, including five separate segments in television shows unplanned success. Within months, the site had generated 426 million hits from 15 million unique visitors averaging six minutes per session. Many visitors learned about the site through word of mouth, both online and offline. More recently, specialized agencies have started to hire word of mouth agents to work for advertisers on a fee basis. Initial research suggests that many consumers react positively to this kind of word of mouth communication. For example, Rock Bottom brew pub chain, reported a 76% jump in 2003 revenues after hired gun Bzz-Agent launched a 13-week word of mouth campaign employing 1,073 of its "agents" to get the word out. These new approaches have altered how media planning works in the advertising process. "Seven years ago media was the last five minutes of the presentation. Now it's reversed," said Rishad Tobaccowala of Publicis Groupe Media, whose fast-growing Starcom division helps clients buy and measure interactive, mobile, and gaming ads. Media planners are playing an increasingly important role in today's advertising industry because of the continuing proliferation of new media options and the increased complexity of media and audience research.

How is a media plan developed? Media planning is a four-step process which consists of

- Setting media objectives in light of marketing and advertising objectives,
- Developing a media strategy for implementing media objectives,
- Designing media tactics for realizing media strategy, and
- Proposing procedures for evaluating the effectiveness of the media plan.

Let's take a look at the planning process through an example: P&G's launch of the Gillette Fusion shaving system for men in early 2006. First, P&G's media objectives called for a $200 million media blitz to reach men in the U.S.

Second, P&G's strategy included a mix of national media to introduce the brands. For example, television advertising, such as a $5 million Super Bowl ad campaign, portrayed Fusion as an advanced technology found in a secret government UFO lab. The TV ads also established the brand's signature orange and blue colour scheme. In store aisles, 180,000 display units promoted Fusion, using the brand's colors to catch consumers' attention. "We're trying to put the product wherever men shop," said Pauline Munroe, marketing director for blades and razors in P&G's Gillette business unit. Third, P&G's media tactics -- such as a Father's Day sweepstakes, an episode of NBC's The Apprentice in which the show's teams competed to promote the razor, and sponsorship of competitive surfing -- helped the company reach men of all ages.

"Fusion will get so much attention that it will drive a lot of men to try these grooming products," said Gary Stibel of New England Consulting Group. Finally, P&G used sales and market share targets to assess the effectiveness of the media plan. P&G expects sales of Fusion to reach $1 billion in sales by year three. P&G knows that the brand has already achieved 25% market share in the U.S. Thus, although $200 million seems like a lot to spend on advertising a new product, it represents a sound financial investment toward the tremendous future profit that P&G will gain from the new shaving system. Now, let's take a deeper look into the media planning process. Media planning, such as planning the marketing communications for the launch of the Fusion new shaving system, starts with setting media objectives. Media objectives usually consist of two key components: target audience and communication goals. The target audience component of the media objectives defines who is the intended target of the campaign. For example, P&G's target audience objective for its Fusion shaving system was men 18-40 years old.

The communications goals component of the media objectives defines how many of the audience the campaign intends to reach and how many times it will reach them. In short, media objectives are a series of statements that specify what exactly the media plan intends to accomplish.

The objectives represent the most important goals of brand message dissemination, and they are the concrete steps to accomplish marketing objectives. You'll learn about sources of data to use to identify your target audience. You'll also learn how to quantify communication plans. The first objective of a media plan is to select the target audience: the people whom the media plan attempts to influence through various forms of brand contact.

Because media objectives are subordinate to marketing and advertising objectives, it is essential to understand how the target audience is defined in the marketing and advertising objectives. The definition may or may not be exactly the same, depending on the marketing and advertising objectives and strategies. A common marketing objective is to increase sales by a specific amount. But this marketing objective does not specify a target audience, which is why the media objective is needed.

Consider Kellogg's Corn Flakes and all the different strategies the advertiser could use to increase sales among different target audiences. For example, one target audience might be current customers -- encouraging people who eat one bowl a day to also "munch" the cereal as a snack.

Or, the advertiser might target competitors' customers, encouraging them to switch brands. Or, the advertiser might target young adults who are shifting from high sugar "kids cereals" to more adult breakfast fare. Finally, the advertiser could target a broader lower-income demographic.

The point is that each campaign could increase sales via a different target audience. Marketers analyse the market situation to identify the potential avenues for boosting sales increase and consider how advertising might achieve those aims. If the advertiser chooses to attract competitors' customers -- like what Sprint does to attract users of other wireless services -- the media plan will need to define the target audience to be brand switchers and will then identify reasons to give those potential switchers to switch, such as greater convenience, lower cost, or additional plan features. For example, in 2006 Sprint Nextel ran an ad campaign urging consumers to switch to Sprint because "no one has a more powerful network."

# 20

# Corporate Communication

Most tangibly, corporate communication is a separate function within a company. The function has close ties to, or includes, investor relations, employee communication, government relations, corporate advertising, corporate philanthropy, business policy, CSR, public relations and media relations. One European Chief Communication Officer described the function as "furthering the strategic goals of the company and removing obstacles to those goals." With historical roots in public relations, the most dramatic change in the corporate communication function has been its changing role from responsibility for "in house" external communication to aligning internal and external messages engaging the company's stakeholders.

At the same time, communicating "the company story" has become a key role of the general manager, not just the responsibility of corporate communication and the CEO. What is really implied by communicating to fully engaging a company's stakeholders?

Corporate communication can also be thought of as the continuous communications that take place within a corporation. Are these communications a help or a distraction? When does communication improve productivity? What kinds of interactions—official and informal— are necessary for people to connect with their work, to feel a sense of purpose? Although business schools teach corporate communication under the umbrella of "management communication," communication for managers can be best understood within the context of an individual organization or industry. Graduate students do not need to be told how quickly and dramatically communication in business is changing, or how difficult it is to predict what will happen in the next few years.

Still, a set of trends can be identified. Taken together, this course suggests the following terms describe a "rhetoric" of corporate communication—the factors that make up the ways in which organizations persuade.

### IDENTITY

An individual manager is said to be communicating effectively when they are acting "naturally" or being "themselves". So too, an organization's messages are most effective when they relate to substantive attributes of the organization, its heritage, and demonstrable behaviour. Johnson and Johnson, for example, is regularly a "most admired" company because managerial decisions can be connected to its credo.

IBM changed its identity from "big blue" to a "solutions" company by changing its business model and communicating the change. At one time, corporate identity was simply a firm's visual identity.

But identity has become a strategic starting point, as well as a way to capture symbolic meaning for stakeholders. Some researchers connect conceptions of individual identity and corporate identity. Do organizations have a personality?

## BRAND

Leveraging the corporate brand might be a sustainable strategy for a one company but not for another. The "brand-power" of a company like Virgin is at once obvious and "intangible". Brand is plainly related to identity and corporate history.

Proctor and Gamble in the U.S. or Unilever in the U.K. are examples of "endorsed identity." The firm's product brands connect to consumers more than the corporate brand. For Coke, product and corporate brand have long been seen as co-terminus. Mitsubishi has a "monolithic" identity although it makes televisions and trucks. Some corporations, like Samsung, have taken on adventurous corporate branding strategies describing what the brand does.

Alfred Sloane of GM invented "endorsed identity," but his company's brand has been struggling to reconnect with American consumers. The phrase "a brand is a promise" to its customers is a familiar one.

Corporate brand extends this notion to mean that a company delivers on the values the brand stands for. This could include: financial performance: treatment of employees: commitment to community: environmental sustainability. What are the similarities and differences between corporate and product brands, their measurement? When is a strong corporate brand a competitive advantage?

## REPUTATION

For some executives, the corporate brand is a key building block for reputation, for others, an end in itself. Investment banks, for example, are dependent on their reputations, on the trust of investors. With each cycle of financial scandals since the mid-20$^{th}$ century, trust has eroded. Reputations take a long time to build and, as we have tragically seen, can vanish in a day. Reputation management has become a major factor in corporate communication.

Attempts to accurately measure an organization's reputation have advanced a good deal in the last ten years. Polls like *Fortune's* "Most Admired

Companies" have taken on a life of their own. Paradoxically, trust in big business is at all time lows, while business is increasingly expected to solve social problems from education to saving the planet. This was not the original purpose of the corporation. What is the role of the corporation in civil society today?

**CRISIS**

Crisis communication is the most widely-known aspect of corporate communication. In a crisis the organization must speak with one voice and speak quickly. Hardly a day passes when a corporate crisis does not prominently appear in the national newspapers. Business is arguable the dominant "fact" of our time, and so always newsworthy. Cable news shows and the web have drastically shortened the time managers have to respond to a crisis.

Since the famous Tylenol and Exxon crises, an extensive literature on crisis management has developed. Sensible "rules" about managing crises can be found, but most crises are particular to themselves, if also related to similar precedents. New kinds of crises (and issues management) have emerged with the growth of Non Governmental Organizations and the web. Concern over social issues from foods safety to the cost of health care has grown in intensity. How can crises be prevented, risk minimized?

*For our purposes, a second set of terms significantly influence the first four*:

1. *Technology and Social Media*: It is difficult to imagine that a relatively short time ago Royal Dutch Shell and Intel were taken by surprise by the power of the web. Greenpeace streamed video of protests against the sinking of the Brent Spar oil rig, images that made the front page of the next day's *Financial Times*. Intel thought a flaw in a complex calculation would not matter to consumers. Following the "Pentium bug crisis", Andy Grove coined the term "inflection point." Companies today wrestle with guidelines for employee blogs. Corporate communication managers become members of product-related chat rooms. Converse posted short films by costumers in a twist on BMW's "The Driver" soon after they were acquired by Nike. New kinds of electronic communication result in new kinds of communities of trust (Face Book and so on) and pose new risks. Some companies have been remarkably adroit at incorporating social media as internal ways to build trust and identity. Can social media be managed?
2. *Blurred Boundaries and shifting stakeholders*: A primary, if not the primary, role of corporate communication has become aligning strategic messages to internal and external stakeholders. Yet, it is increasingly clear that stakeholders are no longer made up of stable or discreet groups. An employee may be, for example, a customer

and a member of an environmental group. CSR will increasingly play a role in corporations. As the millennial generation enters the workplace, some companies strive to make the media environment at work mirror the media environment at home. Are we in a "global village" or should companies still seek to conform to local circumstances? Globalization further blurs boundaries. The Ford Firestone crisis was an exercise in frustration when executives tried to explain arcane technical issues as well as cross-cultural factors in a sound-bite world. How can aligning stakeholders create value?

3. *Trust and Authenticity*: The collapse of trust in legendary institutions that we have just witnessed is still unfolding. But executives like Warren Buffett have long acknowledged that reputation is a company's most valuable asset. How could so many firms lose their bearings on this crucial point? To be sure, recent events are highly complex; yet, it is difficult not to think, or wish, that the council of communication executives could have had some affect at turning points where taking on excessive threatened the reputation of the firm. Authenticity, like transparency, has become something of a "buzzword". What roles do transparency and authenticity play for communication in today's wired world?
4. The origins of modern management can be traced to F.W. Taylor's *Scientific Management*. If business remains in many ways a science, it is one deeply entwined with intangible factors as well as popular culture, that most unpredictable of contexts. How can business best interact with this phenomenon?

Corporate communication is the communication issued by a corporate/ organization/ body/ institute to all its public(s). Publics here can be both internal (employees, stakeholders, i.e. - share and stock holders) and external (agencies, channel partners, media, government, industry bodies and institutes, educational institutes and general public).

An organization needs to talk the same message to all of its stakeholders, in order to transmit coherence, credibility and ethic. If one of these points is broken, the whole community can make this organization disappear.

The Corporate Communication area will help this organization to build its message, combining its vision, mission and values and will also support the organization by communicating its message, activities and practices to all of its stakeholders.

According to the book *Essentials of Corporate Communi-cation* by Cees van Riel and Charles Fombrun the term *Corporate Communication* can be defined as the set of activities involved in managing and orchestrating all internal and external communications aimed at creating favorable starting points with stakeholders on which the company depends. Corporate communication consists of the dissemination of information by a variety of specialists and generalists in an organization, with the common goal of enhancing the organization's ability to retain its license to operate. As Jackson (1987) remarks: Note that it is corporate communication — without a final "s". Tired of being called on to fix the company switchboard, recommend an answering machine or meet a computer salesman, I long ago adopted this form as being more accurate and left communications to the telecommunications specialists.

It's a small point but another attempt to bring clarity out of confusion. Corporate communication serves as the liaison between an organization and its publics.Organizations can strategically communicate to their audiences through public relations and advertising. This may involve an employee newsletter or video, crisis management with the news media, special events planning, building product value and communicating with stockholders, clients or donors.

## CORPORATE COMMUNICATION ENCODES AND PROMOTES

- Strong corporate culture
- Coherent corporate identity
- Reasonable corporate philosophy
- Genuine sense of corporate citizenship
- An appropriate and professional relationship with the press, including quick, responsible ways of commun-icating in a crisis
- Understanding of communication tools and techno-logies
- Sophisticated approaches to global communications

How an organization communicates with its employees, its extended audiences, the press and its customers brings its values to life. Corporate communications is all about managing perceptions and ensuring:

- Effective and timely dissemination of information
- Positive corporate image
- Smooth and affirmative relationship with all stakeholders

Be it a corporate body, company, organization, institution, non-governmental organization, governmental body, all of them need to have a respectable image and reputation. In today's day and age of increasing competition, easy access to information and the media explosion, reputation management has gained even more importance. Therefore, corporate communications as a role has become significant and professional in nature.Gone are the days when corporate communication merely meant 'wining and dining the client' - it has now emerged as a science and art of perception management.

### Key Tasks of Corporate Communication

*The responsibilities of corporate communication are therefore:*

- To flesh out the profile of the "company behind the brand" (corporate branding)

- To develop initiatives that minimize discrepancies between the company's desired identity and brand features;
- To indicate who should perform which tasks in the field of communication;
- To formulate and execute effective procedures in order to facilitate decision making about matters concerning communication;
- To mobilize internal and external support behind corporate objectives.
- To co ordinate with international business firms

## Tools of Corporate Communication

Integrated communication can be achieved in various ways.
*The main four practices are*:

1. Application of visual identity systems (sometimes referred to as "house style")
2. Use of integrated marketing communications;
3. Reliance on coordinating teams;
4. Adoption of a centralized planning system.

## The communication Agenda: To Build Reputation

Corporate communication helps an organization to create distictive and appealing images with its stakeholder groups, build a strong corporate brand, and develop reputation capital. To achieve those ends, all forms of communication must be orchestrated into a coherent whole, and success criteria developed that enable measuring the effects of the organization's communication on its reputation and value.

## External Communication

This involves building and maintaining a positive relationship with the media (television, print, web,). This inclu-des, but is not limited to, drafting and dissemination of press releases, organizing press conferences and meeting with media professionals and organizing events for the media as a group.

### *External Events*

Could involve vendor/ supplier/ distributor meets, channel partner meetings, events related to product launches, important initiatives, et cetera.

### *Company/Spokesperson Profiling*

Ensuring that the company/organization spokesperson is in the public limelight, is well-known and considered as an authority in the respective sector/field.

- Managing content of corporate websites and/or other external touch points

- Managing corporate publications - for the external world
- Managing print media

**Brand Management**

- Development and upkeep of the corporate identity to ensure adherence to corporate brand guidelines

To improve overall business communications so as to clearly and effectively communicate the essence of the company.

**Corporate Identity/Organizational Identity**

There are two approaches for Identity, respectively Corporate Identity and Organizational Identity.

- "Corporate identity is the reality and uniqueness of an organization, which is integrally related to its external and internal image and reputation through corporate communication"
- "Organizational Identity comprises those characteri-stics of an organization that its members believe are central, distinctive and enduring. That is, organiza-tional identity consists of those attributes that members feel are fundamental to (central) and uniquely descriptive of (distinctive) the organization and that persist within the organization over time (enduring)".

## CORPORATE REPUTATION

Reputations are overall assessments of organizations by their stakeholders. They are aggregate perceptions by stakeholders of an organizaitons's ability to fulfil their expectations, whether these stakeholders are interested in buying the company's products, working for the company, or investing in the company's shares.

In 2000, the US based Council of PR Firms identified seven programs that were developed by either media organizations or market research firms, and that were being used by companies to assess or benchmark their corporate reputations. Of these only three are conducted regularly and have broad visibility:

- "America's Most Admired Companies" by Fortune Magazine;
- The "Brand Asset Valuator" by Young & Rubicam;
- "RepTrak" by Reputation Institute.

**Crisis communications**

Crisis has four defining characteristics. Seeger, Sellnow and Ulmer explain that a crises are "specific, unexpected, and non-routine events or series of events that [create] high levels of uncertainty and threat or perceived threat to an organization's high priority goals."

*Thus the first three characteristics are that the event is:*

1. Unexpected (i.e., a surprise),

2. Creates uncertainty,
3. Is seen as a threat to important goals.

Venette argues that "crisis is a process of transformation where the old system can no longer be maintained." Therefore the fourth defining quality is the need for change. If change is not needed, the event could more accurately be described as a failure.

Crisis communication can be broadly defined as the exchange of information before, during, or after a crisis event. Crisis communication is sometimes considered a sub-specialty of the public relations profession that is designed to protect and defend an individual, company, or organization facing a public challenge to its reputation. These challenges may come in the form of an investigation from a government agency, a criminal allegation, a media inquiry, a shareholders lawsuit, a violation of environmental regulations, or any of a number of other scenarios involving the legal, ethical, or financial standing of the entity.

Crisis communication professionals preach that an organization's reputation is often its most valuable asset. When that reputation comes under attack, protecting and defending it becomes the highest priority. This is particularly true in today's 24 hour news cycle, fuelled by government investigations, Congressional or parliamentary hearings, lawsuits, and "gotcha journalism".

When events like these happen, the media firestorm can quickly overwhelm the ability of the entity to effectively respond to the demands of the crisis. To emerge with its reputation intact, an organization must anticipate every move and respond immediately and with confidence. Companies facing such a threat will often bring in experienced crisis communications specialists to help prepare and guide them through the process.

Effectively responding to the challenges of a crisis requires more than the typical skills of the public relations professional, requiring instead experience at the highest levels of the field, such as investigative reporting, politics, and the White House. Crisis communication can include crafting thorough and compelling statements, known as "messages," often tested by research and polling.

A rapid response capability—pioneered by the 1992 Clinton-Gore campaign operatives and refined during Bill Clinton's eight years under attack by his political adversaries while in the White House, has also become an essential element of crisis communication.

Additional tactics may include proactive media outreach to get messages and context to the media, identifying and recruiting credible third-party allies who can attest to the company's side of the story, and striking first, not waiting to be hit. Crisis communication is a part of larger process referred to as crisis management though it may well be a major tool of handling a crisis situation in government, organization or business. Crisis Communication is also sometimes considered a sub-speciality of the Business Continuity area of modern business. The aim of crisis communication in this context is to assist organisations to achieve continuity of critical business processes and information flows under crisis, disaster or event driven circumstances. Responding quickly, efficiently, effectively and in a premeditated way are the primary objectives of an effective crisis communication strategy and/or solution. Harnassing technology and people to ensure a rapid and co-ordinated response to a range of potentially crippling scenarios distinguishes a well thought out and executed plan from a poorly or ill-considered one. The inherent lag time in marshalling responses to a crisis can result in considerable losses to company revenues, reputation as well as substantially impacting on costs.

Effective crisis communication strategies will typically consider achieving most, if not all, of the following objectives:

- Maintain connectivity
- Be readily accessible to the news media
- Show empathy for the people involved
- Allow distributed access
- Streamline communication processes
- Maintain information security
- Ensure uninterrupted audit trails
- Deliver high volume communications
- Support multi-channel communications
- Remove dependencies on paper based processes

By definition a crisis is an unexpected and detrimental situation or event. Crisis communication can play a significant role by transforming the unexpected into the anticipated and responding accordingly.

Some of the most effective recent examples of crisis communication include Richard Branson's (Virgin) and John Armitt's (Network Rail) dignified press conference after the Grayrigg rail disaster of 2007 and US Airways handling of the media after their crashlanding on the Hudson river.

*Employee communication*:

- Sharing information with employees, building employer pride, managing employee issues, et cetera.
- Manage the Intranet and other internal web portals

Organizational communication: Encourage and enable the employees to plan for new ideas and effectively implement them.

*Internal communication*:

- Managing corporate publications for employees and partners
- Organising internal events for staff

**Corporate Communication Officers**

Recent research on the corporate communication function reports that corporate communication officers (CCOs) in Global Fortune 500 companies tend to have average tenures of about 4.5 years and that nearly one-half (48 per cent) report to the Chief Executive Officer.

CCOs say that approximately 42 per cent of their job is strategic and 58 per cent is tactical. Over the next year, they will be focusing more on social responsibility, social media and reputation. The research done by Weber Shandwick and Spencer Stuart found distinct differences between CCOs in Most Admired companies versus Contender companies.

## CORPORATE VIDEO

Corporate video production refers to audio-visual corporate communications material (such as DVD, High-definition video, streaming video or other media) commissioned primarily for a use by a company, corporation or organisation.

A corporate video is often intended for a specific purpose in a corporate or B2B environment and viewed only by a limited or targeted audience. This may include product, service or company promotional videos, training videos and information videos·Corporate video production is frequently the responsibility of a company marketing or corporate communications manager. Examples of corporate video include staff training and safety videos, promotional/brand films, and financial results videos.With the growth of digital technology, there is now often convergence between corporate video and other forms of media communications, such as broadcast television and TV advertising.

For example, a company might feature a promotional video on their website' and is then potentially available to a much wider audience. Also, a corporate video may be produced using the same production techniques and style as a broadcast television programme (such as using outside broadcasting facilities)—as a way of engaging audiences who are used to viewing popular media, a corporate video might even be themed on a well-known television series.

A corporate video production company may typically take the client brief, develop a script or treatment (and sometimes a storyboard), liaise with the client, and agree on a production schedule and delivery date.

The time and scale of a corporate video production can vary greatly. Some videos may use only minimal crew and basic equipment, whilst some large scale corporate videos may have similar (or often higher) budgets and level of production than a broadcast television programme or TV commercial.

*The corporate video production process will frequently involve the following stages*:

- Pre-Production, including script writing and storyboarding. The budget will also be agreed at this stage between the production company and client.

- Production, including location filming with a camera crew and director. This may also include other elements, such as actors and presenters.
- Post-production and video editing - the filmed (live action) footage is edited together. This may also include recording an audio voice-over, adding graphics, composing a music score or soundtrack, and including 2D/3D animation sequences with the finished video.

**Types and Usage**

- Staff training/induction and safety videos
- Investor relations/ financial results
- Company promotional/brand videos
- Video role play (often with actors)
- Client and customer testimonial videos
- Corporate event filming (for example, a new product launch or conference)
- Live and on-demand webcasting
- Technology and product demonstration videos
- Business television

## CORPORATE IMAGE

A corporate image refers to how a corporation is perceived. It is a generally accepted image of what a company stands for. Marketing experts who use public relations and other forms of promotion to suggest a mental picture to the public. Typically, a corporate image is designed to be appealing to the public, so that the company can spark an interest among consumers, create share of mind, generate brand equity, and thus facilitate product sales.

A corporation's image is not solely created by the company: Other contributors to a company's image could include news media, journalists, labour unions, environmental organizations, and other NGOs.

Corporations are not the only form of organization that create these types of images. Governments, charitable organizations, criminal organizations, religious organizations, political organizations, and educational organizations all tend to have a unique image, an image that is partially deliberate and partially accidental, partially self-created and partially exogenous.

## CORPORATE PROPAGANDA

Corporate propaganda are propagandist claims made by a corporation (or corporations), nearly always for the purpose of manipulating market opinion to the benefit of their product or to divide public opinion with regard to controversial issues related to that corporation, and its associated business dealings. Corporate propaganda is distinct from advocacy. Advocacy presents product and service information fully, fairly, and without exploitation of consumer emotions.

Just as the use of these products and services can provide pluses which outweigh the minuses to society and individuals, their advocacy may function more positively than negatively. The most common forms of corporate propaganda are advertising and public relations.

**Examples**

- Decision Earth Procter & Gamble propaganda materials distributed to schools, to influence young children with pseudoscientific notions.
- Bechtel Corporation
- Tobacco industry Long history of advertising and litigation wherein practices of manipulation and deception are common.
- Captain Planet
- Walt Disney's Production of Propaganda for the US Government During World War II

**Marketing Speak**

Marketing speak refers to particular patterns of language often used to promote a product or service to a wide audience by seeking to create the impression that the vendors of the service possess a high level of sophistication, skill, and technical knowledge. Such language is often used in marketing press releases, advertising copy, and prepared statements read by executives and politicians. Marketing speak is characterized by its heavy use of buzzwords, neologisms, and terms appropriated from specialized technical fields which are eventually rendered almost meaningless through heavy repeated use in inappropriate contexts.

*Examples*:

- Unique selling proposition (USP)
- Low hanging fruit (LHF)
- Pushing the envelope
- *Lean forward* and *Lean back* media
- Deep-dive

## ORGANIZATIONAL COMMUNICATION

Organizational communication is a subfield of the larger discipline of communication studies. Organizational communication, as a field, is the consideration, analysis, and criticism of the role of communication in organizational contexts. The field traces its lineage through business information, business communication, and early mass communication studies published in the 1930s through the 1950s. Until then, organizational communication as a discipline consisted of a few professors within speech departments who had a particular interest in speaking and writing in business settings. The current field is well established with its own theories and empirical concerns distinct from other communication subfields and other approaches to organizations. Several seminal publications stand out as works broadening the scope and recognizing the importance of communication in the organizing process, and in using the term "organizational communication". Nobel Laureate Herbert Simon wrote in 1947 about "organization communications systems", saying communication is "absolutely essential to organizations".

In the 1950s, organizational communication focused largely on the role of communication in improving organizational life and organizational output. In the 1980s, the field turned away from a business-oriented approach to communication and became concerned more with the constitutive role of communication in organizing. In the 1990s, critical theory influence on the field was felt as organizational communication scholars focused more on communication's possibilities to oppress and liberate organizational members.

## EARLY ORGANIZATIONAL COMMUNICATION

Some of the main assumptions underlying much of the early organizational communication research were.

- *Humans act rationally*: Sane people behave in rational ways, they generally have access to all of the information needed to make rational decisions they could articulate, and therefore will make rational decisions, unless there is some breakdown in the communication process.
- Formal logic and empirically verifiable data ought to be the foundation upon which any theory should rest. All we really need to understand communication in organizations is:
  - Observable and replicable behaviors that can be transformed into variables by some form of measurement,
  - Formally replicable syllogisms that can extend theory from observed data to other groups and settings
- Communication is primarily a mechanical process, in which a message is constructed and encoded by a sender, transmitted through some channel, then received and decoded by a receiver. Distortion, represented as any differences between the original and the received messages, can and ought to be identified and reduced or eliminated.
- Organizations are mechanical things, in which the parts (including employees functioning in defined roles) are interchangeable. What works in one organization will work in another similar organi-zation. Individual differences can be minimized or even eliminated with careful management tech-niques.
- Organizations function as a container within which communication takes place. Any differences in form or function of communication

between that occurring in an organization and in another setting can be identified and studied as factors affecting the communicative activity.

Herbert Simon introduced the concept of bounded rationality which challenged assumptions about the perfect rationality of communication participants. He maintained that people making decisions in organizations seldom had complete information, and that even if more information was available, they tended to pick the first acceptable option, rather than exploring further to pick the optimal solution.

Through the 1960s, 1970s and 1980s the field expanded greatly in parallel with several other academic disciplines, looking at communication as more than an intentional act designed to transfer an idea. Research expanded beyond the issue of "how to make people understand what I am saying" to tackle questions such as "how does the act of communicating change, or even define, who I am?", "why do organizations that seem to be saying similar things achieve very different results?" and "to what extent are my relationships with others affected by our various organizational contexts?"

In the early 1990s Peter Senge developed a new theories on Organizational Communication. These theories were learning organization and systems thinking. These have been well received and are now a mainstay in current beliefs toward organizational communications.

**Communications Networks**

Networks are another aspect of direction and flow of communication. Bavelas has shown that communication patterns, or networks, influence groups in several important ways. Communication networks may affect the group's completion of the assigned task on time, the position of the de facto leader in the group, or they may affect the group members' satisfaction from occupying certain positions in the network. Although these findings are based on laboratory experiments, they have important implications for the dynamics of communication in formal organizations.

*There are several patterns of communication*:

- "Chain",
- "Wheel",
- "Star",
- "All-Channel" network,
- "Circle".

The Chain can readily be seen to represent the hierarchical pattern that characterizes strictly formal information flow, "from the top down," in military and some types of business organizations. The Wheel can be compared with a typical autocratic organization, meaning one-man rule and limited employee participation. The Star is similar to the basic formal structure of many organizations. The All-Channel network, which is an elaboration of Bavelas's

Circle used by Guetzkow, is analogous to the free-flow of communication in a group that encourages all of its members to become involved in group decision processes. The All-Channel network may also be compared to some of the informal communication networks.

If it's assumed that messages may move in both directions between stations in the networks, it is easy to see that some individuals occupy key positions with regard to the number of messages they handle and the degree to which they exercise control over the flow of information.

For example, the person represented by the central dot in the "Star" handles all messages in the group. In contrast, individuals who occupy stations at the edges of the pattern handle fewer messages and have little or no control over the flow of information.These "peripheral" individuals can communicate with only one or two other persons and must depend entirely on others to relay their messages if they wish to extend their range.

In reporting the results of experiments involving the Circle, Wheel, and Star configurations, Bavelas came to the following tentative conclusions. In patterns with positions located centrally, such as the Wheel and the Star, an organization quickly develops around the people occupying these central positions. In such patterns, the organization is more stable and errors in performance are lower than in patterns having a lower degree of centrality, such as the Circle. However, he also found that the morale of members in high centrality patterns is relatively low. Bavelas speculated that this lower morale could, in the long run, lower the accuracy and speed of such networks. In problem solving requiring the pooling of data and judgments, or "insight," Bavelas suggested that the ability to evaluate partial results, to look at alternatives, and to restructure problems fell off rapidly when one person was able to assume a more central (that is, more controlling) position in the information flow.

For example, insight into a problem requiring change would be less in the Wheel and the Star than in the Circle or the Chain because of the "bottlenecking" effect of data control by central members. It may be concluded from these laboratory results that the structure of communications within an organization will have a significant influence on the accuracy of decisions, the speed with which they can be reached, and the satisfaction of the people involved. Consequently, in networks in which the responsibility for initiating and passing along messages is shared more evenly among the members, the better the group's morale in the long run.

## DIRECTION OF COMMUNICATION

If it's considered formal communications as they occur in traditional military organizations, messages have a "one-way" directional characteristic. In the military organization, the formal communication proceeds from superior to subordinate, and its content is presumably clear because it originates at a higher level of expertise and experience. Military communications also carry the additional assumption that the superior is responsible for making his communication clear and understandable to his subordinates.

This type of organization assumes that there is little need for two-way exchanges between organizational levels except as they are initiated by a higher level. Because messages from superiors are considered to be more important than those from subordinates, the implicit rule is that communication channels, except for prescribed information flows, should not be cluttered by messages from subordinates but should remain open and free for messages moving down the chain of command. "Juniors should be seen and not heard," is still an unwritten, if not explicit, law of military protocol. Vestiges of one-way flows of communication still exist in many formal organizations outside the military, and for many of the same reasons as described above. Although management recognizes that prescribed information must flow both downward and upward, managers may not always be convinced that two-wayness should be encouraged. For example, to what extent is a subordinate free to communicate to his superior that he understands or does not understand a message?

Is it possible for him to question the superior, ask for clarification, suggest modifications to instructions he has received, or transmit unsolicited messages to his superior, which are not prescribed by the rules? To what extent does the one-way rule of direction affect the efficiency of communication in the organization, in addition to the morale and motivation of subordinates?

These are not merely procedural matters but include questions about the organizational climate, pr psychological atmosphere in which communication takes place. Harold Leavitt has suggested a simple experiment that helps answer some of these questions.

À group is assigned the task of re-creating on paper a set of rectangular figures, first as they are described by the leader under one-way conditions, and second as they are described by the leader under two-way conditions.

A different configuration of rectangles is used in the second trial. In the one-way trial, the leader's back is turned to the group. He describes the rectangles as he sees them. No one in the group is allowed to ask questions and no one may indicate by any audible or visible sign his understanding or his frustration as he attempts to follow the leader's directions.

In the two-way trial, the leader faces the group. In this case, the group may ask for clarifications on his description of the rectangles and he can not only see but also can feel and respond to the emotional reactions of group members as they try to re-create his instructions on paper. On the basis of a number of experimental trials similar to the one described above, Leavitt formed these conclusions.

- One-way communication is faster than two-way communication.

- Two-way communication is more accurate than one-way communication.
- Receivers are more sure of themselves and make more correct judgments of how right or wrong they are in the two-way system.
- The sender feels psychologically under attack in the two-way system, because his receivers pick up his mistakes and oversights and point them out to him.
- The two-way method is relatively noisier and looks more disorderly. The one-way method, on the other hand, appears neat and efficient to an outside observer.

Thus, if speed is necessary, if a businesslike appearance is important, if a manager does not want his mistakes recognized, and if he wants to protect his power, then one-way communication seems preferable. In contrast, if the manager wants to get his message across, or if he is concerned about his receivers' feeling that they are participating and are making a contribution, the two-way system is better.

**Interpersonal Communication**

Another facet of communication in the organization is the process of face-to-face, interpersonal communication, between individuals. Such communication may take several forms. Messages may be verbal (that is, expressed in words), or they may not involve words at all but consist of gestures, facial expressions, and certain postures ("body language"). Nonverbal messages may even stem from silence.

Managers do not need answers to operate a successful business; they need questions. Answers can come from anyone, anytime, anywhere in the world thanks to the benefits of all the electronic communication tools at our disposal. This has turned the real job of management into determining what it is the business needs to know, along with the who/what/where/when and how of learning it. To effectively solve problems, seize opportunities, and achieve objectives, questions need to be asked by managers—these are the people responsible for the operation of the enterprise as a whole.

Ideally, the meanings sent are the meanings received. This is most often the case when the messages concern something that can be verified objectively. For example, "This piece of pipe fits the threads on the coupling." In this case, the receiver of the message can check the sender's words by actual trial, if necessary. However, when the sender's words describe a feeling or an opinion about something that cannot be checked objectively, meanings can be very unclear.

"This work is too hard" or "Watergate was politically justified" are examples of opinions or feelings that cannot be verified. Thus they are subject to interpretation and hence to distorted meanings. The receiver's background of experience and learning may differ enough from that of the sender to cause significantly different perceptions and evaluations of the topic under discussion. Nonverbal content always accompanies the verbal content of messages. This is reasonably clear in the case of face-to-face communication. As Virginia Satir has pointed out, people cannot help but communicate symbolically (for example, through their clothing or possessions) or through some form of body language.

In messages that are conveyed by the telephone, a messenger, or a letter, the situation or context in which the message is sent becomes part of its non-verbal content. For example, if the company has been losing money, and in a letter to the production division, the front office orders a reorganization of the shipping and receiving departments, this could be construed to mean that some people were going to lose their jobs — unless it were made explicitly clear that this would not occur.

A number of variables influence the effectiveness of communication. Some are found in the environment in which communication takes place, some in the personalities of the sender and the receiver, and some in the relationship that exists between sender and receiver. These different variables suggest some of the difficulties of communicating with understanding between two people. The sender wants to formulate an idea and communicate it to the receiver. This desire to communicate may arise from his thoughts or feelings or it may have been triggered by something in the environment.

The communication may also be influenced or distorted by the relationship between the sender and the receiver, such as status differences, a staff-line relationship, or a learner-teacher relationship. Whatever its origin, information travels through a series of filters, both in the sender and in the receiver, before the idea can be transmitted and re-created in the receiver's mind. Physical capacities to see, hear, smell, taste, and touch vary between people, so that the image of reality may be distorted even before the mind goes to work. In addition to physical or sense filters, cognitive filters, or the way in which an individual's mind interprets the world around him, will influence his assumptions and feelings.

These filters will determine what the sender of a message says, how he says it, and with what purpose. Filters are present also in the receiver, creating a double complexity that once led Robert Louis Stevenson to say that human communication is "doubly relative". It takes one person to say something and another to decide what he said.

Physical and cognitive, including semantic filters (which decide the meaning of words) combine to form a part of our memory system that helps us respond to reality. In this sense, March and Simon compare a person to a data processing system. Behaviour results from an interaction between a person's internal state and environmental stimuli.

What we have learned through past experience becomes an inventory, or data bank, consisting of values or goals, sets of expectations and preconceptions about the consequences of acting one way or another, and a variety of possible ways of responding to the situation.

This memory system determines what things we will notice and respond to in the environment. At the same time, stimuli in the environment help to determine what parts of the memory system will be activated. Hence, the memory and the environment form an interactive system that causes our behaviour. As this interactive system responds to new experiences, new learnings occur which feed back into memory and gradually change its content. This process is how people adapt to a changing world.

## Communication Approaches in an Organization

Informal and Formal Communication are used in an organization. Informal communication: Informal communi-cation, generally associated with interpersonal, horizontal communication, was primarily seen as a potential hindrance to effective organizational performance. This is no longer the case. Informal communication has become more important to ensuring the effective conduct of work in modern organizations. *Top-down approach*: This is also known as downward communication. This approach is used by the Top Level Management to communicate to the lower levels. This is used to implement policies, gudelines, etc. In this type of organizational communication, distortion of the actual information occurs. This could be made effective by feedbacks.

## Research in Organizational Communication

### *Research Methodologies*

Historically, organizational communication was driven primarily by quantitative research methodologies. Included in functional organizational communication research are statistical analyses (such as surveys, text indexing, network mapping and behaviour modeling). In the early 1980s, the interpretive revolution took place in organizational communication.

*In Putnam and Pacanowsky's 1983 text Communication and Organizations*: An Interpretive Approach. they argued for opening up methodological space for qualitative approaches such as narrative analyses, participant-observation, interviewing, rhetoric and textual approaches readings) and philosophic inquiries. During the 1980s and 1990s critical organizational scholarship began to gain prominence with a focus on issues of gender, race, class, and power/ knowledge. In its current state, the study of organizational communication is open methodologically, with research from post-positive, interpretive, critical, postmodern, and discursive paradigms being published regularly.

Organizational communication scholarship appears in a number of communication journals including but not limited to Management Communication Quarterly, Journal of Applied Communication Research,

Communication Monographs, Academy of Management Journal, Communication Studies, and Southern Communication Journal.

## Current Research Topics in Organizational Communication

The field of organizational communication has moved from acceptance of mechanistic models (e.g., information moving from a sender to a receiver) to a study of the persistent, hegemonic and taken-for-granted ways in which we not only use communication to accomplish certain tasks within organizational settings (e.g., public speaking) but also how the organizations in which we participate affect us.

These approaches include "postmodern", "critical", "participatory", "feminist", "power/political", "organic", etc. and adds to disciplines as wide-ranging as sociology, philosophy, theology, psychology, business, business administration, institutional management, medicine (health communication), neurology (neural nets), semiotics, anthropology, international relations, and music.

*Currently, some topics of research and theory in the field are:*

- Constitution
- Narrative
- Identity
- Interrelatedness
- Power

### *Constitution*

- How communicative behaviors construct or modify organizing processes or products.
- How the organizations within which we interact affect our communicative behaviors, and through these, our own identities.
- Structures other than organizations which might be constituted through our communicative activity (e.g., markets, cooperatives, tribes, political parties, social movements).
- When does something "become" an organization? When does an organization become (an)other thing(s)? Can one organization "house" another? Is the organization still a useful entity/thing/ concept, or has the social/political environment changed so much that what we now call "organization" is so different from the organization of even a few decades ago that it cannot be usefully tagged with the same word—"organization"?

### *Narrative*

- How do group members employ narrative to acculturate/initiate/ indoctrinate new members?

- Do organizational stories act on different levels? Are different narratives purposively invoked to achieve specific outcomes, or are there specific roles of "organizational storyteller"? If so, are stories told by the storyteller received differently than those told by others in the organization?
- In what ways does the organization attempt to influence storytelling about the organization? under what conditions does the organization appear to be more or less effective in obtaining a desired outcome?
- When these stories conflict with one another or with official rules/ policies, how are the conflicts worked out? in situations in which alternative accounts are available, who or how or why are some accepted and others rejected?

### *Identity*

- Who do we see ourselves to be, in terms of our organizational affiliations?
- Do communicative behaviors or occurrences in one or more of the organizations in which we participate effect changes in us? To what extent do we consist of the organizations to which we belong?
- Is it possible for individuals to successfully resist organizational identity? what would that look like?
- Do people who define themselves by their work-organizational membership communicate differently within the organizational setting than people who define themselves more by an avocational (non-vocational) set of relationships?
- For example, researchers have studied how human service workers and firefighters use humor at their jobs as a way to affirm their identity in the face of various challenges Tracy, S.J.; K. K. Myers; C. W. Scott. Others have examined the identities of police organizations, prison guards, and professional women workers.

### *Interrelatedness of Organizational Experiences*

- How do our communicative interactions in one organizational setting affect our communicative actions in other organizational settings?
- How do the phenomenological experiences of participants in a particular organizational setting effect changes in other areas of their lives?
- When the organizational status of a member is significantly changed (e.g., by promotion or expuls-ion) how are their other organizational memberships affected?
- What kind of future relationship between business and society does organizational communication seem to predict?

### *Power*

- How does the use of particular communicative practices within an organizational setting reinforce or alter the various interrelated power relationships within the setting? Are the potential responses of those within or around these organizational settings constrained by factors or processes either within or outside of the organization—(assuming there is an "outside"?

- do taken-for-granted organizational practices work to fortify the dominant hegemonic narrative? Do iDndividuals resist/confront these practices, through what actions/agencies, and to what effects?
- Do status changes in an organization (e.g., promotions, demotions, restructuring, financial/social strata changes) change communicative behaviour? Are there criteria employed by organizational members to differentiate between "legitimate" (i.e., endorsed by the formal organizational structure) and "illegitimate" (i.e., opposed by or unknown to the formal power structure)? Are behaviors? When are they successful, and what do we even there "pretenders" or "usurpers" who employ these communicativemean by "successful?"

## COMMUNICATION STUDIES

Communication studies is an academic field that deals with processes of communication, commonly defined as the sharing of symbols over distances in space and time. Hence, communication studies encompasses a wide range of topics and contexts ranging from face-to-face conversation to speeches to mass media outlets such as television broadcasting. Communication studies, as a discipline, is also often interested in how audiences interpret information and the political, cultural, economic, and social dimensions of speech and language in context.

The field is institutionalized under many different names at different universities and in various countries, including "communications", "communication studies", "speech communication", "rhetorical studies", "communications science", "media studies", "communication arts", "mass communication", "media ecology," and sometimes even "mediology" although this latter is a different area of study. Communication studies often overlaps with academic programs in journalism, film and cinema, radio and television, advertising and public relations and performance studies. Recently, institutions have migrated towards the common term of "communication studies" to encapsulate and cohere the vast depth and breadth of the field.

In the United States, the National Communication Associ-ation (NCA) recognizes nine distinct but often overlapping sub-disciplines within the broader communi-cation discipline: Communication & Technology, Critical-Cultural, Health, Intercultural-International, Inter-personal-Small Group, Mass Communication, Organizational, Political, and Rhetorical.

The International Communication Association (ICA) recognizes a much larger and evolving list of sections, including among others Communication

History; Commun-ication Law and Policy; Ethnicity and Race in Communication; Feminist Scholarship; Gay, Lesbian, Bisexual and Transgender Studies; Global Communication and Social Change; Informa-tion Systems; Instructional/Developmental Communication; Journalism Studies; Language and Social Interaction; Organizational Communication; Philosophy of Communi-cation; Political Communication; Popular Communication; Public Relations; and Visual Communication Studies.

Communication studies is often considered a part of both the social sciences and the humanities, drawing heavily on fields such as sociology, psychology, anthropology, political science, and economics as well as rhetoric, literary studies, linguistics, and semiotics.

The field can incorporate and overlap with the work of other disciplines as well, however, including engineering, architecture, mathematics, computer science, gender and sexuality studies.

The vast breadth and interdisciplinary nature of commun-ication studies has understandably made it difficult for both students and institutions to place it within the broader educational system. Despite intellectual incoherence, the field attracts and sustains large numbers of students, scholarly journals, professional associations, and lively discussions across the academy for researchers, educators, lawmakers, businesses, and reformers.

Broadly understood, the contemporary study of communication per se interfaces and overlaps with areas such as business, organizational development, philosophy, languages, composition, theatre, debate (often called "forensics"), literary criticism, sociology, psychology, history, anthropology, semiotics, international policy, economics and political science, among others. The breadth and the primacy of communication in many areas of life is responsible for the ubiquity of communication studies, as well as for the resulting confusion about what does and does not constitute communication. Ongoing debates rage whether commun-ication studies can best be understood as a discipline, a field, or simply a topic.

Most U.S. graduate programs in Communication today trace their history through speech to ancient rhetoric. Programs in Communication, Communication Arts or Communication Sciences often include Organizational Communication, Interpersonal Communication, Speech Communication (or Rhetoric), Mass Communication, and sometimes Journalism, Film criticism, Theatre, Political science (e.g., political campaign strategies, public speaking, effects of media on elections), or Radio, Television or Film production.

Graduates of formal communication programs can be found in a wide range of fields working as university professors, marketing researchers, media editors and designers, speech therapists, journalists, human resources managers, corporate trainers, public relations practitioners, and media managers and consultants in a variety of fields including, media production, life coaching, public speaking, organizational, political campaign/issue management and public policy. Communication is often recognized as a cornerstone of modern society—it would be hard to conceive of modern life without it. However, communication as an English-language field of study and a subject of social thought took off only in the first part of the twentieth century, and is thus a relatively recent and thus unsettled discovery.

In what is sometimes called the "transmission" view, communication is a process by which messages are sent, transmitted, filtered, and received. At core, the transmission view maps closely onto information theory inspired by Shannon's 1948 "a Mathematical Theory of Communication." A more recent "ritual" view, proposed by the late James W. Carey, holds that communication partakes in central daily rituals that forge meaningful human relationships and communities. While transmission proposes a model of communication as transportation (across space, in one time), the ritual model proposes that meaning can be constituted in repeated media events (across times, in one space). The newspaper, for instance, does not only transmit messages to the reader through text, but reminds and reassures the reader through repeated and meaningful events, such as its morning appearance on the doorstep and a familiar page layout. A fuller conceptualization of communication activity, many scholars contend, lies somewhere between and beyond these two views.

## History, pre-20th Century

Various aspects of communication have long been the subject of human study. In ancient Greece and Rome, the study of rhetoric, the art of oratory and persuasion, was a vital subject for students. One significant ongoing debate was whether one could be an effective speaker in a base cause (Sophists) or whether excellent rhetoric came from the excellence of the orator's character (Socrates, Plato, Cicero). Through the European Middle Ages and Renaissance grammar, rhetoric, and logic constituted the entire trivium, the base of the system of classical learning in Europe.

## History, North America

### *1900s–1920s*

Though the study of communication reaches back to antiquity and beyond, early twentieth-century work by Charles Horton Cooley, Walter Lippmann, and John Dewey has been of particular importance for the academic discipline as it stands today in the United States. In his 1909 *Social Organization: a Study of the Larger Mind,* Cooley defines communication as "the mechanism through which human relations exist and develop—all the symbols of the mind, together with the means of conveying them through space and preserving them in time."

This view, which has subsequently been largely marginalized in sociology, gave processes of communication a central and constitutive place in the study of social relations. *Public Opinion,* published in 1922 by Walter Lippmann, couples this view of the constitutive importance of communication with a fear that the rise of new technologies and institutions of mass communication allowed for the manufacture of consent and generated dissonance between what he called 'the world outside and the pictures in our heads' on a scale that made democracy as classically conceived almost impossible to realise.

John Dewey's 1927 The Public and its Problems drew on the same view of communications, but coupled it instead with an optimistic progressive and democratic reform agenda, arguing famously "communication can alone create a great community". Cooley, Lippmann, and Dewey capture themes like the central importance of communication in social life, the rise of large and potentially powerful media institutions and the development of new communications technologies in societies undergoing rapid transformation, and questions regarding the relationship between communication, democracy, and community.

All these remain central to the discipline of communication studies. Many of these concerns are also central to the work of writers such as Gabriel Tarde and Theodor W. Adorno, which has been central to the development of communication studies elsewhere. The first decades of the twentieth century also saw the development of parallel currents of cultural criticism that drew less on the social sciences and more on the humanities. Though trained as a sociologist, the work of W. E. B. Du Bois on art and spirituals stands out here.

The study of American public address began during this time frame. In 1925, Herbert A. Wichelns published the essay "The Literary Criticism of Oratory" in the book *Studies in Rhetoric and Public Speaking in Honour of James Albert Winans.* ' Wicheln's essay attempted to "put rhetorical studies on par with literary studies as an area of academic interest and research." Wichelns wrote that oratory should be taken as seriously as literature, and therefore, it should be subject to criticism and analysis. Although the essay is now standard reading in most rhetorical criticism courses, it had little immediate impact on the field of rhetorical studies.

### *1930s–1950s*

The institutionalization of communication studies in U.S. higher education and research has often been traced to Columbia University, the University of Chicago, and the University of Illinois Urbana-Champaign, where early pioneers and institutionalizers like Paul F. Lazarsfeld, Harold Lasswell, and Wilbur Schramm worked.

The Bureau of Applied Social Research was established in 1944 at Columbia University by Paul F. Lazarsfeld. It was a continuation of the Rockefeller Foundation-funded Radio Project that he had led at various institutions from 1937, which had been at Columbia as the Office of Radio

Research since 1939. In its various incarnations, the Radio Project had involved Lazarsfeld himself, and people like Adorno, Hadley Cantril, Gordon Allport, and Frank Stanton (who went on to be president of CBS).

Lazarsfeld and the Bureau mobilized substantial sums for research, and produced, with various co-authors, a series of books and edited volumes that helped define the discipline, such as *Personal Influence* which remains a classic in what is called the 'media effects'-tradition. At Columbia, communications studies have traditionally been closely aligned with sociology, and people like Robert Merton and others from the sociology programme were at times involved. The university did only recently, in the 1990s, establish an actual degree-granting graduate programme in communications, illustrating how much important research on communications continues to take place outside the discipline that carries the name. The Bureau, and Lazarsfeld's research more generally, exemplifies the close relations that have sometimes existed between communication studies and the media industries.

From the 1940s and onwards, the University of Chicago was home to several temporary but important committees and commissions on communications, programs that also educated several leading communication scholars. In contrast to what took place at Columbia, these programs explicitly claimed the name 'communications' for themselves. The Committee on Communication and Public Opinion, also funded by the Rockefeller Foundation, was staffed with, in addition to Lasswell, people such as Douglas Waples, Samuel A. Stouffer, Louis Wirth, and Herbert Blumer, all of whom held positions elsewhere at the university.

They formed a committee that essentially served as a scholarly and educational extension of the federal government's increasing interest in communications during times of war, and was in particular closely linked to the Office of War Information. The committee is a reminder of connection as important as the Bureau's with the industry, namely the connection between communication studies and government interests and funding.

Chicago later provided an institutional home for The Hutchins Commission on the Freedom of the Press and the Committee on Communication. The latter was a degree-granting programme that counted Elihu Katz, Bernard Berelson, Edward Shils, and David Riesman amongst its faculty, and produced graduates like Herbert J. Gans and Michael Gurevitch. The committee also produced publications like Berelson and Janowitz' *Public Opinion and Communication* and the journal *Studies in Public Communication.* The Institute for Communications Research was founded at the University of Illinois at Urbana-Champaign in 1947 by Wilbur Schramm, who was a key figure in the post-war institutionalization of communication studies in the U.S. Like the various Chicago committees, the Illinois programme claimed the name 'communications' and granted graduate degrees in the subject. Schramm, who, in contrast to the more social science-inspired figures at

Columbia and Chicago, had a background in English literature, developed communication studies partly by merging existing programs in speech communication, rhetoric, and, especially, journalism under the aegis of communication. He also edited a textbook *The Process and Effects of Mass Communication* that helped define the field, partly by claiming the Lazarsfeld, Lasswell, Carl Hovland, and Kurt Lewin as its founding fathers.

He also wrote several other manifestos for the discipline, including *The Science of Human Communication* 1963. Schramm and the Institute moved on to Stanford University in 1955. Many of Schramm's students, such as Everett Rogers, went on to make important contributions of their own.

### *1950s–1960s*

From the 1950s onwards, communications studies branched out in several new and often very different directions. Numerous new programs opened up at various universities, and new journals were established. The work of what has been called 'medium theorists', arguably defined by Harold Innis' (1950) *Empire and Communications* grew increasingly important, and was popularized by Marshall McLuhan in his *Understanding Media.* This perspective informs the later work of Joshua Meyrowitz.

Two developments in the 1940s shifted the paradigm of communication studies in the 1950s and thereafter toward a more-quantitative orientation, or at least the inescapable need to consider such an orientation. One was cybernetics, as formulated by Norbert Wiener in his *Cybernetics: Or the Control and Communication in the Animal and the Machine.*

The other was information theory, as recast in quantitative terms by Claude E. Shannon and Warren Weaver in their *Mathematical Theory of Communication.* These works were widely appropriated to, and offered for some the prospect of, a general theory of society.

The tradition of critical theory associated with the Frankfurt School was, as in Europe, an important source of influence for many researchers. While done out of sociology departments, the work of Jürgen Habermas, the US-based Leo Löwenthal, Herbert Marcuse, and Siegfried Kracauer, as well as earlier figures like Adorno and Max Horkheimer continued to inform a whole tradition of cultural criticism that often focused both empirically and theoretically on the culture industry. In 1953, to address growing needs in industry, Rensselaer Polytechnic Institute began offering a master of science degree in technical writing. In the 1960s, partly because of the need to represent that the degree incorporated training in oral and audiovisual communication, the degree title became technical communication. It was the brainchild of longtime RPI professor and administrator Jay R. Gould.

### *1960s–1970s*

In the 1960s Gould and his colleagues experienced increasing demand for doctoral-level studies in technical and business communication. As result, in 1965 RPI began its Ph.D. programme in communication and rhetoric. This Ph.D. degree programme became a prototype for other technologically oriented Ph.D. communication programs in the United States and other industrialized countries.

The 1960s and 1970s saw the development of cultivation theory, pioneered by George Gerbner at the Annenberg School for Communication at the University of Pennsylvania. This approach shifted emphasis from the short-term effects that had been the central interest of many earlier works on the media, and instead tried to track the effect of exposure to, for instance, television over time on viewers' perceptions of reality.

### *1970s–1980s*

Neil Postman founded the media ecology programme at New York University in 1971. Media ecologists draw on a wide range of inspirations in their attempts to study entire media environments in an even broader and more cultural fashion than the work done in the Canadian medium theory tradition. This perspective is the basis of a separate professional association, the Media Ecology Association.

In 1972, Maxwell McCombs and Donald Shaw published a path-breaking article that offered an agenda-setting theory of media effects that gave new ways of conceptualizing the short-term media effects that earlier work had generally deemed limited. This approach, organized around additional ideas such as framing, priming, and gatekeeping, has been highly influential, especially in the study of political communication and news coverage.

The 1970s also saw the development of what became known as uses and gratifications research, developed by scholars such as Elihu Katz, Jay G. Blumler, and Michael Gurevitch. Instead of looking at communications processes simply as a one-way flow from senders to receivers, this approach began scrutinizing what audiences get out of communications, what they do with it, why they engage with it—especially with mass media.

### History, Germany

Communication studies in Germany has a rich hermeneutic heritage in philology, textual interpretation, and historical studies. The post-world war II era, however, has seen the rise of a number of new paradigms. Elisabeth Noelle-Neumann pioneered work on the spiral of silence in a tradition that has been widely influential across the world and has proven to be easily compatible with the dominant paradigms in, for instance, the United States.

In the 1970s, Karl Deutsch came to West Germany, and his cybernetics inspired work has been widely influential there as elsewhere. The work of the Frankfurt School has been a cornerstone of much German work on communication, in addition to Horkheimer, Adorno, and Habermas, figures like Oskar Negt and Alexander Kluge has been important in the development of this strand of thought. An important competing paradigm has been the systems theory developed by Niklas Luhmann and his students, such as Dirk Baecker and others.

Finally, from the 1980s and onwards, people like Friedrich Kittler has led the development of a 'new German medium theory', aligned partly with the Canadian medium theory of Innis and McLuhan and partly with post-structuralism.

### *Professional Associations*

- National Communication Association (NCA): The main national professional organization covering many of the areas of communication studies in the U.S.
- International Communication Association is the main international association for communication studies, which combines an older focus on quantitatively based social science studies with newer critical and cultural studies of communicative phenomena.
- Association for Education in Journalism and Mass Communication.
- Association for Business Communication (ABC).
- International Association of Business Communicators (IABC).
- Society for Technical Communication (STC).
- Public Relations Society of America (PRSA).
- European Communication Research and Education Association (ECREA) is the main European association for communication studies.
- European Association for the Teaching of Academic Writing (EATAW) is the main European association for writing studies.
- Association for Teachers of Technical Writing (ATTW).
- International Association for Media and Communi-cations Research (IAMCR) is also a large international association for communication studies.
- IEEE Professional Communication Society.

## ASSOCIATION FOR BUSINESS COMMUNICATION

The Association for Business Communication (ABC) is the primary academic organization for the field of business communication scholarship, research, education and practice. The mission statement on its website reflects this: "The Association for Business Communication (ABC) is an international organization committed to fostering excellence in business communication scholarship, research, education, and practice."

Much of the strength of the organization rests in its interdisciplinary nature. Members belong to such varied academic fields as Management, Marketing, English, Foreign Languages, Speech, Communication, Linguistics, and Information Systems. Additionally the organization brings together university academicians, business practitioners, and business consultants.

**Organizational Structure**

ABC is an international organization, divided into eight regional divisions, each with its own separate academic conferences. The regions are Europe, Asia and Pacific Rim, Caribbean and Central America, and five North American regions (Canada plus Eastern, Midwest, Southeast, and Southwest United States).

Each year the entire membership meets at the International Convention in October or November. Midyear, two regional conferences are held—one in the European region and the other in one of the North American regions. The Asia and Pacific Rim region holds a conference every two years. At the International Convention and at the regional conferences, members come together to share research in business communication, participate in workshops, and network.

A Board of Directors and an Executive Committee lead the ABC. The Board of Directors is directly elected with a Vice President elected from each of 8 regions and 12 directors at large, with staggered terms. The executive committee consists of a permanent position of Executive Director and four officers of the Association. The members of the executive committee serve for four years in rotating capacity, beginning as second vice president in the first year, then first vice president the next, president the next, and past president the last year on the committee.

The organization as a whole elects the second vice president position from among candidates on the Board of Directors.The current Executive Director of the ABC is Dr. Betty S. Johnson of (Stephen F. Austin State University). She took office in 2007, succeeding Robert J. Myers of Baruch College in that position. When she took office, the headquarters of the ABC moved with her from New York City to Nacogdoches, Texas where Stephen F. Austin State University is located.

For 2007-2008 the Executive Committee consists of President Dr. Roger Conaway, First Vice President Dr. James Dubinsky (Virginia Tech), Second Vice President, Deborah Valentine (Emory University, Atlanta, Georgia, USA), and Immediate Past President Dr. Jackie Harrison (AUT University, Auckland, New Zealand).

***Journal of Business Communication***

*JBC* was founded in 1963. At the time (and for several decades) it remained the only journal devoted solely to business communication theory. In its own words on the ABC website *JBC* "publishes manuscripts that contribute to knowledge and theory of business communication as a distinct, multifaceted field approached through the administrative disciplines, the liberal arts, and the social sciences."

*JBC* summarizes its research focus as devoted to articles which contribute to knowledge and theory of business communication as a distinct, multifaceted field approached through the administrative disciplines, the liberal arts, and the social sciences. Accordingly, JBC seeks manuscripts that address all areas of business communication including but not limited to business composition/technical writing, information systems, international business communication, management commu-nication, and organizational and corporate communication. In addition, JBC welcomes submissions concerning the role of written, verbal, nonverbal and electronic communi-cation in the creation, maintenance, and performance of profit and not for profit business.

The current editor-in-chief of the *JBC* is Dr. Margaret Baker Graham of Iowa State University. The last several editors-in-chief of *JBC* have been in Iowa State University's English Department, which also devotes office space and resources to *JBC* and to the *Journal of Business and Technical Communication.*

### *Business Communication Quarterly*

*Business Communication Quarterly* was founded in 1937. In its earlier years, *BCQ* was known as the *Bulletin of the ABCA* and later the *Bulletin of the ABC.* It took on its present name in 1994. In its own words on the ABC website, *BCQ* is "devoted to the teaching of business communication, which is a broad, interdisciplinary field.

" *BCQ summarizes the focus of its articles as*:

- Discussions of issues and methods for teaching business communication in a variety of settings: two–year college, technical institute, four-year college, university, corporate or agency training programme, and the like
- Case studies of specific classroom techniques
- Tutorials on business communication processes or products, especially innovations in electronic technology that need to be introduced into the classroom
- Research on classroom teaching or assessment
- Summary reviews of literature on teaching business communication
- Book reviews—reviews of both textbooks and other items of interest to teachers
- Reports on strategies for programme development

The current editor of *BCQ* is Dr. Kathryn Riley of Illinois Institute of Technology.

### Standing Committees, Ad Hoc Committees and Interest Groups

*The ABC has 17 standing committees, as follow*:

1. Association to Advance Collegiate Schools of Business (AACSB) Liaison
2. Business Practices Committee
3. Community College Committee

4. Convention Procedures Committee
5. Diversity Initiative Committee
6. Employment Opportunities Committee
7. Intercultural Communication Committee
8. International Issues Committee
9. Modern Language Association (MLA) Liaison Committee
10. Nominations Committee
11. Publications Board
12. Research Committee
13. Review of the Executive Director Committee
14. Student Competition Committee
15. Teaching Committee 16. Undergraduate Studies Committee
17. Web Board

The ABC has Ad Hoc Committees for interests that have not yet warranted a Standing Committee, but may in the future become so. Many of the Standing Committees began as Ad Hoc Committees. In 2006 has four Ad Hoc Committees:

- Marketing of ABC
- Non-Tenure Track Faculty
- Professional Ethics
- Retired Members

Additionally, ABC members pursue a number of professional objectives through voluntary interest groups. Interest group may be convened by the First Vice President or by members' current interest groups. In 2006, the ABC had the following five Interest Groups:

- MBA Consortium
- Business Practices
- Consultants' Interest Group
- Intercultural Communication
- Rhetoric Special Interest Group

ABC was founded in 1936, beginning with a modest membership of 72 members, all but one from the United States (the only exception being from Canada). The organization, based at the University of Illinois, was then named the "Association of College Teachers of Business Writers." The next year, 1937, that name changed to the "American Business Writing Association."

By the 1960s, the field had grown considerably and became heavily interested in areas well beyond business writing (such as oral presentations, negotiations, and nonverbal communication among others). In 1967, the Board of Directors voted to change the name of the organization to the "American Business Communication Association" to reflect this change.

By the late 1970s, as the membership of the organization grew to include more member from outside the Americas and as the focus of research expanded heavily into the fields of intercultural communication and cross-cultural business communication practice, the term "American" became increasingly inaccurate of both the membership and focus of the organization. In 1985, the Board of Directors voted to change the name to its current "Association for Business Communication."

## International Association of Business Communicators

The International Association of Business Communicators (IABC) is a leading association for business communication professionals. IABC has approximately 16,000 members in more than 100 chapters in 70 countries.

IABC members hold positions in a variety of communication professions, including: public relations, media relations, corporate communications, employee communi-cations, public affairs, investor relations, government relations, marketing communication, community relations, writing, editing, advertising, graphic design, human resources and teaching. IABC's headquarters are located in San Francisco, California, United States. IABC was founded in 1970 from a merger of the American Association of Industrial Editors and the International Council of Industrial Editors. Its initial focus was on internal communication. However, IABC expanded its mission after research showed that members would leave after being promoted into positions with wider public relations responsibilities.

### *Accreditation*

IABC members can seek accreditation as Accredited Business Communicators (post-nominal ABC). Accreditation is offered as an IABC professional development programme. It offers communicators a way of demonstrating their ability to think and plan strategically and to successfully manage those skills essential to effective organizational communi-cation, which could include internal communications, media relations, crisis communications and external relations.

To receive accreditation, applicants must meet education and experience requirements, submit a portfolio that includes work samples with measurable outcomes, and pass both written and oral examinations. Accreditation recognizes communicators who have reached a standard of knowledge and proficiency that is globally accepted among the communication profession.

### *Code of Ethics*

The organization has a code of ethics for those professionals in public relations. The themes of its values are that business communications must be "legal... ethical, and... in good taste". Members are required to follow the IABC Code of Ethics.

However, it has been observed that there is not an enforcement programme in place that can realistically punish breaches of its code.

### *Research Foundation*

Founded in 1982, IABC Research Foundation serves as the research and development arm of the International Association of Business Communicators. The Foundation supports and advances the practice of organizational communication by providing IABC members with research that bridges the divide between communication theory and practice by offering in-depth knowledge and tools that improve organizational communication performance and strengthen the commun-ication profession as a whole.

### **Awards Programs**

Every year, IABC sponsors three levels of communication awards programs for members and nonmembers: Bronze Quill awards, Silver Quill awards, and Gold Quill awards.. Communicators can choose to enter their best professional work produced during the prior year in these Quill communications contests.

The specific divisions and categories for each contest can vary, but typical categories include marketing communi-cations, member/employee communi-cations, media relations, crisis communications, social responsibility, writing, graphic design, publication design, social media, interactive/web design, and photography. Bronze Quill (BQ) awards programs are hosted by local IABC chapters. The respective chapter's board of directors plans and executes a BQ communications contest open to business communicators working with a specific city and/or a small region of a state/province. Silver Quill is sponsored by regional divisions, such as IABC's Heritage and Pacific Plains regions, and are open to communicators in the respective geographic area.

Open to all communicators worldwide, Gold Quill typically receives entries from over 25 countries. The programme aims to cross communication disciplines and reviews entries from professional communicators, ranging from strategists to tacticians. All Gold Quill Awards winners receive international recognition in IABC's magazine, Communication World; are eligible to participate in an awards ceremony at IABC's annual international conference, are mentioned on the IABC website, and are considered for publication in IABC's resource materials. In 2008, the programme attracted over 1,000 entries across 26 categories.

IABC awards programs are open to both members and non-members of the organization. Global Leadership Awards include the Fellow Award and the Chairman's Award. The IABC Fellow designation is the highest honour IABC can bestow on an individual and acknowledges outstanding leadership, professional accomplishment and service to IABC and the communication profession. Criteria for the Fellow Award include contribution to the organizational communication field and profession; career achievement; authorship, speaking and lecturing; contribu-tions to IABC; and other professional recognition such as community activities and other business-related activities. The Chairman's Award recognizes IABC members who have made selfless contributions and worked behind the scenes at the international level to enhance the association's image, facilitate member development and benefit the communication profession.

### Annual Conference and Networking Opportunities

IABC holds a world conference each year. In 2006, the host city was Vancouver, Canada. In 2007, the host city was New Orleans, Louisiana and IABC partnered with Wells Fargo to volunteer and provide financial support to build homes through Habitat for Humanity for the city's hurricane-damaged Ninth Ward.

The 2008 conference was in New York City, and the 2009 event will be held in San Francisco from June 7 to June 10, 2009. Eurocomm 2009 will be held in Lugano, Switzerland February 9 - 10, 2009

IABC's world conference is open to communicators, regardless of membership. As a professional association, IABC offers networking opportunities for students and other people entering the industry. As the United States Department of Labour notes, IABC "provides an opportunity for students to exchange views with public relations specialists and to make professional contacts that may help them find a full-time job in the field."

## THE EVOLUTION OF CORPORATE COMMUNICATIONS

Trying to get a message across to every employee in an organization is a lot like trying to control kids in a school bus: some will listen; some will hear but misunderstand the message; and some will ignore the message altogether and later complain, "But nobody told me."

Communicating to hundreds, sometimes thousands, of employees within an organization is no small feat. This challenge is further complicated in organizations with a global presence, where corporate headquarters is responsible for delivering the same message to satellite offices in geographically dispersed locations. But it's not enough to just create the message.

Effective corporate communication involves not only the message itself, but also the medium that carries and delivers it. It's these two components of a communication that dictate whether employees will receive and understand it. But don't fool yourself in thinking that there's some long process of deliberation when they receive one of these messages. Most corporate communications will grab the attention of an employee for no more than a few seconds — if at all. It's within that very narrow window of opportunity that they will decide whether to read something or toss it aside. Employees are processing more information than ever before — information dealing with their projects, their clients, and their industry as a whole. With all this information competing for employees' attention, does a single corporate communication stand a chance of making it through?

## EFFECTIVE COMMUNICATION

Organizations have struggled to find the best way to get company communications to their employees for years. These communications can range from notices of service interruptions to announcements of corporate events. But is anyone really listening? Communication is a two-way street; it requires a sender and a receiver. If no one is listening, you're just a crazy person talking to yourself.

Anyone involved with corporate communications needs to be aware of their receivers' habits and idiosyncrasies before deciding on message and medium. It wouldn't make sense to use technology-based communications with an audience who's not tech-savvy without first providing them with adequate training; or to post an important announcement on a bulletin board when most users rely solely on their intranet for news. An understanding of the audience will help determine the best medium to use in order to get your message across.

Communication mediums can be classified into two methods: the sender pushes the message to the receiver (e.g., sending an e-mail) or the receiver pulls the message from a source (e.g., reading an intranet post). In the '90s, the IT industry was abuzz with the concept of push technology, a method of delivering content to users' desktop without requiring them to actively seek it out. The technology, however, never lived up to its hype and communications fell back to old stalwarts: the intranet and e-mail. But they have their problems too.

Posting corporate communications on an intranet requires employees to access the system repeatedly because they won't know when new information will be posted. There's a good chance that some employees will miss an important announcement because they were busy with other things and don't get the chance to check when the communication was posted. E-mail has the ability to alert every employee once a communication is sent, but there are uncontrollable factors that hinder its effectiveness as a corporate communications medium. E-mail failed through no fault of its own, and was perhaps a victim of its own success.

### E-Mail

The advent of e-mail changed the way organizations communicated with their employees in a big way. Rather than post and send out large quantities of paper-based announcements, a single e-mail message could be sent to all employees at the same time, regardless of their geographic location. At the time, e-mail was the biggest advancement in corporate communication — until users just stopped reading them. So what happened? Has e-mail outlived its usefulness as an internal corporate communications medium? The answer is yes and no. It's still a big part of corporate communication, but it's lost a lot of its effectiveness. There's perhaps no bigger contributor to this decline than spam. E-mail has been contaminated by so much junk that it's difficult to get an important message across. Users might give a company announcement a cursory glance and pass it by thinking it's just more unsolicited mail; or they might set-up e-mail filters so restrictive that the message never even makes it through. With the sheer volume of e-mail that comes pouring in daily, employees may simply treat these types of internal communications as white noise and ignore them. And with the time-sensitive nature of corporate communications, it might be too late when users finally discover the message.

**RSS, the New E-mail**

Many news Web sites and bloggers are already using RSS feeds to "broadcast" their content. Even marketers and advertisers are realizing the advantages of RSS as a means to attract potential customers. It's an easy, unintrusive way to syndicate frequently changing Web content such as daily blog entries or news headlines.

Momentum is also growing in the corporate environment for RSS. Organizations are beginning to see that RSS can be used to pick up where e-mail left off (or, some would say, failed) as an internal corporate communicator. One of the problems with corporate-wide e-mail announcements is that they can't be categorized. An important announcement concerning network downtime will end up in users' inbox, sandwiched between joke mail and spam. There's no context to e-mail messages short of the subject header, which is not always easily noticeable. RSS, however, offers more communication control on the part of both the sender and the receiver.

Senders can create topical RSS feeds based on different types of corporate communications, and receivers have the choice of which feeds they subscribe to. This ensures that employees only receive content that's relevant to them. It's up to organizations to decide how to best categorize its RSS feeds, but some examples might include:

- *Important announcements*: Crucial, time-sensitive information requiring immediate attention such as scheduled downtimes for IT and facility infrastruc-tures
- *Executive communications*: Messages from manage-ment.
- *Corporate events listings*: Details of special events such as company sponsored fundraisers, family days, and holiday parties.
- *Intranet changes and upgrades*: Announcements of new features and changes to the corporate intranet.
- *Corporate policy changes*: Updates to internal corporate policies such as flex hours, Internet usage and etiquette, and employee benefits.

- *Personnel changes*: Announcements of promotions, departmental transfers, and retirements.

Migrating to RSS is also a relatively simple proposition when compared to other types of IT implementations. It's not necessary to install standalone RSS readers (known as aggregators) throughout the company.

RSS readers are becoming standard features in many e-mail clients and Web browsers, or they can be installed as plug-ins to existing applications that don't already have them. This allows employees to get the benefits of RSS without having to learn a whole new interface.

### Advantages of RSS Over E-mail for Corporate Communication

- RSS separates important internal communications from all the "chatter" that can pollute e-mail: spam, jokes from friends, and newsletter subscriptions.
- RSS doesn't overwhelm users. RSS presents users with a headline and a short synopsis so they can decide if it's worth following the link to the full message stored on the corporate intranet. Many RSS readers will also give users the option of viewing only this summary information or the entire document.
- Unlike corporate-wide e-mail, RSS is completely opt-in. If you're not interested in hearing about the company's special events, you simply don't subscribe to that feed.
- RSS feeds won't be blocked by any filters so the message is sure to get through.
- RSS feeds don't compete with hundreds of e-mail messages for the users' attention. RSS has a singular focus so important announcements will stand out more clearly than an e-mail that's buried in a list of other messages.
- RSS standardizes the formating and display of the internal communications since it's stored on the intranet (Some users don't like to receive HTML-based e-mail so organizations had to develop both a formatted message and a text-only message to cover all its employees).

## PODCASTING AND VODCASTING

Podcasting (audio) and vodcasting (video) are other methods that can be used for corporate communications, although they haven't been widely adopted yet. Contrary to popular misconception, podcasting and vodcasting are not simply multimedia files stored on a server for users to download.

Like RSS, they're based on a subscription model. Users subscribe to podcast and vodcast feeds through similar aggregator software that can be set-up to automatically download new content when it's available. But instead of reading the message, they listen to it or watch it. Podcasting and vodcasting are ideal ways to get messages — especially lengthy messages — across to large corporate audiences since it presents them with a much more convenient (and some would say, more natural) form of communication.

It's far more convenient to listen to an audio podcast of a CEO's quarterly results presentation on a portable media player while going to work than it is to sit at a desk reading through the twenty page equivalent. But there might be an annoyance factor when it comes to using a multimedia approach to corporate communications. Users who decide to listen to podcasts or watch vodcasts at their desks without the use of headphones might irritate their neighbors. What's worse is if several people were to access a podcast or vodcast at the same time, raising the noise pollution and tempers of the office.

## CLOSING THOUGHTS

There's no perfect solution when it comes to corporate communications. You'll never be able to reach every employee all the time because even if the solution is rock solid, there will always be someone who just doesn't bother — regardless of the medium used. It's the responsibility of the organization to inform its employees, and to provide the means by which it gets its communications across easily and efficiently. But as the sender, organizations can only do so much. They can only make sure that it's not the message and the medium that fails the user community. The receiver of the communication also has a part to play. Each individual employee must be receptive to the message when it arrives. This is their responsibility. If they continually disregard corporate communications and claim, "But nobody told me," perhaps the response to that should be, "Why didn't you listen?"

## INTERNAL COMMUNICATIONS STRATEGY

*There are 12 essential elements of a successful internal communications strategy*:

1. *Effective employee-directed communications must be led from the top*: Effective communications require the active commitment and endorsement of senior managers. It is not enough simply to develop a 'vision statement' or formulate in general terms the values by which the company lives. Behaviour is what counts. Managers must be seen to behave in a manner that is consistent with the ethos they are promoting.
2. *The essence of good communications is consistency*: At all costs, avoid following fashion and tinkering. If you try to improve communications and then fail—because your messages are inconsistent or are 'good news only'—things will not quietly settle back into the way they used to be. You will inevitably have created expectations, and may have to live with the consequences of having disappointed those expectations.

3. Successful employee communications owe as much to consistency, careful planning and attention to detail as they do to charisma or natural gifts: We might not all be another Zig Ziglar, Tony Robbins or Bill Clinton. But even such communication 'giants' slip up if they fail to plan, fail to pay attention to detail and fail to project a consistent message.
4. *Communication via the line manager is most effective*:' Line Manager to employee' communication is an opportunity for people to ask questions and check that they have understood the issues correctly. However, be aware that business urgency and reality may dictate the need, on many occasions, to inform employees directly rather than relying entirely on the cascade process. (Though managers will still need to answer people's questions and listen to their views.)
5. *Employee communications are not optional extras, they are part of business as usual and should be planned and budgeted for as such:* An employee communications plan—key themes, targets, objectives and resources—provides a context in which to deliver initiatives that arise at short notice.
6. *There must be integration between internal and external communications:* There must be a fit between what you are telling your people and what you are telling your customers, shareholders and public. (By the same token, there must be a fit between what you are telling your people, and what the external media are telling them.)
7. *Timing is critical*: However clearly expressed and well-presented your message may be, if it arrives at the wrong time you might as well not have bothered. Old news is often worse than no news. Consequently, it is important to ensure that the channels you use can really deliver at the time you need them to.
8. *Tone is important*: Expressing overly-gushing enthusiasm about a technical change of little real significance to your staff or public at large is scarcely calculated to make people take your message to heart. If they don't take that message to heart, why would they take the rest of what you say to their bosoms?
9. *Never lose sight of the 'what's in it for me?' factor*: We are self-interested creatures. I may have invented the most amazing gadget ever, but unless I get you emotionally involved you are never likely to listen to my message about it. But if I can show you how my gadget will revolutionise your life, add dollars to your wallet, free up your time, fix your smelly feet, wash your car for you, stop your kids arguing with you, bring peace with your spouse, bring world peace...
10. *Communication is a two-way process*: Employee communications are NOT a one-way information dump. Capturing feedback is of critical importance, and if you are not seen to be listening and acting on what you are told, why should people bother telling you?

11. *A single key theme or a couple of key themes is a means of giving coherence to a range of diverse employee communications initiatives:* In recent years, the overriding theme of many corporate employee communications has been the impact on the business of competition, regulation and economic forces. Many messages and initiatives can therefore be evaluated according to the light they shed on one or more of these key themes.
12. *Set your standards and stick to them*: Determine which channels should be mandatory and which should be optional; establish quality standards for all channels and review these at least annually.

Whether you are working for a small business, large corporation, or are a student, there are numerous sources that you can turn to for help with writing. Businesses need to be able to effectively communicate with their customers, their employees and their potential customers. Effective verbal communication is equally important, but nonverbal communication in the form of copy writing, article writing, press release writing, and more requires a certain level of expertise and experience.

The typical small business wants to focus their efforts on their core business activities without spending too much time on projects that can easily be outsourced to consultants or freelance professionals. Many small businesses turn to freelancers to help them save time and money.

For example, a certified public accountant opened his own accounting practice after working in another accounting firm for the last ten years. One of the ways he decided to search for new clients was to embark on an advertising and promotional campaign. Although some of his previous clients followed him to his new practice, he wanted to increase the number of accounts he currently handled.

These accounts included various individuals and small businesses from around the town. Rather than hire new employees or handle the projects himself, he decided to hire a consultant through a freelance web site to work on copy writing for a local newspaper ad campaign as well as to help with press releases and company news distribution. By outsourcing these non-core business activities to an independent consultant, he is able to save himself time and money and also gets the expertise of an established professional who specializes in the types of writing that he needs assistance with.

He decides to list his writing projects in a freelance marketplace and receives bids from independent consultants and freelance writers. He was able to choose a service provider based on factors related to cost, the service provider experience, references, and previous feedback from clients.

All small businesses have a decision to make about whether to outsource certain projects or to complete the work in house. Using economics as a deciding factor, it makes sense economically for businesses to outsource writing projects when the projects are non-core business activities that do not contribute to the company bottom line. Small businesses also need to be able to effectively communicate with their current customers. Some of the more effective ways to get help writing effective communication for current customers involve using tools such as newsletters, email lists, and articles written by outsourced consultants. Newsletters are very effective ways to keep customers informed of current events and happenings within the company.

They also offer you the opportunity to gain new clients as the newsletter gets passed around and is often seen by more than one person during its life cycle. It makes sense and is a smart move to outsource corporate communications instead of keeping it in-house. Hiring a separate professional will save your business money and time.

For less than the cost of hiring a full time employee, and because it will contribute to allowing more concentration on the activities that will earn your business money, contracting with a consultant or freelancer for your corporate communications (writing of press releases to distribute company news, getting publicity through pieces in newspapers and magazines, and getting help writing newsletters or articles) simply makes sense. An expert in the field who has amassed many years of experience with business writing, persuasive writing, and copy writing in addition to having experience writing press releases, articles, essays, and possibly academic or technical research and term papers will have a lot to offer you and your business.

Large corporations use writing to effectively communicate on all levels of business. Business writing and corporate communications are essential elements that keep the public informed and give companies their corporate image. A company image, or its publicly perceived notion of credibility and reliability is extremely important to its bottom line. For example, upon its introduction many years ago an American car company introduced a car known as the "Nova".

After some time, it was discovered that the car was not selling well in many Spanish speaking countries. Because in Spanish, "No va" translates to "doesn't go", the car sales in these countries were dismal. Effective corporate communication can have far reaching effect. Ineffective corporate communication can result in lower sales as shown in the car sales example.

Large corporations also need to be effective communi-cators with their current employees. Internal corporate communications are equally important and keep your employees abreast of company accomplishments, events and human resource issues. Finally, students also need to be able to write effectively as well. Writing assignments can include writing essays, writing term papers, report writing, and thesis writing not to mention having to demonstrate writing ability in other subjects outside of English class.

For example, law students need to be able to write not only persuasive but argumentative writing as well. Foreign language students need to be able to translate into their native language and then back again. Science and technology students need to be able to demonstrate scientific writing ability. Taking writing tips from college professors that teach correct formatting and usage, including APA style, and improving your proofreading and editing skills will result in quality writing assignments. For the student that is looking for writing help and homework assistance for their assignments, freelance marketplaces that allow you to hire a consultant or tutor could be a productive and time saving solution. From a freelance or independent consultant's standpoint, marketing writing skills to potential service buyers is important to keeping any consulting business thriving. Registering with freelance marketplaces will enable you to showcase your writing skills, talents and abilities. Previous experience with all kinds of writing ranging from grant writing, fiction writing and interactive writing to writing short stories, articles and ebooks or even technical pieces, in addition to all forms of business writing will enable you to prove your varied background and skills.

All of which can be showcased in your freelance marketplace profile. Creating and managing a profile is important to make you stand out from the crowd of freelance writers competing for new writing projects. All in all, those looking for writing help can find a vast array of resources in the form of consultants who are more than willing to lend a helping hand.

## The Nature of Corporate Communication

This article looks at the way organisations communicate with their employees, drawing parallels with the highly sophisticated means of communication that nature has developed, to see if these can be applied in business. It is argued that few organisations currently communicate effectively and by adopting some of nature's techniques many could get closer to achieving 'corporate homeostasis'.

Ensuring that communication within an organisation is as efficient as possible is the key to its success. Maintaining staff satisfaction and empowering people to feel informed and confident in their work should lead to smoother running, better customer experience and, in turn, increased activity. Therefore it is vital for management to understand how this can be implemented to best effect. Areas for discussion and improvement are identified in this article as: adapting organi-sations to suit the environment, communicating clearly and effectively with staff, making adjustments to find the right balance, knowing the limits of productivity and responding to threats. Focusing on these areas, suggestions are made as to how businesses can adopt specific communication techniques to improve operations.

It is potentially easier for organisations to look at current communication methods in place and compare to examples from nature than to those of competitors. By looking at their fundamental needs and how these are best met through natural means, businesses should avoid the unnecessary complications and complexities that come from the corporate environment.

## Techniques for Effective Corporate Communication

Corporate communication today is the result of phenomenal progress in the electronic technology. Gadgetry such as the mobile phone and the Internet connectivity have harnessed the boon of electronic communication for the employer as well as the employee. The success of corporate workplace communication largely depends on the speed at which important information is disseminated, the accuracy of vocabulary, proper use of business etiquette and that of communication and of course, optimum use of technological development available at hand.

Even though most corporate communication is in-house, among the employees and between associates and affiliates among the executives, effective communication plays a critical role in the response generated. Effective communication skills are developed over a period of time and/or learned extensively at dedicated corporate training workshops and as a part of business management. However, they are expected to be tweaked within the work environment.

Depending on the organizational culture developed and observed within work stations and the business premised at large, communication styles differ. There are many work environs that prefer the informal communication style, while some are strictly formal. This way or that, at grass root level the core components remain the same. At all times and within all preferred communication styles, effective communication skills need to be regularly updated and upgraded because in the modern corporate world there is no scope for stagnancy.

To keep up with the rest of the work force, establish a strong corporate identity and harness the ever-evolving corporate communication techniques, you need to consider applying the paradigm shifts as you adhere to the basic essentials that have stood the test of time. Effective corporate communication helps to address the need to span across physical boundaries and deliver vital information at a click, as a part of the business growth strategy. The technology is a part of every work station today, but are you using it to capacity?

## Techniques for Effective Corporate Communication

### *Timelines*

It is crucial to remember that your business interests and business relationships may be spanning the continents and hence, respecting timelines and calculating deadlines are of utmost importance. You need to devise a technique to try out and confirm to the best communication 'space' that works for you. Always focus on saving time and ensuring timely execution of important strategies and business plans. In order to save time and meet organizational goals amidst the workforce in one physical arena as well as across the globe, you should capitalize on the communication media like efax and internet telephone at hand.

### *Protocol*

Formal, as well as informal work environs demand respect for protocol. It is very important to follow the same when communicating too and ensure that the chosen communication technique or techniques are designed to meet specifications. Irrespective of whether you are personally communicating at a presentation or using some form of communication media, acknowledging seniors within the hierarchy chart over those on lower rungs ensures that you don't rub sore shoulders. If this strategy is applied all the time, you will notice easier follow-through and much more clarity in the delegation and execution of work within the community.

### *Technology*

Make the most of corporate communication mediums available at your disposal to build strong business relationships. You should optimize the use of online publications, Ezines and even automated responses to make your presence felt within the business community. This highly effective corporate communication technique or strategy helps you to literally 'be' at two or more places at the same time! Businesses around the world today, capitalize on the efficiency of electronic communication and internet technology. Don't be left behind.

Techniques for good corporate communication have a number of tangible and intangible benefits including optimized increased revenue, improved customer retention and service and lead examples of corporate leadership to colleagues and new recruits. As you sway between the frustration and by-the-minute exerted stress of responsibilities, focusing on a positive mental attitude and keeping the tried and tested techniques for successful corporate communication in mind helps a lot.

## Communication in Corporate Affairs

Globalization of economy is the basic trend of 21st century. Most of the academic discussions concentrating on corporate communication which is important in the application of marketing techniques in the industry. The relevance of successful and coordinated corporate communication is unquestionable. Theoretically supported corporate communications are effective in the successful business and its effects identified by the leading companies. It is equally important as technology since application of technology need to communicate effectively in the corporate world. With out effective communication corporate relationship will be impossible. Proper communication will enable the business growth in an organization.

Now a days Information Technology and management are the recent trend in the career field. Most of the company is looking for the people who are able to make some changes. Communication skill is an essential element in this new generation job. Also employees should be able to take new challenges and to perform the job responsibility effectively. In this competitive world, employees should be able to understand the situation and to communicate the meaningful information in time.

The purpose of communication management is the accessibility of information flow from top management to bottom. It will be effective only when officials are communi-cating information effectively to all the employees. Thus all parties should be communicate and transfer the necessary information meaningfully and resourcefully. The development of the organization depends on its commun-ication process.

Since each and every business process communication is inevitable. It is an exchange of information and knowledge with the internal groups as well as stakeholders who have direct relationship with the organization, which will enhance the growth of the organization.

Corporate communication is the strong and consistent message which is influencing and motivating its employees and stakeholders and also it aims to attain business development success. If there is any change or business crisis, corporate communication plays a very vital role to handle it effectively. Every body is looking forward how will the change or crisis affect the organization and how it handled by the authorities.

They also have the curiosity to know how a company tackles the situations even after the event is over. In corporate life it is very indispensable; you need to put into words what ever you did. Moreover you need to communicate confidently. Communication is the cornerstone function of every organization to buildup its status in the corporate world as well as its stakeholders. Their work is very concerned with internal communications management from the standpoint of sharing knowledge and decisions from the enterprise with employees, suppliers, investors and partners. Communications is one of the most important link between an organization and the public.

Major companies are considered communication as an effective tool to intensifying its scope and rationalizing its service. They have renewed their communication strategy to expand their branches in various parts of the country. Organization interaction with the community, its stakeholders, staff and other interested groups always channel its progress. Leading organizations have their own communication team with efficient communicators who are responsible for communication function with various national and international organizations.

Each communication department has its own Communi-cators and communications director is the head of the board. They have communication teams and department has its own right. Certain other organizations communications happen in the areas of public involvement, clients and the corporate affairs department. Communication can be a part of someone's job. Time demands are not concerned in the case of important communications.

Communications professional's role is different based on their seniority and designation. It may also depend on whether they are working individually or group based. Usually their role is to make information about their organization which is to be accessed by their staff and public. It also aims to the accountability and their involvement in the reforms that are taking place.

Early management theories assumed bosses should be dominant, paternal, and rational in the use of communication to direct employees' work. The body of knowledge relevant to that managerial philosophy can be reduced to one directive: Give instructions clearly and firmly. From that limited beginning, research and theory progressed to explain the impact organizations have on how people communicate and why communication helps or harms organizations. Many research studies revealed that human relationship empower-ing employee's interest in their work and a positive attitude about themselves and about the organization. This leads to the use of advanced management philosophy.

Employee's involvement in the design and execution of work recognized by the managers and researchers and they emphasized bosses cannot control workers as per human resource approach. There is a cooperative balance between bosses and employees in the Revolutionizing management theory, where the human resources shifted the locus of control. A recent version of this approach reduces organizational excellence and productivity to the axiom "Work smarter, not harder." That approach to management treats employees and organizational processes as being thoughtful.

Corporate Communications is the processes a company uses to communicate all its messages to key constituencies. It encodes and promotes a strong corporate culture, a coherent corporate identity, an appropriate and professional relationship with the media, and quick, responsible ways of communicating in a crisis. It also defines how an organization communicates with its stakeholders and how that brings a company's values to life. Corporate Communications are often defined as the products of communications, memos, letters, reports, Web sites, community engagement, social and environmental initiatives or programs. These make up most importantly an aggregate of messages that a company sends to its constituencies whether internal or external.

It is important to build up an image of a company by demonstrating its integrity and to listen and speak to its stakeholders honestly. This makes corporate social responsibility as a vital component of Corporate Communications, making it as a strategic tool in which a company stand out by creating competitive advantage Interpersonal communication in an organization, realise the fact that the interpersonal communication transpires when people inside a company interact with out side people like products sale and services to customers or clients. All means of communication occurs in large companies, employees routinely communicate interpersonally with one another, for instance by phone or writing, without ever meeting face to face.

A variety of new electronic innovations offer many possibilities for interpersonal contact through mediated channels. "Interpersonal communication," Weick observed, "is the essence of organization because it creates structures that then affect what else gets said and done and by whom" Organizational performances are interactional, contextual, episodic, and improvisational. Interpersonal communication is important for the exchange of information and coordination of activities. Employees' perception of the quality of communication in their organization depends on their interaction with their supervisors, the climate in the company, and appraisal others make of their work performance.

Employees are approaching their immediate head to get job related information which will affect their performance, satisfaction, team work and turn over. They are also seeking information from the top management to extent the scope of their efforts in the outcome especially productivity, commitment, morale, loyalty and trust.

The crisis issues of the company like risk management, environment, social investment and community engagement are forcing companies to become more deliberately engaged through communicators. Communication is the key factor in the creation, implementation, monitoring and reporting on all corporate activities.

Through communication, stakeholders understand company's purpose, goals and values. Communication also aimed to influence employee's attitude toward the workplace loyalty and pride in the company in which they are working. Theoretically speaking, Corporate Communication plays a critical role in building and maintaining relationships with the stakeholders of a corporation. Communication is an unavoidable tool in the corporate sector. Media communi-cations are an essential channel through which all stakeholders receive information and develop perceptions of a company.

*Specific responsibilities of a corporate communicator include*:

- Supervise the status of the organization
- Develop, execute and evaluate communications strategies
- Ensuring effective two-way internal communications
- Taking the lead on media handling, proactively placing good news stories, dealing with enquiries and producing media releases
- Developing links with other departments, which enhances the smooth functioning.
- Planning proactive communications
- Leading public relations, including customer services
- Playing a key role in issue management and planning

- Ensuring that other health organizations are kept fully briefed on developments, plans and any incidents in your organization
- Producing high quality information service
- Advising senior colleagues on strategic communi-cations and related issues
- Engaging in business promotion campaigns

*Typically, the following skills would be necessary for a communications role:*

- Ability to work equally well both on your own and within a team
- Ability to write, speak and brief others clearly
- Ability to assess and select appropriate communi-cations routes for different messages and audiences
- Ability to remain calm under pressure
- Ability to recognize sensitive situations and act appropriately
- Negotiating and influencing skills
- Ability to work well with others at all levels both within and outside your company
- Ability to gain the trust and respect of senior colleagues
- Ability to provide creative input to projects
- Ability to think strategically

Now a days communication professional are facing lot of challenges in the areas of global corporate and brand positioning, internal relations in change situations, corporate identity shaping, and brand management. All communication is based on organizational strategy and the communication professionals are expected to fulfill the objectives of the organization.

Corporate Communication experts are the advocates for an organisations in managing the complex communications that take places between organisations and their external and internal audiences.

These specialist communicators are representing the organisation and make the organisation to aware of public views and attitudes. Other responsibilities of corporate communicators include media contacts, drafting press release,arrange and conduct programmes of internal and external communications. The process of corporate communication includes both theory and practice. It is important to identify the role of communication in corporate relationship for the effective functioning as well as to provide organisational objectives.

Apart from these to create a personal portfolio which portrait the skills across the range of professional communication areas. Other areas like skills in managing and planning projects in the areas of corporate communication is also essential. Enhance the knowledge of corporate communication to an advanced level, developing and presenting plans for corporate communication in a range of different scenarios, including crisis management and the development of corporate brands. Effective communication is closely related to the suceess of the organisation. Through which company's reputation, survival and its success is communicating to the public as well as its own employees and stakeholders. Communication is closely linked to business objectives and strategies. It is essential if organisations are to inform and influence external stakeholders including their customers, and to harness the efforts of all their members towards the successful accomplish-ment of organisational objectives. In conclusion, corporate communications represents the corporation's voice, its reputation, integrity and the images it projects of itself on a global and regional stage populated by its various audiences and stakeholders.

## CORPORATE COMMUNICATION: AN ESSENTIAL TOOL IN AN ORGANIZATION

A company resident reviews a feasibility study for an environment protection project in a small community where the company's headquarters building is located. A personnel manager discusses with union leaders the forthcoming collective bargaining agreement. A marketing manager reviews videos of proposed media campaigns. A group of employees discuss the latest changes in the top management over coffee at the cafeteria.

What do each of these activities share? They all involve corporate communication. Some have this notion that corporate communication is the same as organizational communication. Others think it is a mere "rehash" of public relations. Still there are those who equate it with advertising, company publications, and management information systems.

If corporate communication is not generally well understood, it may be because corporate communication is still evolving. The concept is an offshoot of the growing recognition by top management of communication as a strategic resource in achieving corporate goals and objectives.

As the term implies, corporate communication encompas-ses all the communication activities undertaken within the corporate context, whether formal or informal, regardless of direction or flow of information (i.e. top-down, bottom-up, horizontal). What corporate communication aims to achieve is to integrate the various communication activities within the corporate organization and recognize them as key management functions.

It seeks to upgrade public relations. It seeks to upgrade public relations, organizational communication, and advertising into the level of scientific discipline quite removed from the level of gut feel. As the International Management Magazine noted, corporate communication-related activities a common direction or framework. The growth of corporate communication can be attributed to the trend among progressive companies to appoint a communication man to top managerial positions (and even in the executive board). Corporate Executive Officers (CEOs) are beginning to realise that the success or failure of corporate strategies depends on how communication resources are harnessed.

## COMMUNICATION: THE NERVOUS SYSTEM OF ORGANIZATIONS

A review of definitions of the term organization indicates how critical communication is the very existence of an organization. Koontz and O'Donnel define organization as a communication decision-making network. Peter Drucker states, "The organization is above all, an information decision-making system." Communication is not a secondary or derived aspect of an organization, but rather the essence of organized activity and is the basic process out of which all functions derive. It is quite clear then that communication links the various parts of an organization; it is the principal tool of managers. Through communication, the manager receives the information needed in making the right decision, and once the decision is made, manager must communicate it to others. Perhaps you often hear managers saying, "Our problem is communication."

Indeed, many managers use communi-cation as an excuse if they are not able to achieve their goal or objective. While it is true that communication as an excuse if they are not able to achieve their goal or objective. While it is true that communication is a vital skill of managers, it would be wrong to conclude that an effective communicator alone makes a good manager. An effective communication for a wrong decision will not do any good to the company. Conversely, for a manager to be an effective planner and decision-maker is not enough. A good decision (or action plan) must be translated into action.

# 21

# Brand Extension

Brand extension or brand stretching is a marketing strategy in which a firm marketing a product with a well-developed image uses the same brand name in a different product category. The new product is called a spin-off. Organizations use this strategy to increase and leverage brand equity (definition: the net worth and long-term sustainability just from the renowned name). An example of a brand extension is Jello-gelatin creating Jello pudding pops.

It increases awareness of the brand name and increases profitability from offerings in more than one product category. A brand's "extendibility" depends on how strong consumer's associations are to the brand's values and goals. Ralph Lauren's Polo brand successfully extended from clothing to home furnishings such as bedding and towels. Both clothing and bedding are made of linen and fulfill a similar consumer function of comfort and hominess. Arm & Hammer leveraged its brand equity from basic baking soda into the oral care and laundry care categories.

By emphasizing its key attributes, the cleaning and deodorizing properties of its core product, Arm & Hammer was able to leverage those attributes into new categories with success. Another example is Virgin Group, which was initially a record label that has extended its brand successfully many times; from transportation (aeroplanes, trains) to games stores and video stores such a Virgin Megastores.

In 1990s, 81% of new products used brand extension to introduce new brands and to create sales. Launching a new product, is not only time consuming but also needs a big budget to create awareness and to promote a product's benefits. Brand extension is one of the new product development strategies which can reduce financial risk by using the parent brand name to enhance consumers' perception due to the core brand equity.

While there can be significant benefits in brand extension strategies, there can also be significant risks, resulting in a diluted or severely damaged brand image. Poor choices for brand extension may dilute and deteriorate the core brand and damage the brand equity. Most of the literature focuses on the consumer evaluation and positive impact on parent brand. In practical cases, the failures of brand extension are at higher rate than the successes. Some studies show that negative impact may dilute brand image and equity. In spite of the positive impact of brand extension, negative association and wrong communication strategy do harm to the parent brand even brand family.

Product extensions are versions of the same parent product that serve a segment of the target market and increase the variety of an offering. An example of a product extension is Coke vs. Diet Coke in same product category of soft drinks. This tactic is undertaken due to the brand loyalty and brand awareness they enjoy consumers are more likely to buy a new product that has a tried and trusted brand name on it. This means the market is catered for as they are receiving a product from a brand they trust and Coca Cola is catered for as they can increase their product portfolio and they have a larger hold over the market in which they are performing in.

## TYPES OF PRODUCT EXTENSION

Brand extension research mainly focuses on the consumer evaluation of extension and attitude of the parent brand. Following the Aaker and Keller's model, they provide a sufficient depth and breadth proposition to examine consumer behaviour and conceptual framework. They use three dimensions to measure the fit of extension. First of all, the "Complement" is that consumer takes two product (extension and parent brand product) classes as complement to satisfy their specific needs. Secondly, the "Substitute" indicates two products have same user situation and satisfy their same needs which means the products class is very similar so that can replace each other. At last, the "Transfer" is the relationship between extension product and manufacturer which "reflects the perceived ability of any firm operating in the first product class to make a product in the second class". The first two measures focus on the consumer's demand and the last one focuses on firm's ability.

From the line extension to brand extension, however, there are many different way of extension such as "brand alliance", co-branding or "brand franchise extension".Tauber suggests seven strategies to identify extension cases such as product with parent brand's benefit, same product with different price or quality, etc. In his suggestion, it can be classified into two category of extension; extension of product-related association and non-product related association. Another form of brand extension, is a licensed brand extension. Where the brand-owner partners (sometimes with a competitor) who takes on the responsibility of manufacturer and sales of the new products, paying a royalty every time a product is sold.

## CATEGORISATION THEORY

Researchers tend to use "categorisation theory" as their fundamental theory to explore the links about the brand extension. When consumers face thousands of products, they not only are initially confused and disorderly in mind, but also try to categorise the brand association or image with their existing memory. When two or more products exit in front of consumers, they might reposition memories to frame a brand image and concept toward new introduction. A consumer can judge or evaluate the extension by their category memory. They categorise new information into specific brand or product class label and store it. This process is not only related to consumer's experience and knowledge, but also involvement and choice of brand. If the brand association is highly related to extension, consumer can perceive the fit among brand extension. Some studies suggest that consumer may ignore or overcome the dissonance from extension especially flagship product which means the low perceived of fit does not dilute the flagship's equity.

## BRAND EXTENSION FAILURE

Literature related to negative effect of brand extension is limited and the findings are revealed as incongruent. The early works of Aaker and Keller find no significant evidence that brand name can be diluted by unsuccessful brand extensions. Conversely, Loken and Roedder-John indicate that dilution effect do occur when the extension across inconsistency of product category and brand beliefs. The failure of extension may come from difficulty of connecting with parent brand, a lack of similarity and familiarity and inconsistent IMC messages.

"Equity of an integrated oriented brand can be diluted significantly from both functional and non-functional attributes-base variables", which means dilution does occur across the brand extension to the parent brand. These failures of extension make consumers create a negative or new association relate to parent brand even brand family or to disturb and confuse the original brand identity and meaning.

In addition, Martinez and de Chernatony classify the brand image in two types: the general brand image and the product brand image. They suggest that if the brand name is strong enough as Nike or Sony, the negative impact has no specific damage on general brand image and "the dilution effect is greater on product brand image than on general brand image". In consequence, consumer may maintain their belief about the attributes and feelings from parent brand. On the other hand, their study shows that "brand extension dilutes the brand image, changing the beliefs and association in consumers' mind".

The flagship product is a money-spinner to a firm. Marketer spends budget and time to create maximum exposure and awareness for the product. Theoretically speaking, flagship product is usually had the top sales and highest awareness in its product category. In spite of Aaker and Keller's research reported that the prestige brand do no harm from failure of extension. Evidence shows that the dilution effect has great and instant damage to the flagship product and brand family. But in some findings, even overall parent belief is diluted; the flagship product would not be harmed. In addition, brand extension is also "diminish consumer's feelings and beliefs about brand name." To establish a strong brand, it is necessary to build up a "brand ladder".

Marketers may go behind the order and model created by Aaker and Keller which they are authorities on brand management. But branding does not always follow a rational line. One mistake can damage all brand equity. A classic extension failure example would be Coca Cola launching "New Coke" in 1985. Although initially accepted a backlash against "New Coke" soon emerged among consumers. Not only did Coca Cola not succeed in developing a new brand but sales of the original flavour also decreased. Coca Cola were had to make considerable efforts to regain customers who had turned to Pepsi cola.

Although there are few works about the failure of extensions, literature still provides sufficient in depth research around this issue. Studies also suggest that brand extension is a risky strategy to increase sales or brand equity. It should consider the damage of parent brand no matter what types of extension are used. Example. BIC Pens tried to produce BIC pantyhose.

## BRAND EQUITY

Brand equity is defined as the main concern in brand management and IMC campaign. Every marketer should pursue the long term equity and pay attention to every strategy in detail. Because a small message dissonance would cause great failure of brand extension. On the other hand, consumer has his psychology process in mind.

The moderating variable is a useful indication to evaluate consumer evaluation of brand extension. Throughout the categorisation theory and associative network theory, consumer does have the ability to process information into useful knowledge for them. They would measure and compares the difference between core brand and extension product through quality of core brand, fit in category, former experience and knowledge, and difficulty of making.

Consequently, in this article may conclude some points about consumer evaluation of brand extension:

- Quality of core brand creates a strong position for brand and low the impact of fit in consumer evaluation.
- Similarity between core brand and extension is the main concern of consumer perception of fit. The higher the similarity is the higher perception of fit.
- Consumer's knowledge and experience affect the evaluation before extension product trail.
- The more innovation of extension product is, the greater positive fit can perceive.

A successful brand message strategy relies on a congruent communication and a clear brand image. The negative impact of brand extension would cause a great damage to parent brand and brand family. From a manager and marketer's perspective, an operation of branding should maintain brand messages and associations within a consistency and continuum in the long way. Because the effects of negative impact from brand extension are tremendous and permanently. Every messages or brand extension can dilute the brand in nature.

## BRAND IMPLEMENTATION

Brand implementation refers to the physical application of brand identity across visual identity carriers. This can include signage, uniforms, liveries and branded merchandise. Brand implementation encompasses facets of architecture, product design, industrial design, quantity surveying, engineering, procurement, project management and retail design.

Brand implementation emerged as a discipline in the 1990s when brand owners recognized the need for consistency across branded estates. Traditionally, brand implementation was handled by various parties, including shop-fitters, interior designers and sign companies. Lack of centralized project management led to inconsistencies, while information dissymmetry meant suppliers had too much control over brand issues. Brand implementation was thus coined as an umbrella term for all aspects of the application and maintenance of physical brand assets.

### Today

Brand implementation is now a critical discipline focused on binding the relationship between the target audience and the brand. This allows brand implementation firms to identify the best possible manufacturing solution for each project.

### Magic and Logic

Brand implementation does not involve the design or creation of brand identity. Instead, brand implementation agencies work closely with branding agencies to ensure that the latter's work is applied accurately and consistently. This relationship is referred to as Magic and Logic (RTM of Marketing Supply Chain International). Branding agencies look after the Magic (creative) and brand implementation agencies look after the Logic (implementation).

## BRAND LOYALTY

Brand loyalty, in marketing, consists of a consumer's commitment to repurchase or otherwise continue using the brand and can be demonstrated by repeated buying of a product or service or other positive behaviors such as word of mouth advocacy.

Brand loyalty is more than simple repurchasing, however. Customers may repurchase a brand due to situational constraints (such as vendor lock-in), a lack of viable alternatives, or out of convenience. Such loyalty is referred to as "spurious loyalty". True brand loyalty exists when customers have a high relative attitude toward the brand which is then exhibited through repurchase behaviour. This type of loyalty can be a great asset to the firm: customers are willing to pay higher prices, they may cost less to serve, and can bring new customers to the firm. For example, if Joe has brand loyalty to Company A he will purchase Company A's products even if Company B's are cheaper and/or of a higher quality.

An example of a major brand loyalty programme that extended for several years and spread worldwide is Pepsi Stuff. Perhaps the most significant contemporary example of brand loyalty is the dedication that many Mac users show to the Apple company and its products. From the point of view of many marketers, loyalty to the brand — in terms of consumer usage — is a key factor.

**Usage Rate**

Most important of all, in this context, is usually the 'rate' of usage, to which the Pareto 80-20 Rule applies. Kotler's 'heavy users' are likely to be disproportionately important to the brand (typically, 20 per cent of users accounting for 80 per cent of usage — and of suppliers' profit).

As a result, suppliers often segment their customers into 'heavy', 'medium' and 'light' users; as far as they can, they target 'heavy users'.

**Loyalty**

A second dimension, however, is whether the customer is committed to the brand.

*Philip Kotler, again, defines four patterns of behaviour:*

- *Hardcore loyals*: Who buy the brand all the time.
- *Softcore loyals*: Loyal to two or three brands.
- *Shifting loyalty*: Moving from one brand to another.
- Switchers: With no loyalty (possibly 'deal-prone', constantly looking for bargains or 'vanity prone', looking for something different).

***Factors Influencing Brand Loyalty***

It has been suggested that loyalty includes some degree of pre-dispositional commitment toward a brand. Brand loyalty is viewed as multidimensional construct. It is determined by several distinct psychological processes and it entails multivariate measurements. Customers' perceived value, brand trust, customers' satisfaction, repeat purchase behaviour, and commitment are found to be the key influencing factors of brand loyalty. Commitment and repeated purchase behaviour are considered as necessary conditions for brand loyalty followed by perceived value, satisfaction, and brand trust. Fred Reichheld, one of the most influential writers on brand loyalty, claimed that enhancing customer loyalty could have dramatic effects on profitability.

Among the benefits from brand loyalty — specifically, longer tenure or staying as a customer for longer — was said to be lower sensitivity to price. This claim had not been empirically tested until recently. Recent research found evidence that longer-term customers were indeed less sensitive to price increases.

**Industrial Markets**

In industrial markets, organizations regard the 'heavy users' as 'major accounts' to be handled by senior sales personnel and even managers; whereas the 'light users' may be handled by the general salesforce or by a dealer.

**Portfolios of Brands**

Andrew Ehrenberg, then of the London Business School said that consumers buy 'portfolios of brands'. They switch regularly between brands, often because they simply want a change.

Thus, 'brand penetration' or 'brand share' reflects only a statistical chance that the majority of customers will buy that brand next time as part of a portfolio of brands they favour. It does not guarantee that they will stay loyal.

Influencing the statistical probabilities facing a consumer choosing from a portfolio of preferred brands, which is required in this context, is a very different role for a brand manager; compared with the — much simpler — one traditionally described of recruiting and holding dedicated customers. The concept also emphasises the need for managing continuity.

**Market Inertia**

One of the most prominent features of many markets is their overall stability — or inertia. Thus, in their essential characteristics they change very slowly, often over decades — sometimes centuries — rather than over months. This stability has two very important implications. The first is that those who are clear brand leaders are especially well placed in relation to their competitors and should want to further the inertia which lies behind that stable position.

This, however, still demands a continuing pattern of minor changes to keep up with the marginal changes in consumer taste (which may be minor to the theorist but will still be crucial in terms of those consumers' purchasing patterns as markets do not favour the over-complacent). These minor investments are a small price to pay for the long term profits which brand leaders usually enjoy. The second, and more important, is that someone who wishes to overturn this stability and change the market (or significantly change one's position in it), massive investments must be expected to be made in order to succeed. Even though stability is the natural state of markets, sudden changes can still occur, and the environment must be constantly scanned for signs of these.

## EXAMPLES OF BRAND LOYALTY PROMOTIONS

### My Coke Rewards

My Coke Rewards is a customer loyalty marketing campaign for the Coca-Cola soft drink. Customers enter codes found on specially marked packages of Coca-Cola products on a website. Codes can also be entered "on the go" by texting them from a cell phone.

These codes are converted into virtual "points" which can in turn be redeemed by members for various prizes or sweepstakes entries. The programme was first launched in 2006. By November of that year, more than one million prizes had been redeemed. The programme has since been extended every year for the past four years with the current extension announced on November 6th, 2009 until 2010.

### Limitations

The programme has always featured limits on the number of codes and points that could be redeemed at one time. Prior to February 17, 2009, members were limited to entering 10 codes per day, regardless of the number of points that this represented. Members who entered 10 codes from 24-can packages could, under this system, earn a total of 200 points per day, or 1400 per week. This represented that maximum rate at which points could be accrued without the use of bonus points and similar promotions.

On February 17, 2009, this system was changed. Members are now limited to entering 120 points per week, regardless of the number of codes redeemed per week. Bonus points and promotional offers such as "Double Points Days" are still not subject to this weekly limit. My Coke Rewards now has a meter that tells the member how many points they earned during the current week, and whether they have reached the 120 point-per-week limit. Attempts to enter codes that exceed the limit (for example, entering 10-point code once you have accumulated 119 points) do not cause overflow; the participant is told to "hold on to that code".

In addition, MyCokeRewards features an expiration date of codes that are entered. Currently, points expire after 90 days of user account inactivity, meaning a customer must either add points to their account or claim a prize within 90 days to ensure their points do not expire.

### Code Reuse

There are two types of codes: single-use and multi-use codes. Single-use codes like those found on Coke products contain a mix of letters and numbers. These codes can only be used once; if they have been entered in any account they will not work again. By contrast, multi-use codes are identified by being all numeric and may be entered by multiple users. Thus far the multi-use codes have all started with the digits 10008. They have been distributed through email, including during the 2006 Christmas holiday season, as well as through direct mail and print advertising campaigns in various magazines and other publications. Both Blockbuster and Disney (with Pirates of the Caribbean) have participated in such special promotions.

**Controversy**

The programme is one of several marketing campaigns that have come under fire from the Centre for Digital Democracy, an advocacy group interested in regulating how food products are marketed to children.

Coca-Cola's online marketing techniques are included in a 98-page report issued in May 2007 by the centre and the American University called "Interactive Food & Beverage Marketing: Targeting Children and Youth" which criticizes the programme for collecting personal information from children and for promoting obesity.

Childhood obesity was also a concern for weight-loss instructor Julia Griggs Havey who sued Coca-Cola over the programme in 2006, but dropped her lawsuit a few weeks later. The lawsuit was dropped for the specific reason of it being frivolous, since there was a misinterpretation as to what was required of a user in order to accumulate Coke points and obtain the currently available reward prizes.

The first assumption—that those who have Coke codes must purchase the product in order to redeem them—was shown to be untrue, as Coke stated they took into consideration that users may obtain codes from others. Second, it was pointed out that the CocaCola Company has other products besides Coca-Cola, including Powerade and Dasani water that are available for those who do not wish to consume high amounts of high fructose corn syrup or caffeine.

Some customers have further accused Coca-Cola of utilizing "bait-and-switch" tactics in the programme. They claim that the prizes for which they had been saving are either constantly out of stock or are no longer available. Some items have experienced steep unexpected price increases, as well; for example the coupons for a free 20 ounce bottle of Coke increased 25% (from 24 points to 30), a $75 Blockbuster gift card which used to cost 722 points went up to 1020 points (a 41% increase), and the price of a GPX docking station went up from 975 points to 1820 (an 87% increase).

These increases, it should be noted, took place at the same time as Coca-Cola was taking drastic measures to decrease the number of points awarded (through its February 2009 rule changes which reduced the maximum number of points from 1400 per week to 120 per week). For its part, Coca Cola has maintained that all prizes in the My Point Rewards programme are available "while supplies last," and that there is no guarantee expressed or intended that a given prize will either continue to be offered or continue to be offered at the same price. Some prizes are advertised as "free."

For example, you may redeem points for a "free 20 oz. sparkling product." What you receive is a manufacturers coupon. These coupons are not accepted at all retailers who sell Coca-Cola products, which can be frustrating to customers. Also, when you find a retailer who does accept the coupons, you are responsible for sales tax on the retail price of the product plus any state container deposits.

In California, for example, redeeming a "free" coupon for a 20 oz. beverage will cost the consumer $.20. Ounce-for-ounce, that is only slightly less than paying full retail for bulk packaging of the same product.

**Pepsi Stuff**

Pepsi Stuff refers to a promotion launched by PepsiCo, first in North America and then around the world, in the 1990s and continuing into the 2000s featuring merchandise that could be purchased with Pepsi Points. Customers can acquire points from specially marked Pepsi packages and fountain cups. Additional points have been sold both by Pepsi and by consumers, the latter mainly enabled by eBay.

***1990s Campaigns***

Points were distributed on billions of packages and cups and millions of consumers participated. According to some sources, the first Pepsi Stuff campaign significantly outperformed The Coca-Cola Company's much-anticipated Atlanta Olympics Summer with growth 3 times larger than Coca-Cola's and 2 points of share gained by Pepsi.

Pepsi Stuff continued to run throughout North America due to consumer and bottler demand, and was eventually expanded to include Mountain Dew and other drinks, and into many international markets. In response to the campaign, The Coca-Cola Company accelerated and extended its discount pricing programs.

Pepsi Stuff was one of the first major consumer promotions to feature a dedicated interactive Web site. Celebrities like Andre Agassi, David Beckham, Beyoncé, Cindy Crawford, Jimmy Fallon, Jeff Gordon, Derek Jeter, John Lee Hooker, Shaquille O'Neal, Deion Sanders, Shakira, Britney Spears, and the Spice Girls appeared in TV, print, and Internet advertising promoting Pepsi Stuff. PepsiCo produced over 200 million catalogs each year, billions of Pepsi points, and an extensive line of free merchandise.

***2000s Campaigns***

In the years after the initial Pepsi Stuff promotion, both Pepsi and Coca-

Cola have introduced other promotions in a similar vein to the original campaign. Some promotions involved a variety of merchandise, while others involved specific products, such as Cash or MP3s.

Permanent merchandise campaigns began in 2005 when The Coca-Cola Company launched iCoke, a very similar programme in which consumers collect points printed on packages, in Canada, with its introduction in the United States in 2006 as "My Coke Rewards."

Also in 2006, Pepsi introduced Pepsi Access in Canada to compete with iCoke, although that campaign ended in 2007. In 2008, Pepsi relaunched the programme, this time in partnership with Amazon MP3 and with a dedicated website that provides a "shopping" experience modeled on the Amazon website. Amazon's partnership follows to Amazon's actual website, where the option to pay for certain designated items with Pepsi Points instead of traditional payment methods, is available. Pepsi is once again relying on celebrities to advertise the promotion, including a Super Bowl spot starring Justin Timberlake and featuring Andy Samberg from Saturday Night Live.

Different product have codes worth different point values; single bottles generally have one point while can 12-packs have two and 24-packs have four. Codes from Pepsi NFL Kickoff 12-packs are worth four points. Items available for redemption through the promotion range in value from 5 points (MP3 song download) to 175 points (Vintage Pepsi logo hoodie sweatshirt). Customers can also redeem points for entry in various sweepstakes.

## BRAND ORIENTATION

Brand orientation is a deliberate approach to working with brands, both internally and externally. The most important driving force behind this increased interest in strong brands is the accelerating pace of globalization. This has resulted in an ever-tougher competitive situation on many markets. A product's superiority is in itself no longer sufficient to guarantee its success. The fast pace of technological development and the increased speed with which imitations turn up on the market have dramatically shortened product lifecycles. The consequence is that product-related competitive advantages soon risk being transformed into competitive prerequisites. For this reason, increasing numbers of companies are looking for other, more enduring, competitive tools – such as brands. Brand orientation refers to "the degree to which the organization values brands and its practices are oriented towards building brand capabilities".

## BRAND MANAGEMENT

Brand management is the application of marketing techniques to a specific product, product line, or brand. It seeks to increase the product's perceived value to the customer and thereby increase brand franchise and brand equity. Marketers see a brand as an implied promise that the level of quality people have come to expect from a brand will continue with future purchases of the same product. This may increase sales by making a comparison with competing products more favorable. It may also enable the manufacturer to charge more for the product. The value of the brand is determined by the amount of profit it generates for the manufacturer. This can result from a combination of increased sales and increased price, and/or reduced COGS (cost of goods sold), and/or reduced or more efficient marketing investment.

All of these enhancements may improve the profitability of a brand, and thus, "Brand Managers" often carry *line-management* accountability for a brand's P&L (Profit and Loss) profitability, in contrast to marketing *staff* manager roles, which are allocated budgets from above, to manage and execute. In this regard, Brand Management is often viewed in organizations as a broader and more strategic role than Marketing alone.

The annual list of the world's most valuable brands, published by Interbrand and *Business Week*, indicates that the market value of companies often consists largely of brand equity. Research by McKinsey & Company, a global consulting firm, in 2000 suggested that strong, well-leveraged brands produce higher returns to shareholders than weaker, narrower brands. Taken together, this means that brands seriously impact shareholder value, which ultimately makes branding a CEO responsibility. The discipline of brand management was started at Procter & Gamble PLC as a result of a famous memo by Neil H. McElroy.

### *Principles*

*A good brand name should*:

- Be protected (or at least protectable) under trademark law.
- Be easy to pronounce.
- Be easy to remember.
- Be easy to recognize.
- Be easy to translate into all languages in the markets where the brand will be used.
- Attract attention.
- Suggest product benefits (e.g.: Easy-Off) or suggest usage (note the tradeoff with strong trademark protection.)
- Suggest the company or product image.
- Distinguish the product's positioning relative to the competition.
- Be attractive.
- Stand out among a group of other brands.

### *Types of Brands*

A number of different types of brands are recognized. A "premium brand" typically costs more than other products in the same category. These are sometimes referred to as 'top-shelf' products. An "economy brand" is a brand targeted to a high price elasticity market segment. They generally position themselves as offering all the same benefits as a premium product, for an 'economic' price.

A "fighting brand" is a brand created specifically to counter a competitive threat. When a company's name is used as a product brand name, this is referred to as corporate branding. When one brand name is used for several related products, this is referred to as family branding. When all a company's products are given different brand names, this is referred to as individual branding. When a company uses the brand equity associated with an existing brand name to introduce a new product or product line, this is referred to as "brand extension." When large retailers buy products in bulk from manufacturers and put their own brand name on them, this is called private branding, store brand, white labelling, private label or own brand (UK). Private brands can be differentiated from "manufacturers' brands" (also referred to as "national brands"). When different brands work together to market their products, this is referred to as "co-branding". When a company sells the rights to use a brand name to another company for use on a non-competing product or in another geographical area, this is referred to as "brand licensing."

An "employment brand" is created when a company wants to build awareness with potential candidates. Earlier it was not existing but now we see commodities being branded, this is called commodity branding.

## Brand awareness

### *Functions of Brand*

For Consumers Identification of source of product, Assignment of responsibility to product maker, Risk reducer, Search cost reducer, Symbolic device, Signal of quality. For Manufacture Means of identification to simplify handling or tracing, Means of legally protecting unique features, Signal of quality level to satisfied customers, Means of endowing products with unique associations, Source of competitive advantage, Source of financial returns.

### *Brand Architecture*

The different brands owned by a company are related to each other via brand architecture. In "product brand architecture", the company supports many different product brands with each having its own name and style of expression while the company itself remains invisible to consumers. Procter & Gamble, considered by many to have created product branding, is a choice example with its many unrelated consumer brands such as Tide, Pampers, Abunda, Ivory and Pantene.

With "endorsed brand architecture", a mother brand is tied to product brands, such as The Courtyard Hotels (product brand name) by

Marriott (mother brand name). Endorsed brands benefit from the standing of their mother brand and thus save a company some marketing expense by virtue promoting all the linked brands whenever the mother brand is advertised.

The third model of brand architecture is most commonly referred to as "corporate branding". The mother brand is used and all products carry this name and all advertising speaks with the same voice. A good example of this brand architecture is the UK-based conglomerate Virgin. Virgin brands all its businesses with its name

**Techniques**

Companies sometimes want to reduce the number of brands that they market. This process is known as "Brand rationalization." Some companies tend to create more brands and product variations within a brand than economies of scale would indicate. Sometimes, they will create a specific service or product brand for each market that they target.

In the case of product branding, this may be to gain retail shelf space (and reduce the amount of shelf space allocated to competing brands). A company may decide to rationalize their portfolio of brands from time to time to gain production and marketing efficiency, or to rationalize a brand portfolio as part of corporate restructuring.

A recurring challenge for brand managers is to build a consistent brand while keeping its message fresh and relevant. An older brand identity may be misaligned to a redefined target market, a restated corporate vision statement, revisited mission statement or values of a company.

Brand identities may also lose resonance with their target market through demographic evolution. Repositioning a brand (sometimes called rebranding), may cost some brand equity, and can confuse the target market, but ideally, a brand can be repositioned while retaining existing brand equity for leverage. Brand orientation is a deliberate approach to working with brands, both internally and externally.

The most important driving force behind this increased interest in strong brands is the accelerating pace of globalization. This has resulted in an ever-tougher competitive situation on many markets. A product's superiority is in itself no longer sufficient to guarantee its success. The fast pace of technological development and the increased speed with which imitations turn up on the market have dramatically shortened product lifecycles. The consequence is that product-related competitive advantages soon risk being transformed into competitive prerequisites.

For this reason, increasing numbers of companies are looking for other, more enduring, competitive tools – such as brands. Brand Orientation refers to "the degree to which the organization values brands and its practices are oriented towards building brand capabilities".

## Challenges

There are several challenges associated with setting objectives for a brand or product category.

- Brand managers sometimes limit themselves to setting financial and market performance objectives. They may not question strategic objectives if they feel this is the responsibility of senior management.
- Most product level or brand managers limit themselves to setting short-term objectives because their compensation packages are designed to reward short-term behaviour. Short-term objectives should be seen as milestones towards long-term objectives.
- Often product level managers are not given enough information to construct strategic objectives.
- It is sometimes difficult to translate corporate level objectives into brand- or product-level objectives. Changes in shareholders' equity are easy for a company to calculate. It is not so easy to calculate the change in shareholders' equity that can be attributed to a product or category. More complex metrics like changes in the net present value of shareholders' equity are even more difficult for the product manager to assess.
- In a diversified company, the objectives of some brands may conflict with those of other brands. Or worse, corporate objectives may conflict with the specific needs of your brand. This is particularly true in regard to the trade-off between stability and riskiness. Corporate objectives must be broad enough that brands with high-risk products are not constrained by objectives set with cash cows in mind. The brand manager also needs to know senior management's harvesting strategy. If corporate management intends to invest in brand equity and take a long-term position in the market (i.e. penetration and growth strategy), it would be a mistake for the product manager to use short-term cash flow objectives (ie. price skimming strategy). Only when these conflicts and tradeoffs are made explicit, is it possible for all levels of objectives to fit together in a coherent and mutually supportive manner.
- Brand managers sometimes set objectives that optimize the performance of their unit rather than optimize overall corporate performance. This is particularly true where compensation is based primarily on unit performance. Managers tend to ignore potential synergies and inter-unit joint processes.
- Overall organisation alignment behind the brand to achieve Integrated Marketing is complex.
- Brands are sometimes criticized within social media web sites and this must be monitored and managed (if possible)

### Online Brand Management

Companies are embracing brand reputation management as a strategic imperative and are increasingly turning to online monitoring in their efforts to prevent their public image from becoming tarnished. Online brand reputation protection can mean monitoring for the misappropriation of a brand trademark by fraudsters intent on confusing consumers for monetary gain.

It can also mean monitoring for less malicious, although perhaps equally damaging, infractions, such as the unauthorized use of a brand logo or even for negative brand information (and misinformation) from online consumers that appears in online communities and other social media platforms. The red flag can be something as benign as a blog rant about a bad hotel experience or an electronic gadget that functions below expectations.

## DIGITAL BRAND ENGAGEMENT

Due to the way the Internet is fast evolving, especially through the social web and social media, there is now a plethora of digital channels which can be used to hold a dialogue between a Brand and a Consumer, or groups of consumers. Digital brand engagement is brand engagement with a key focus on communication via the web.

The Cluetrain Manifesto written by four visionaries in 1999 (which is now a very long time ago) predicted the Internet would evolve to a point where the consumer holds the "power" and no longer could the corporate world continue to communicate to their markets (the people they wish to interact with) in a push marketing or broadcast manner.

How right they were. The Internet has evolved and people/consumers can now be very selective about which brands they choose to interact with; and have the ability to communicate their thoughts and feelings globally.

Such mediums on the social web including blogs, micro-blogs, forums, social networks, groups within social networks, bookmarking sites, imagery and video sites can all be utilised by consumers; and they are doing just this in their thousands. Brands can take notice of what is being said about them, their product or service by monitoring conversations taking place outside of their own website, through "buzz monitoring" tools and there are a number of tools to chose from. The value of the information provided is proportional to the time and expertise dedicated to configuring and analysing the data provided.

This value can be increased further when the buzz monitoring data is correlated with onsite web analytics data. It's important to listen and observe the buzz, and analyse its impact prior to engaging. The key elements to consider when listening and observing, before formulating a digital engagement strategy, are:

*People/Consumer*:
- Who are they?
- What are their values?
- What motivates them?
- How do they behave?

*Location*:
- Where are they?
- Are they just an Observer?
- Are they a Participant?
- Or are they Active Contributor?

*Influence*:
- Reach of conversation?
- Authority of dialogue and site?
- Volume and amount of buzz?
- Sentiment - (positive, negative, neutral)?
- Brand Association
- Are they inquisitive and looking for info?
- Are they about to commit to the Brand?
- Are they loyal brand advocates?
- Are they brand opponents?

Once you have an overview of what the current brand/consumer situation is online, you are far better informed to create an engagement strategy. The information above will provide a "Factual" position as it is based upon what people are actually doing and saying. There is another level of research that can be carried out which adds a "Predictive" element. i.e. undertake some consumer testing prior to implementing and engagement approach.

Typically, and traditionally this is carried out in a conscious level manner of research, such as focus groups, surveys and interviews. However, it is becoming recognised that conscious level research on its own can be flawed, as it is based upon the assumption that people are prepared to and are able to articulate what they are think on all levels. Therefore a combination of research at the conscious and unconscious level is recommended. Having obtained meaningful and valuable information from all the research and analysis, the time should now be right to start formulating the digital engagement strategy. In order to put some structure and process around this, the following approach is recommended, although there may be other methods which can be used.

*People/Consumer*:
- Create virtual representative consumer groups
- Understand why they need your brand
- Outline what aspects of the brand appeal to them
- Create content that has a value to each group

*Location*:
- Be present and available in the relevant online areas

- Be visible and offer free information
- Provide a platform/mechanism for interaction
- Engage with them observing the right etiquette

*Influence*:

- Prioritise the key influences
- Stimulate inter consumer dialogue
- Provide status and recognition for influencers
- Address negative comments by helping

*Brand Association* :

- Maximise your advocacy into creating interest
- Encourage inter consumer dialogue to minimise risk of commitment
- Reward your advocates and people loyal to your brand
- Reduce brand opponency where possible

The other key area to consider is full integration with "offline" brand engagement/marketing strategy. To maximise the returns, these need to be full synchronised and complemen-tary. Typically, offline marketing can be used to drive online interaction. Encouraging people to communicate with the brand.

# Index

## E



## F



## H



## I



## J



## L



## M



## N



## P



## Q



## R



## S